Decoding the TOEFL® iBT

Basic

READING Answers & Explanations

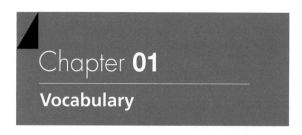

Chapter 01
Vocabulary

Basic Practice
p. 15

| Answers | A ⓒ | B Ⓐ | C Ⓑ |

Practice with Short Passages
p. 16

A | The Steel Plow

| Answers | Ⓐ |

Answer Explanation

When a creation is practical, it is effective since it works well.

Vocabulary

- **primitive** = basic; simple
- **ideal** = the best; working very well for a particular situation
- **stick** = to become attached to

B | The Brown-Headed Cowbird

| Answers | ⓒ |

Answer Explanation

When some birds reject the eggs, it means that they do not care for the eggs.

Vocabulary

- **hatch** = to come out of an egg and to be born
- **vocalization** = the act of making a sound or noise from one's mouth
- **maturity** = adulthood

Practice with Long Passages
p. 18

A | The Formation of the Grand Canyon

| Answers |
| 1 ⓓ 2 ⓓ 3 Ⓐ 4 Initial Formation: ①, ④ Widening of the Canyon: ②, ③ |

Answer Explanation

1 ⓓ The passage reads, "The canyon stretches for 446 kilometers and is twenty-nine kilometers across at its widest point. In some places, it descends more than 1,800 meters from its rim."

2 ⓓ When the canyon cliffs have colorful bands, there are colorful strips of rocks in layers.

3 Ⓐ The author writes about how ice erosion widened the Grand Canyon in writing, "In addition, ice eroded its walls. First, water seeped into cracks in the rocks. At night, when it got cooler, the water froze, became ice, and expanded. That caused rocks to break away from the canyon walls."

4 Initial Formation: ①, ④
Widening of the Canyon: ②, ③
About the initial formation of the Grand Canyon, the author writes, "Over a period of five or six million years, the river's water eroded the soft sedimentary rocks. Layers of these rocks are visible today as colorful bands in the canyon's cliffs, (①)" and adds, "The Colorado River, which flows through the Colorado Plateau, is mostly responsible for the formation of the Grand Canyon. (④)" Regarding the widening of the canyon, the passage reads, "When it rains, flashfloods often result. This creates numerous streams that carry away large amounts of soil and rock. This is exactly what happened to the Grand Canyon. (③) In addition, ice eroded its walls. First, water seeped into cracks in the rocks. At night, when it got cooler, the water froze, became ice, and expanded. That caused rocks to break away from the canyon walls. (②)" Answer choices ⑤ and ⑥ contain incorrect information, so they are wrong answers.

Vocabulary

- **rim** = the outer edge of something
- **uplifting** = the process of picking up something
- **sunbaked** = heated, dried, and hardened by the sun
- **flashflood** = a sudden flood with fast-moving water

B | The Benefits of Sleep

| Answers |
| 1 Ⓑ 2 Ⓑ 3 ⓒ 4 ①, ④, ⑤ |

Answer Explanation

1 Ⓑ In writing, "When there is darkness, most animals sleep," the author implies that some animals are active during the night.

2 Ⓑ When a body resists certain diseases, it fights against them to keep the body healthy.

3 ⓒ The sentence points out that large prey animals sleep for a short amount of time while smaller prey animals sleep longer. This thought is best expressed in the sentence in answer choice Ⓒ.

4 ① , ④ , ⑤ The summary sentence points out that animals get many benefits from sleep. This thought is best expressed in answer choices ① , ④ , and ⑤ . Answer choices ② and ③ are minor points, so they are incorrect answers.

Vocabulary

- cycle = a series of actions or events that are repeated
- restore = to bring back to an original condition
- suffer = to have a loss or disadvantage
- nocturnal = active at night

iBT Practice Test   p. 22

Answers

PASSAGE 1

1 Ⓐ   2 Ⓐ   3 Ⓒ   4 Ⓒ
5 Ⓑ   6 Ⓐ   7 ②   8 ② , ④ , ⑥

PASSAGE 2

9 Ⓓ   10 Ⓒ   11 Ⓐ   12 Ⓑ
13 Ⓓ   14 Ⓑ   15 Ⓒ   16 ② , ③ , ④

PASSAGE 1

Answer Explanation

1 Vocabulary Question

Ⓐ When a people's origin remains a mystery, it means that it is not confirmed where the people came from.

2 Rhetorical Purpose Question

Ⓐ It is written, "The first contact made between the Algonquin people and the Europeans happened in Quebec in 1603. French explorer Samuel de Champlain met them then."

3 Sentence Simplification Question

Ⓒ The sentence points out that the leader of each clan had to be supported by the people, but the clans lacked a single overall leader. This thought is best expressed in the sentence in answer choice Ⓒ.

4 Vocabulary Question

Ⓒ When local river systems are extensive, they are broad, so there are many of them.

5 Negative Factual Information Question

Ⓑ There is no mention in the passage of how many tribes belonged to the Iroquois Confederacy.

6 Factual Information Question

Ⓐ The passage reads, "Many of them take an active interest in preserving their culture. While a lot of them lead modern lives, there are others that engage in traditional practices. In doing so, they hope to preserve their heritage for future generations."

7 Insert Text Question

② The sentence before the second square reads, "The Algonquins soon became close allies of the French and fought alongside them in several wars against the British." The sentence to be added mentions the relationship between the Algonquins and the French and points out how long they remained "close allies." The two sentences therefore go well together.

8 Prose Summary Question

② , ④ , ⑥ The summary sentence points out that the Algonquins have had various relationships with the Europeans ever since they met each other in North America. This thought is best reflected in answer choices ② , ④ , and ⑥ . Answer choices ① , ③ , and ⑤ are minor points, so they are all incorrect.

PASSAGE 2

Answer Explanation

9 Vocabulary Question

Ⓓ When glaciers carve up the land beneath them, they cut it.

10 Factual Information Question

Ⓒ The passage reads, "They normally form in the Arctic and Antarctic regions but may also be created in mountain ranges at high altitudes."

11 Factual Information Question

Ⓐ The author notes, "The most notable effect of glaciers is how they depress the land under them. Depending upon the composition of the soil and the rock, the land may retain its former shape. However, the passing of a glacier typically leaves large depressions in the soil. These fill with water and form lakes."

12 Negative Factual Information Question

Ⓑ The passage points out, "The famous long fjords of Scandinavia were created in this manner during the last ice age thousands of years ago," so it is not true that some fjords are several million years old.

13 Inference Question

Ⓓ The author writes, "Three other major types of land formations occur due to glacial erosion. They are cirques, arêtes, and horns. A cirque forms when a glacier erodes a mountainside. It is a bowl-shaped depression which has a steeper side facing uphill, giving it a tilted appearance. Cirques are especially common in the Alps Mountains of Europe." Since cirques are "especially common in the Alps Mountains" and are formed "when a glacier erodes a mountainside," it can be inferred that many of the Alps Mountains were eroded by the actions of glaciers.

14 Vocabulary Question

Ⓑ When a glacier halts its movement, it stops.

15 Sentence Simplification Question

Ⓒ The sentence points out that the movement of a glacier forms a drumlin, which looks like a long hill of soil or rock and has the shape of a teardrop. This thought is best expressed by the sentence in answer choice Ⓒ.

16 Prose Summary Question

②, ③, ④ The summary sentence notes that glaciers change the land beneath them in many ways when they move. This thought is best described in answer choices ②, ③, and ④. Answer choice ⑥ is a minor point, so it is an incorrect answer. Answer choice ① contains information not mentioned in the passage, so it is also incorrect. And answer choice ⑤ contains incorrect information, so it is wrong.

Vocabulary Review   p. 30

Answers

A
1 maturity   2 hatch
3 tribe   4 flashflood
5 nocturnal
B
1 a   2 b   3 b   4 b   5 a
6 b   7 b   8 a   9 b

Chapter 02
Reference

Basic Practice   p. 33

Answers   A Ⓑ   B Ⓐ   C Ⓐ

Practice with Short Passages   p. 34

A | The Life Cycle of the Grasshopper

Answers   Ⓑ

Answer Explanation

The "they" that remain underground for around ten months are their eggs, which are the eggs that most grasshoppers lay.

Vocabulary

- **lifespan** = the length of time an organism lives
- **stage** = a level
- **shed** = to get rid of

B | Crowd Psychology

Answers   Ⓑ

Answer Explanation

The "it" that takes place is mob behavior.

Vocabulary

- **account for** = to explain; to be responsible for
- **mob** = a large group of people who behave badly and are often violent
- **delusion** = a false belief or opinion

Practice with Long Passages   p. 36

A | Orca Hunting Methods

Answers
1 Ⓒ   2 Ⓒ   3 Ⓓ
4 Herring: ④, ⑤   Seal: ②, ⑥

1 Ⓒ There is no mention in the passage of where the orca prefers to hunt animals.

2 Ⓒ The "it" that is hit on the head and stunned is the shark.

3 Ⓓ The passage reads, "It slaps the shark on the head to stun it, and then the orca flips the shark upside down. This makes the shark defenseless, so the orca can easily kill and eat it." Since the shark is stunned, it cannot move.

4 Herring: ④, ⑤
 Seal: ②, ⑥
 About herring, the passage reads, "The orca utilizes a method called the carousel to hunt herring. Hunting in groups, several orcas surround the herring, (④) move their bodies rapidly, and create air bubbles in the water. These actions herd the herring into a tightly rotating ball like a carousel. (⑤) The orcas then slap the ball with their tails to stun large numbers of herring, making it easy for the orcas to eat them." As for seals, the author writes, "Sometimes seals climb onto an ice sheet to escape from a group of orcas. The orcas then swim together toward the ice sheet, which creates a wave of water as they move. Occasionally, the wave rocks the ice sheet enough so that it knocks the seals into the water. (②, ⑥)" Answer choice ① is not mentioned in the passage, so it is incorrect. Answer choice ③ refers to sharks, so it is a wrong answer as well.

Vocabulary

- **feed on** = to eat
- **prey** = to hunt other animals
- **defenseless** = unable to protect oneself
- **rock** = to move from side to side

B │ The Evolution of the Romance Languages

Answers

1 Ⓓ	2 Ⓑ	3 Ⓐ	4 ①, ②, ⑤

Answer Explanation

1 Ⓓ The author points out how Classical Latin was different from Vulgar Latin in writing, "Vulgar Latin was the language of common people, soldiers, and merchants. Classical Latin, on the other hand, was the language of upper-class Romans."

2 Ⓑ The "these" that changed into individual languages such as French and Spanish are regional dialects.

3 Ⓐ When some similarities are retained, they are kept.

4 ①, ②, ⑤ The summary sentence points out that the Romance languages developed from Latin over many years. This thought is best described in answer choices ①, ②, and ⑤. Answer choice ③ contains incorrect information, so it is a wrong answer. And answer choice ④ is a minor point, so it is also incorrect.

Vocabulary

- **collapse** = to fall apart
- **merchant** = a person who sells things to others
- **distinct** = unique; individual
- **dialect** = a local variation of a language

iBT Practice Test   p. 40

Answers

PASSAGE 1

1 Ⓓ	2 Ⓐ	3 Ⓒ	4 Ⓓ
5 Ⓐ	6 Ⓒ	7 Ⓒ	8 ①, ④, ⑥

PASSAGE 2

9 Ⓑ	10 Ⓒ	11 Ⓑ	12 Ⓐ
13 Ⓐ	14 Ⓒ	15 Ⓓ	16 ③, ④, ⑤

PASSAGE 1

Answer Explanation

1 **Negative Factual Information Question**

 Ⓓ The passage mentions that some of the islands on Lake Victoria are inhabited, but there is no mention of how many people live on the islands.

2 **Factual Information Question**

 Ⓐ About the haplochromine cichlid, the author writes, "This large number of species was the result of adaptive radiation. This is an evolutionary process in which many new species develop from a single species in the past."

3 **Reference Question**

 Ⓒ The "it" that evolved in Lake Victoria is the cichlid.

4 **Vocabulary Question**

 Ⓓ When new species were introduced to Lake Victoria, it means that they were put in the lake on purpose.

5 **Rhetorical Purpose Question**

 Ⓐ In the passage, the author points out what kind of harm the Nile perch is causing in writing, "However, rather than helping, they have had a devastating impact on the ecosystem of the lake. The first fish introduced was the Nile perch. This giant fish can grow up to two meters long and weigh around 200 kilograms. It has an enormous appetite and devours numerous small fish."

6 Sentence Simplification Question

Ⓒ The sentence points out that hundreds of species of cichlids and many other types of fish have disappeared from Lake Victoria. This thought is best expressed by the sentence in answer choice Ⓒ.

7 Reference Question

Ⓒ The "They" that increase the nitrogen level of the lake are chemical fertilizers.

8 Prose Summary Question

①, ④, ⑥ The summary sentence points out that there are many reasons that large numbers of fish are disappearing from Lake Victoria. This thought is best reflected in answer choices ①, ④, and ⑥. Answer choices ② and ③ contain incorrect information, so they are wrong answers. And answer choice ⑤ is not mentioned in the passage, so it is also incorrect.

PASSAGE 2

Answer Explanation

9 Reference Question

Ⓑ The "them" that scientists first examined were fossilized remains of the archaeopteryx.

10 Negative Factual Information Question

Ⓒ According to the passage, "The archaeopteryx lived about 150 million years ago during the Late Jurassic Period." So it is not true that it lived for more than 150 million years.

11 Vocabulary Question

Ⓑ When the small feathers decomposed, they rotted, so they disappeared.

12 Inference Question

Ⓐ The author writes, "The archaeopteryx's feathers had the same appearance and structure as modern bird feathers. Other hints from the fossils show certain birdlike features. These include a similar bone structure with modern birds." The author therefore implies that the archaeopteryx was probably a relative of modern-day birds.

13 Factual Information Question

Ⓐ It is written, "It is possible that the animal used its wings and feathers to glide from a high position to a lower one. Perhaps it climbed to high places and then did controlled glides to attack prey beneath it."

14 Rhetorical Purpose Question

Ⓒ The author describes another animal similar to the archaeopteryx in writing, "Yet recent discoveries in China of a new birdlike animal appear to dispute this finding. The new species, named the xiaotingia, lived five million years before the archaeopteryx. Whether it and other birdlike dinosaurs evolved from the xiaotingia is disputed."

15 Sentence Simplification Question

Ⓓ The sentence points out that there is a debate between people who think the animals were birds and others who think they only resembled birds. This thought is best expressed by the sentence in answer choice Ⓓ.

16 Prose Summary Question

③, ④, ⑤ The summary sentence notes that the archaeopteryx was a prehistoric animal that resembled a bird and may or may not have been the animal that birds evolved from. This thought is best described in answer choices ③, ④, and ⑤. Answer choices ① and ② are minor points, so they are incorrect answers. Answer choice ⑥ contains wrong information, so it is also incorrect.

⎮ Vocabulary Review   p. 48

Answers

A
1	mob	2	erosion
3	merchants	4	lifespan
5	impact		

B
| 1 a | 2 b | 3 b | 4 a | 5 a |
| 6 b | 7 a | 8 a | 9 b | |

Chapter 03

Factual Information

Basic Practice

p. 51

Answers	A 1T 2T 3F	B 1T 2F 3F
	B 1F 2T 3T	

Practice with Short Passages

p. 52

A | Taylorism

Answers	Ⓑ

Answer Explanation

The passage reads, "Taylorism had many critics. They disliked the way that it treated workers."

Vocabulary

- **efficient** = making the best use of time, money, or other resources
- **stress** = to emphasize
- **critic** = a person who comments on something, often in a negative way

B | Mosaics

Answers	Ⓓ

Answer Explanation

The author writes, "They often decorated walls in temples or made mosaic floors on tiles in villas." Since people lived in villas, then mosaics were sometimes made in people's homes.

Vocabulary

- **glue** = to connect two things together by using a sticky substance
- **feature** = to be a main part of
- **extravagant** = wild; flashy

Practice with Long Passages

p. 54

A | The Rings of Saturn

Answers	1 Ⓓ	2 Ⓐ	3 Ⓐ
	4 ①, ④, ⑤		

Answer Explanation

1 Ⓓ About Galileo Galilei, the author notes, "The first person to see them was Italian astronomer Galileo Galilei. He used a telescope to observe them in 1601 but was not certain what they were." Thus, he is mentioned to point out that he was the first person to see the rings of Saturn.

2 Ⓐ The passage reads, "In addition, the particles making up the rings are different sizes. Some are tiny grains of sand while others are massive rock and ice formations."

3 Ⓐ The "some" that believe the rings of Saturn are the remains of a moon are astronomers.

4 ①, ④, ⑤ The summary sentence points out that Saturn has many rings that orbit it. This thought is best described in answer choices ①, ④, and ⑤. Answer choices ② and ③ are minor points, so they are wrong answers.

Vocabulary

- **prominent** = obvious; apparent
- **band** = a thin, flat strip
- **extensive** = widespread
- **gravity** = the force of attraction that causes things to fall to the ground

B | Atoll Formation

Answers			
1 Ⓑ, Ⓒ	2 Ⓐ	3 Ⓒ	4 ①, ③, ④

Answer Explanation

1 Ⓑ, Ⓒ It is written, "As more time passes, the island forms a ring of coral around it. Coral is a living organism which grows in warm waters in large colonies. As the coral grows, it releases secretions of calcium carbonate. They form a hard, rocklike structure that the coral anchors onto. This structure is a coral reef."

2 Ⓐ When something emerges from the water, it rises from beneath the surface.

3 Ⓒ The sentence points out that the coral reef becomes flat and sandy due to wind and water erosion. This thought is best expressed by the sentence in answer choice Ⓒ.

4 ①, ③, ④ The summary sentence points out that

atolls form when volcanoes rise above the surface but then later sink beneath it. This thought is best described in answer choices ①, ③, and ④. Answer choice ② is a minor point, so it is incorrect. Answer choice ⑤ contains information that is not included in the passage, so it is a wrong choice as well.

Vocabulary

- **naturalist** = a person who studies nature
- **secretion** = something that is released from an organism
- **anchor** = to connect one thing to another to keep the first thing from moving
- **sparse** = rare; uncommon

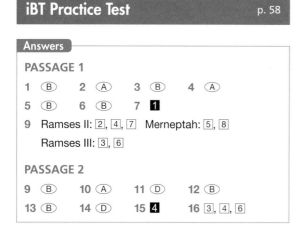

p. 58

Answers

PASSAGE 1

| 1 | Ⓑ | 2 | Ⓐ | 3 | Ⓑ | 4 | Ⓐ |
| 5 | Ⓑ | 6 | Ⓑ | 7 | ■1 | | |

9 Ramses II: ②, ④, ⑦   Merneptah: ⑤, ⑧
   Ramses III: ③, ⑥

PASSAGE 2

| 9 | Ⓑ | 10 | Ⓐ | 11 | Ⓓ | 12 | Ⓑ |
| 13 | Ⓑ | 14 | Ⓓ | 15 | ■4 | 16 | ③, ④, ⑥ |

PASSAGE 1

Answer Explanation

1 Factual Information Question

Ⓑ The passage reads, "They suddenly appeared in the second millennium B.C., and their attacks lasted for roughly a century. They sailed in ships and raided large numbers of coastal cities and towns."

2 Factual Information Question

Ⓐ It is mentioned, "One detailed text claims that the Sea Peoples were the allies of the Hittites, who were enemies of Egypt during the reign of Ramses II."

3 Vocabulary Question

Ⓑ When Merneptah had to deal with the Sea Peoples, he had to handle them.

4 Rhetorical Purpose Question

Ⓐ About Kadesh, the author mentions that the Sea Peoples successfully assaulted it in writing, "They attacked and destroyed the great Egyptian trading center of Kadesh."

5 Inference Question

Ⓑ In noting, "However, after the Egyptians defeated them at the Nile delta, the Sea Peoples were barely heard from again," the author implies that the Sea Peoples did not recover after losing a battle to the Egyptians.

6 Negative Factual Information Question

Ⓑ There is no mention in the passage of the name of the attackers that the Sea Peoples might have been escaping from.

7 Insert Text Question

■1 The sentence before the first square reads, "The reason for their disappearance is uncertain." The sentence to be added begins with "but," so it provides a counterpoint to the previous sentence. It then explains why the Sea Peoples might have disappeared. The two sentences therefore go well together.

9 Fill in a Table Question

Ramses II: ②, ④, ⑦
Merneptah: ⑤, ⑧
Ramses III: ③, ⑥
About Ramses II, the passage reads, "According to writings found in the nineteenth century, the attackers arrived from the sea with no warning, and nobody was able to stop them. One detailed text claims that the Sea Peoples were the allies of the Hittites, who were enemies of Egypt during the reign of Ramses II. In 1274 B.C., Ramses II managed to defeat the Hittites. He stopped a naval attack on Egypt by the Sea Peoples as well. (②, ④, ⑦)" As for Merneptah, the author writes, "Ramses II's son, Merneptah, also had to deal with the Sea Peoples. They allied themselves with another Egyptian enemy, the Libyans. (⑧) Merneptah defeated both in a great sea battle in which the Egyptians killed more than 6,000 of their enemies. (⑤)" Regarding Ramses III, it is written, "However, they returned yet again during the rule of Ramses III. They attacked and destroyed the great Egyptian trading center of Kadesh. (⑥) The Sea Peoples then raided several places along the Egyptian coast. Finally, they attacked the Nile River delta region. During the Battle of the Delta in 1175 B.C., the Egyptians ambushed the Sea Peoples. (③)" The information in answer choices ① and ⑨ is not mentioned in the passage, so they are both incorrect answer choices.

PASSAGE 2

Answer Explanation

9 Factual Information Question

Ⓑ The author writes, "A series of laws, called the Calico Acts, banned the importing of cotton textiles. These laws were directed at cheap imports from

India. The major purpose of the Calico Acts was to protect England's domestic cotton spinning and weaving industries."

10 Vocabulary Question

(A) When a process is laborious, it is very difficult to do.

11 Rhetorical Purpose Question

(D) The author names the spinning wheel as the first cotton fiber spinning machine in writing, "Cotton fiber spinning machines had been around for centuries. The first was the spinning wheel, which had been invented in the Islamic world in the 1000s."

12 Factual Information Question

(B) It is written, "In 1738, Lewis Paul and John Wyatt invented the rolling spinning wheel. It spun cotton yarn faster and made it a more even thickness."

13 Inference Question

(B) First, the author writes, "In 1738, Lewis Paul and John Wyatt invented the rolling spinning wheel. It spun cotton yarn faster and made it a more even thickness. Their invention became the basis for later spinning machines." Then, the author points out, "The first of these was James Hargreaves's spinning jenny, which he invented in 1764. It allowed cotton spinners to spin eight threads of cotton yarn at one time." It can therefore be inferred that the spinning jenny that Hargreaves invented was inspired by the invention of Paul and Wyatt.

14 Negative Factual Information Question

(D) There is no mention in the passage of the number of people needed to run the water frame.

15 Insert Text Question

■4 The sentence before the fourth square reads, "This final invention led to the explosion of textile manufacturing and was a major step forward in the Industrial Revolution." The sentence to be added mentions another result of the cotton gin, which was that cotton became a huge cash crop in the southern part of the United States. Thus the two sentences go well together.

16 Prose Summary Question

3, 4, 6 The summary sentence notes that several inventions helped the textile industry during the Industrial Revolution. This thought is best described in answer choices 3, 4, and 6. Answer choices 2 and 5 are minor points, so they are incorrect answer. Answer choice 1 contains information not mentioned in the passage, so it is also incorrect.

Vocabulary Review
p. 66

Answers

A
1 sparse 2 reign
3 flee 4 efficient
5 ally
B
1 a 2 b 3 b 4 a 5 a
6 b 7 a 8 b 9 a

Chapter 04
Negative Factual Information

Basic Practice
p. 69

| Answers | A 1T 2T 3F | B 1T 2F 3F |
| | B 1F 2T 3F | |

Practice with Short Passages
p. 70

A | Patagonia

Answers ⓒ

Answer Explanation

There is no mention in the passage of there being three distinct regions in Patagonia. There are only two main parts.

Vocabulary

• **rugged** = rocky; hilly
• **vast** = extensive; very large
• **inhabitant** = a person who lives in a certain area

B | Walking Fish

Answers ⓓ

Answer Explanation

There is no mention in the passage regarding when the

climbing perch is expected to make its way to Australia.

Vocabulary

- **aggressive** = tending to attack others without being attacked first
- **ecosystem** = all the living and nonliving things in a certain area
- **disrupt** = to cause problems; to interrupt

Practice with Long Passages   p. 72

A | Art Deco in New York City

Answers

| 1 Ⓒ | 2 Ⓑ | 3 Ⓓ | 4 ①, ②, ④ |

Answer Explanation

1 Ⓒ When skyscrapers are towering, they are very high.

2 Ⓑ The sentence points out that the buildings are wide at their bottoms but get taller layers as they become higher. This thought is best expressed by the sentence in answer choice Ⓑ.

3 Ⓓ There is no mention in the passage of how much shorter the Chrysler Building is than the Empire State Building.

4 ①, ②, ④ The summary sentence points out that the Art Deco Movement influenced many skyscrapers in New York City. This thought is best reflected in answer choices ①, ②, and ④. Answer choices ③ and ⑤ are both minor points, so they are wrong answers.

Vocabulary

- **characterize** = to describe something; to mark or distinguish something
- **prohibit** = not to allow; to ban
- **spire** = a tall, thin, pointed top of a building
- **massive** = very large; enormous

B | Economic Bubbles

Answers

| 1 Ⓐ | 2 Ⓑ | 3 **4** | 4 ②, ③, ⑤ |

Answer Explanation

1 Ⓐ Prominent historical examples are those which are notable for some reason.

2 Ⓑ There is no information in the passage about how long an economic bubble lasts before it bursts.

3 **4** The sentence before the fourth square reads,

"Only a few, such as Amazon.com, survived when the bubble burst." The sentence to be added covers the one of the results of "when the bubble burst." The two sentences therefore go well together.

4 ②, ③, ⑤ The summary sentence points out that in an economic bubble, an asset's price rises and then suddenly bursts. This thought is best reflected in answer choices ②, ③, and ⑤. Answer choice ① is a minor point, so it is incorrect. Answer choice ④ contains information that is not mentioned in the passage, so it is a wrong answer as well.

Vocabulary

- **asset** = anything that has value
- **burst** = to explode; to blow up
- **investor** = a person who puts money into a business in the hope of earning more money
- **profit** = money a person or company makes from doing business

iBT Practice Test   p. 76

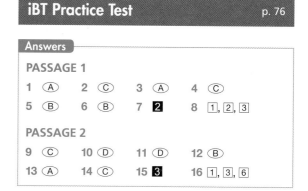

Answers

PASSAGE 1

| 1 Ⓐ | 2 Ⓒ | 3 Ⓐ | 4 Ⓒ |
| 5 Ⓑ | 6 Ⓑ | 7 **2** | 8 ①, ②, ③ |

PASSAGE 2

| 9 Ⓒ | 10 Ⓓ | 11 Ⓓ | 12 Ⓑ |
| 13 Ⓐ | 14 Ⓒ | 15 **3** | 16 ①, ③, ⑥ |

PASSAGE 1

Answer Explanation

1 **Negative Factual Information Question**

Ⓐ There is no mention in the passage of which of the works of Thales have survived.

2 **Inference Question**

Ⓒ In writing, "His work heavily influenced those who came after him, including Socrates, Plato, and Aristotle," the author implies that Socrates, Plato, and Aristotle all read some of the writing of Thales since they were influenced by him.

3 **Negative Factual Information Question**

Ⓐ It is not true that Thales knew how to use electricity as a source of energy. According to the passage, he only discovered static electricity but did not use it.

4 **Rhetorical Purpose Question**

Ⓒ In discussing the First Cause, the author shows how it relates to the philosophy of Thales in the entire paragraph.

5 Factual Information Question

Ⓑ The passage reads, "One part of his theory was that the Earth was floating on a vast ocean of water. He further believed that earthquakes were caused by the motion of this ocean's waves."

6 Vocabulary Question

Ⓑ When Thales overtly rejected the influence of the gods on nature, he openly denied that they had an effect on it.

7 Insert Text Question

2 The sentence in front of the second square reads, "Others claim he meant that a person must know his or her inner self before everything else." This sentence and the one before it provide possible interpretations of a saying. The sentence to be added explains that people support both of those interpretations. The two sentences therefore go well together.

8 Prose Summary Question

①, ②, ③ The summary sentence points out that Thales was talented in many fields. This thought is best reflected in answer choices ①, ②, and ③. Answer choices ④ and ⑥ are minor points, so they are both incorrect. And answer choice ⑤ has incorrect information, so it is a wrong answer as well.

PASSAGE 2

Answer Explanation

9 Vocabulary Question

Ⓒ When farmers cleared new trees from their land, they removed them from their fields.

10 Factual Information Question

Ⓓ The passage reads, "In many places, there were thick forests and numerous rocks in the soil."

11 Negative Factual Information Question

Ⓓ There is no mention in the passage of the sizes of the harvests that farmers reaped from their fields.

12 Rhetorical Purpose Question

Ⓑ In writing, "Many New England colonists turned to the Atlantic Ocean for extra food. The nearby water had enormous schools of cod and haddock as well as lobsters, crabs, and other shellfish," the author names some of the animals that colonists caught for food in the Atlantic Ocean.

13 Factual Information Question

Ⓐ The author writes, "As for residences, the typical colonial farmer's home in New England in

the seventeenth century was a log cabin with a dirt floor. It was often a single room in which the entire family cooked, ate, and slept."

14 Inference Question

Ⓒ The passage reads, "There were many rivers and waterfalls in the area to run machines, so sawmills eventually began turning out cut wood for building houses." The author therefore implies that sawmills used water power to run.

15 Insert Text Question

3 The sentence before the third square reads, "They practiced crop rotation if they had enough cleared land to make it practical." The sentence to be added explains how crop rotation worked and why the colonists did it. Thus the two sentences go well together.

16 Prose Summary Question

①, ③, ⑥ The summary sentence notes that the lives of the colonists who farmed land in New England during the colonial period were hard. This thought is best described in answer choices ①, ③, and ⑥. Answer choice ④ is a minor point, so it is an incorrect answer. Answer choices ② and ⑤ contain information not mentioned in the passage, so they are also incorrect.

| Vocabulary Review

p. 84

Answers

A

1	disrupted	2	aggressive
3	substance	4	predict
5	investors		

B

1	a	2	a	3	b	4	a	5	b
6	a	7	b	8	b	9	a		

Chapter 05

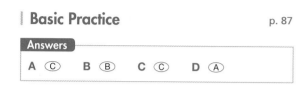

Sentence Simplification

| Basic Practice   p. 87

Practice with Short Passages   p. 88

A | The Renaissance of the Twelfth Century

Answer Explanation

The sentence points out that people in the West got knowledge from the East. This thought is best expressed by the sentence in answer choice ⓒ.

Vocabulary

• **eager** = willing to do something
• **flock** = to go somewhere in great numbers
• **theology** = the study of religion

B | Robert Goddard

Answer Explanation

The sentence points out that Goddard thought a liquid fuel-powered rocket could go to the moon even though others did not think that way. This thought is best expressed by the sentence in answer choice ⓑ.

Vocabulary

• **patent** = the legal right to an invention
• **mock** = to make fun of
• **abandon** = to give up

Practice with Long Passages   p. 90

A | Sediment in Rivers

Answer Explanation

1   ⓓ The author writes, "Sediment is a combination of soil particles and organic matter. It typically consists of clay, silt, sand, gravel, and decaying plant and animal matter."

2   ⓓ The sentence points out that when a river bends, the water moves slowly, thereby causing sediment to make wide banks. This thought is best expressed by the sentence in answer choice ⓓ.

3   ⓒ There is no mention in the passage of how sediment makes deltas and marshes too big.

4   ①, ②, ④ The summary sentence points out that sediment can get into rivers in various ways and then affect them. This thought is best reflected in answer choices ①, ②, and ④. Answer choices ③ and ⑤ are minor points, so they are both incorrect.

Vocabulary

• **decay** = to rot
• **suspend** = to be held up in the air or in another substance; to be above the ground
• **estuary** = the part of a river where it meets the ocean
• **clog** = to block

B | Venomous Insects

Answer Explanation

1   ⓐ About the horsefly, the author notes, "The horsefly is one such insect. This predator captures prey and then injects it with a powerful venom that paralyzes its victim. The horsefly can then feed upon its victim at its leisure."

2   ⓓ The "them" that are prevented from getting the bees' supplies of honeys are attackers.

3   ⓑ The sentence points out that the venom of the ant can kill small mammals and cause pain in humans. This thought is best expressed in answer choice ⓑ.

4   Offensive Purposes: ②, ④
     Defensive Purposes: ①, ⑤

Regarding offensive purposes, the author writes, "Flies, beetles, and wasps are some insects that use their venom for offensive purposes. (④) The horsefly is one such insect. This predator captures prey and then injects it with a powerful venom that paralyzes its victim (②)." As for defensive purposes, the passage reads, "Many more insects utilize their venom for defensive purposes, (①)" and adds, "Honeybees, for instance, protect their hives by stinging attackers. This prevents them from getting the bees' supplies of honey, which they need to survive. (⑤)" Answer choices ③ and ⑥ are not mentioned in the passage, so they are incorrect answer choices.

Vocabulary

- **inject** = to put some sort of liquid into a person or animal
- **paralyze** = to prevent someone or something from moving
- **deadly** = able to kill
- **larva** = insects that have just hatched

iBT Practice Test   p. 94

Answers

PASSAGE 1

1 Ⓑ	2 Ⓓ	3 Ⓓ	4 Ⓐ
5 Ⓐ	6 Ⓑ	7 Ⓒ	8 ③, ④, ⑥

PASSAGE 2

9 Ⓐ	10 Ⓒ	11 Ⓐ	12 Ⓑ
13 Ⓐ	14 Ⓓ	15 Ⓑ	16 ③, ④, ⑤

PASSAGE 1

Answer Explanation

1 Reference Question

Ⓑ The "It" that is known for its beautiful and diverse landscape is Norwich.

2 Sentence Simplification Question

Ⓓ The sentence points out that the exhibition made the school better known and was the first one in England that did not take place in London. This thought is best expressed by the sentence in answer choice Ⓓ.

3 Inference Question

Ⓓ In writing, "Crome was interested in examining the state of painting, architecture, and sculpture. He wanted to do that to discover the best methods to achieve perfection in those arts. Despite his

lofty goal, the society primarily became a school of landscape painters," the author implies that the original goals of John Crome regarding the school were not met.

4 Factual Information Question

Ⓐ The author notes, "He preferred to send other artists to sketch places and then used their drawings to make paintings of his own."

5 Rhetorical Purpose Question

Ⓐ About *Woody Landscape*, the author writes, "A more vibrant example is James Stark's *Woody Landscape*, whose date of completion is unknown." In writing that, the author is using the painting as a typical one made by the Norwich School.

6 Negative Factual Information Question

Ⓑ There is no mention in the passage regarding why so many landscapes were painted by members of the Norwich School.

7 Vocabulary Question

Ⓒ When a school begins to lose favor with people, it becomes less popular than it was before.

8 Prose Summary Question

③, ④, ⑥ The summary sentence points out that John Crome founded the Norwich School of Art and that its members painted many landscapes. This thought is best reflected in answer choices ③, ④, and ⑥. Answer choices ① and ⑤ are minor points, so they are incorrect answers. Answer choice ② contains information not mentioned in the passage, so it is a wrong answer as well.

PASSAGE 2

Answer Explanation

9 Negative Factual Information Question

Ⓐ The author writes, "The reason is that bees are responsible for pollinating many crops people eat. They also pollinate numerous species of wild plants." So it is not true that bees pollinate all of the wild plants growing in forests.

10 Factual Information Question

Ⓒ It is written, "As they do so, their bodies brush up against the pollen in flowers and trees. While they move from flower to flower, the pollen gathered on their bodies is spread around. This starts the reproductive cycles of plants."

11 Negative Factual Information Question

Ⓐ There is no mention in the paragraph about bees pollinating nuts planted by people.

12 Vocabulary Question

Ⓑ When bears and other wild animals ravage entire hives, they destroy the hives to get to the honey.

13 Rhetorical Purpose Question

Ⓐ About moths, dragonflies, and praying mantises, the author notes that they hunt and kill bees by writing, "Large numbers of bird species consume them. So do spiders and insects such as moths, dragonflies, and praying mantises."

14 Sentence Simplification Question

Ⓓ The sentence points out that many species of plants would die if it were not for bees that keep them alive. This thought is best expressed by the sentence in answer choice Ⓓ.

15 Inference Question

Ⓑ The author writes, "In some places, entire colonies are dying in what biologists call colony collapse disorder. Experts are struggling to understand why this is happening." The author therefore implies that the reason colony collapse disorder is happening is not fully understood by scientists yet.

16 Prose Summary Question

③, ④, ⑤ The summary sentence notes that there are many reasons that bees are important in their ecosystems. This thought is best described in answer choices ③, ④, and ⑤. Answer choices ① is a minor point, so it is an incorrect answer. Answer choices ② and ⑥ contain information not mentioned in the passage, so they are also incorrect.

| Vocabulary Review   p. 102

Answers

A
1 patent   2 Decaying
3 mocked   4 theology
5 exhibition
B
1 a   2 b   3 b   4 a   5 b
6 b   7 a   8 b   9 a

Chapter 06
Inference

| Basic Practice   p. 105

Answers   A Ⓐ   B Ⓒ   C Ⓐ

Practice with Short Passages   p. 106

A | The Kangaroo

Answers   Ⓐ

Answer Explanation

The author writes, "It is also vulnerable to periods of extreme heat and drought." This implies that the kangaroo can be killed by extreme weather conditions.

Vocabulary

· **hind** = back
· **pouch** = a pocket
· **vulnerable** = able to be hurt or killed by

B | James Fenimore Cooper

Answers   Ⓐ

Answer Explanation

The passage reads, "His family moved to Cooperstown in upstate New York. Growing up there, he was tremendously influenced by the land and the people. They would feature in the novels that made him famous." It also notes, "Three years later, he authored *The Pioneers*, the first of the five books in *The Leatherstocking Tales*. It featured the woodsman Natty Bumppo. This book told a tale about life on the American frontier." The author therefore implies that *The Pioneers* was inspired by Cooper's life as a child.

Vocabulary

· **woodsman** = a person who spends a lot of time in the forest and is skilled at hunting
· **frontier** = the land at the edge of a country that has few people living in it
· **subsequently** = later; next

Practice with Long Passages   p. 108

A | Language Acquisition by Children

Answers

| 1 | ⓒ | 2 | Ⓑ | 3 | Ⓑ | 4 | ②, ③, ⑤ |

Answer Explanation

1 ⓒ An interactive aspect is a cooperative one between two or more people.

2 Ⓑ The passage reads, "Baby talk utilizes short, simple sentences. It also uses basic structures, includes repetitions, and employs exaggerated pronunciation."

3 Ⓑ In writing, "As children grow older, they need to play with others their age. Doing so can improve their language skills. Play activities are dynamic situations, so children must use language to do activities with others," the author implies that children with more friends can develop better language skills.

4 ②, ③, ⑤ The summary sentence points out that there are several ways that children learn to speak over time. This thought is best reflected in answer choices ②, ③, and ⑤. Answer choice ① is a minor point, so it is incorrect. Answer choice ④ is incorrect information, so it is a wrong answer as well.

Vocabulary

- **dynamic** = active
- **static** = inactive
- **exaggerated** = overstated
- **complexity** = how complicated something is

B | The Effects of Public Transportation on Urban Life

Answers

| 1 | Ⓐ | 2 | ⓒ | 3 | Ⓐ | 4 | ②, ③, ④ |

Answer Explanation

1 Ⓐ In writing, "City streets also tended to be narrow and were not maintained well," the author implies that the streets were often in very poor condition.

2 ⓒ About Coney Island, the author mentions, "Coney Island in New York and Brighton Beach in England were connected to big cities by railways. Thus, people living in nearby cities were easily able to visit them."

3 Ⓐ It is written, "These forms of public transportation could carry people long distances for low prices."

4 ②, ③, ④ The summary sentence points out that as public transportation developed, cities changed a

lot. This thought is best reflected in answer choices ②, ③, and ④. Answer choice ① is a minor point, so it is incorrect. Answer choice ⑤ contains information that is not in the passage, so it is a wrong answer as well.

Vocabulary

- **relatively** = fairly; quite
- **workplace** = the location where a person's job is
- **establish** = to start, found, or create
- **lane** = a part of a road wide enough for vehicles to drive on

iBT Practice Test   p. 112

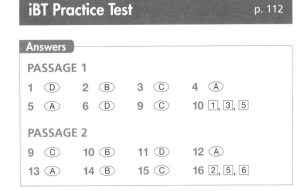

Answers

PASSAGE 1

| 1 | Ⓓ | 2 | Ⓑ | 3 | ⓒ | 4 | Ⓐ |
| 5 | Ⓐ | 6 | Ⓓ | 9 | ⓒ | 10 | ①, ③, ⑤ |

PASSAGE 2

| 9 | ⓒ | 10 | Ⓑ | 11 | Ⓓ | 12 | Ⓐ |
| 13 | Ⓐ | 14 | Ⓑ | 15 | ⓒ | 16 | ②, ⑤, ⑥ |

PASSAGE 1

Answer Explanation

1 **Vocabulary Question**

   Ⓓ The endeavors that the people of Venice had to be creative in were their efforts.

2 **Vocabulary Question**

   Ⓑ Because the cistern bottoms were slanted, they were angled so that water would flow down to the wells.

3 **Negative Factual Information Question**

   ⓒ It is not true that fresh water was stored in barrels. The barrels were only used to transport water from rivers to the city.

4 **Inference Question**

   Ⓐ In writing, "It was also locked because control of the wells was strict. Local officials or priests from nearby churches controlled the keys to the wells," the author implies that local priests were considered people to be trusted since they were given keys to the wells.

5 **Inference Question**

   Ⓐ The author writes, "In addition, during the periodic times of flooding, the manholes and wellheads were protected from the floodwaters. This prevented salt water from seeping into the cisterns."

In writing this, the author implies that seawater covered the streets of the city when there were floods.

6 Sentence Simplification Question

Ⓓ The sentence points out that the Venetians acted like the Romans did and built an aqueduct to bring in water. This thought is best expressed by the sentence in answer choice Ⓓ.

7 Factual Information Question

Ⓒ The author notes, "The aqueduct was completed in 1886 and became the main source of fresh water for Venice. Soon afterward, many cisterns were closed down and their manholes covered over."

8 Prose Summary Question

①, ③, ⑤ The summary sentence points out that Venice had an effective system to provide water for the people living there. This thought is best reflected in answer choices ①, ③, and ⑤. Answer choices ② and ④ are minor points, so they are wrong answers. Answer choice ⑥ contains incorrect information, so it is incorrect as well.

PASSAGE 2

Answer Explanation

9 Factual Information Question

Ⓒ The passage reads, "Portraiture is one of the oldest forms of art and dates back to ancient Egypt."

10 Vocabulary Question

Ⓑ When a portrait artist has an aim, the portrait artist has a specific intention.

11 Rhetorical Purpose Question

Ⓓ About scars, moles, a large nose, and a weak chin, the author writes, "The artist also had to protect the subject from ridicule. Any ugly features, such as scars, moles, a large nose, and a weak chin, were overlooked." So the author mentions them as features not painted by portrait artists.

12 Negative Factual Information Question

Ⓐ The passage reads, "To capture an image of an individual requires the person or people to sit for the artist. This means posing for a long time, often in a certain position, wearing certain clothing, or holding an object. This is tiring and may require several sessions before the artist is satisfied. The subject may be painted standing, sitting, or reclining." So it is not true that artists make their subjects take identical positions when posing for a portrait.

13 Vocabulary Question

Ⓐ When having a portrait is deemed important, it is considered important by people.

14 Sentence Simplification Question

Ⓑ The sentence points out that a person who likes the portrait an artist makes will hang it up so that others can see it. This thought is best expressed by the sentence in answer choice Ⓑ.

15 Inference Question

Ⓒ The author writes, "One famous example of this is Graham Sutherland's 1954 portrait of Winston Churchill. Churchill had his portrait burned after a public viewing left him unhappy." Since Churchill had the portrait burned, it is implied that the painting no longer exists.

16 Prose Summary Question

②, ⑤, ⑥ The summary sentence notes that artists paint portraits, which focus on people's heads, of important people during their times. This thought is best described in answer choices ②, ⑤, and ⑥. Answer choices ①, ③, and ④ are all minor points, so they are incorrect answers.

| Vocabulary Review

p. 120

Answers

A
1	frontier	2	flow
3	complexity	4	aqueduct
5	pouch		

B
1 b	2 b	3 a	4 a	5 b
6 b	7 a	8 a	9 a	

Chapter 07

Rhetorical Purpose

Basic Practice

p. 123

Answers	A Ⓑ B Ⓐ C Ⓒ

Practice with Short Passages

p. 124

A | Whirlpools

Answers	Ⓐ

Answer Explanation

The passage reads, "One of the largest natural whirlpools in the world is the Old Sow Whirlpool." The author mentions it as an example of a very large whirlpool.

Vocabulary

- **swirl** = to move around in a circle
- **temporary** = lasting a short amount of time; not permanent
- **harm** = to cause damage or injury to

B | The Composition of Comets

Answers	Ⓒ

Answer Explanation

In mentioning "frozen water" in the passage, the author points out, "The rest of the nucleus is comprised mostly of frozen water."

Vocabulary

- **substance** = a material
- **melt** = to change from a solid to a liquid
- **extend** = to stretch; to reach from one place to another

Practice with Long Passages

p. 126

A | The Golden Age of Piracy

Answers	1 Ⓒ 2 Ⓑ 3 Ⓓ 4 ①, ④, ⑤

Answer Explanation

1 Ⓒ When trade routes were vulnerable to pirate attacks, they were exposed to pirates and were likely to get attacked.

2 Ⓑ There is no mention in the passage of what pirates did when they attacked ships on the sea.

3 Ⓓ About the British Royal Navy, the passage reads, "However, in the end, most pirate captains were captured and executed. The British Royal Navy played a major role in doing that."

4 ①, ④, ⑤ The summary sentence points out that there were many pirate attacks on ships during the Golden Age of Piracy. This thought is best reflected by answer choices ①, ④, and ⑤. Answer choices ② and ③ are minor points, so they are both incorrect.

Vocabulary

- **plunder** = to steal something after attacking a person or place
- **conception** = an idea, belief, or thought about something
- **homeland** = the place where a person is from
- **execute** = to kill, often for committing a crime

B | Trout Streams

Answers	1 Ⓓ 2 Ⓓ 3 Ⓒ 4 ②, ③, ④

Answer Explanation

1 Ⓓ The passage reads, "However, trout only live in water which is cold or cool. Most trout thrive when the water temperature ranges between ten and sixteen degrees Celsius."

2 Ⓓ The "those" that are flying above the water are insects.

3 Ⓒ In writing, "Another feature of trout streams is that trout prefer pools where the current does not move too swiftly. This allows trout to rest without having to swim against the current," the author explains why trout like living in pools.

4 ②, ③, ④ The summary sentence points out that trout living in streams have many common features. This thought is best reflected by answer choices ②, ③, and ④. Answer choice ① is a minor point, so it is incorrect. And answer choice ⑤ is not mentioned in

the passage, so it is a wrong answer as well.

Vocabulary

Vocabulary

- **thrive** = to do well
- **exceed** = to go past or beyond
- **shade** = to cast a shadow over something to block it from the sun
- **strike** = to hit; to attack

iBT Practice Test   p. 130

Answers

PASSAGE 1

1 Ⓑ	2 Ⓓ	3 Ⓒ	4 Ⓐ
5 Ⓑ	6 Ⓒ	7 ③	

8 Safety: ②, ③, ⑨   Belongingness: ①, ⑥
   Esteem: ⑤, ⑧

PASSAGE 2

9 Ⓒ	10 Ⓐ	11 Ⓑ	12 Ⓓ
13 Ⓑ	14 Ⓒ	15 ③	

16 Effusive Eruption: ③, ④
   Explosive Eruption: ②, ⑥, ⑦

PASSAGE 1

Answer Explanation

1 Inference Question

Ⓑ In writing, "American psychologist Abraham Maslow first presented the theory named after him in 1943 in a paper entitled 'A Theory of Human Motivation,'" the author implies that Maslow printed his theory in a journal.

2 Negative Factual Information Question

Ⓓ It is not true that physiological needs are difficult to obtain for people since they are basic needs all people require.

3 Rhetorical Purpose Question

Ⓒ The author writes, "Individuals can also take steps to ensure their economic safety by getting job security, by purchasing health insurance, and by accumulating savings in banks."

4 Vocabulary Question

Ⓐ The "sense" of security that people may not have is a feeling of security.

5 Factual Information Question

Ⓑ The passage reads, "This sense of belongingness can be negatively affected when people are ignored by others."

6 Rhetorical Purpose Question

Ⓒ Most of the paragraph about esteem explains how people can obtain it.

7 Insert Text Question

❸ The sentence before the third square reads, "They can then try to fulfill their potential." The sentence to be added then mentions that people can fulfill their potential "in a variety of ways." The two sentences therefore go well together.

8 Fill in a Table Question

Safety: ②, ③, ⑨
Belongingness: ①, ⑥
Esteem: ⑤, ⑧

About safety, the author writes, "Safety needs deal with obtaining freedom from fear, (②)" and also adds, "People begin to concern themselves with their physical safety once their basic needs have been met. Among them are protection from natural disasters, criminals, and enemies. (⑨) In modern society, firefighters, police, and military forces provide a great amount of this protection. (③)" As for belongingness, the passage reads, "Most people get this through their families. (⑥) In addition, as they grow older, they make friends and expand their circles of belongingness. (①)" Regarding esteem, the author comments, "To be esteemed, people do their best to be recognized for their achievements. (⑧) Being successful in their work, education, and community activities can bring respect from others. (⑤)" Answer choice ④ refers to self-actualization while answer choice ⑦ refers to physiological needs, so both of them are incorrect answer choices.

PASSAGE 2

Answer Explanation

9 Rhetorical Purpose Question

Ⓒ In writing, "Hawaiian eruptions also see lava slowly coming out of the ground. They tend to make low, wide cones, called shield cones," the author focuses on how shield cones are a land formation created by Hawaiian eruptions.

10 Factual Information Question

Ⓐ The author points out, "Effusive eruptions are mild and often involve lava oozing out of the ground. The lava ejected has a low viscosity and a low gas content."

11 Vocabulary Question

Ⓑ When large gas bubbles violently hurl lava, ash, and rocks high into the air, the gas bubbles throw them into the air.

12 Rhetorical Purpose Question

Ⓓ The author explains how a certain type of eruption got its name in writing, "Plinian eruptions are the most violent of all. They are named for Pliny the Younger, a Roman who recorded the eruption of Mount Vesuvius in Italy in 79 A.D."

13 Inference Question

Ⓑ First, the author writes, "Lava from explosive eruptions has a higher gas content and higher viscosity. These volcanoes tend to erupt with massive ejections of lava, gas, ash, and sometimes steam. The mildest is the Strombolian type." Then, the author mentions, "The most violent explosive eruptions are the Peléan and Plinian types. Peléan eruptions are named for Mount Pelée on the island of Martinique." It can therefore be inferred that Peléan eruptions are more destructive in nature than Strombolian ones.

14 Factual Information Question

Ⓒ The passage reads, "This happens in shallow water when a volcano forms near the surface. As gas bubbles up, it bursts and shoots lava into the water. The interaction of hot lava and cool water causes the water to flash into steam."

15 Insert Text Question

3 The sentence before the third square reads, "A more violent eruption is the Vulcanian one." The sentence to be added points out how the Vulcanian eruption got its name. Thus the two sentences go well together.

16 Fill in a Table Question

Effusive Eruption: ③, ④
Explosive Eruption: ②, ⑥, ⑦
About effusive eruptions, the author notes, "The lava ejected has a low viscosity and a low gas content," (③) and, "Hawaiian eruptions also see lava slowly coming out of the ground. They tend to make low, wide cones, called shield cones. As they progress, lava flows from both the summit and from cracks in the mountains' sides. This type is named for volcanoes found in Hawaii such as Mauna Loa." (④) As for explosive eruptions, the author points out, "Lava from explosive eruptions has a higher gas content and higher viscosity. These volcanoes tend to erupt with massive ejections of lava, gas, ash, and sometimes steam. The mildest is the Strombolian type," and, "The most violent explosive eruptions are the Peléan and Plinian types." (②) The author also mentions, "They are characterized by massive ejections of ash and gas in pyroclastic flows. These are thick clouds of hot ash, rocks, and gas that flow down the slopes of volcanoes and that destroy everything in their path," (⑥) and,

"The eruptions involve huge explosions that shoot masses of ash, lava, gas, and rocks into the air." (⑦)

Vocabulary Review　　　　　　p. 138

Answers

A
1 conception　　2 swirl
3 exceeds　　　4 homeland
5 melt
B
1 a　　2 b　　3 a　　4 b　　5 b
6 a　　7 b　　8 a　　9 a

Chapter 08
Insert Text

Basic Practice　　　　　　p. 141

Answers　A Ⓓ – Ⓐ – Ⓒ – Ⓑ – Ⓔ
　　　　　　B Ⓐ – Ⓓ – Ⓔ – Ⓒ – Ⓑ
　　　　　　C Ⓑ – Ⓒ – Ⓔ – Ⓐ – Ⓓ

Practice with Short Passages　　p. 142

A ｜ Terrestrial Planets

Answers　　**4**

Answer Explanation

The sentence before the fourth square reads, "Mercury's is almost eighty-eight days while that of Mars is 687 days." The sentence to be added also refers to how long it takes a planet to orbit the sun. The two sentences therefore go well together.

Vocabulary

- **giant** = someone or something that is much larger than normal
- **apparent** = clear; obvious

- **rocky** = made of rocks and stones

B | Stalactites and Stalagmites

Answers　❷

Answer Explanation

The sentence before the second square reads, "In the process, it dissolves calcite." The sentence to be added provides an explanation of what calcite is. The two sentences therefore go well together.

Vocabulary

- **emerge** = to come out from
- **dissolve** = to break down when exposed to a liquid
- **drip** = to fall in drops, as in water

Practice with Long Passages　p. 144

A | The Human Eye

Answers

| 1 Ⓒ | 2 Ⓐ | 3 ❸ | 4 ②, ④, ⑤ |

Answer Explanation

1　Ⓒ The "they" that can be interpreted as images are signals.

2　Ⓐ About the iris, the author writes, "The iris acts like a muscle as it opens and closes to allow more or less light into the eye."

3　❸ The sentence before the third square reads, "Cones are in the center of the retina." The sentence to be added creates a contract by using "unlike rods." The "they" in the sentence to be added refers to cones. The two sentences therefore go well together.

4　②, ④, ⑤ The summary sentence points out that all of the parts of the eye work together to let people see. This thought is best reflected in answer choices ②, ④, and ⑤. Answer choice ① is a minor point, so it is a wrong answer. And answer choice ③ is not mentioned in the passage, so it is also incorrect.

Vocabulary

- **interpret** = to understand
- **fluid** = a liquid
- **absorb** = to soak up; to take in
- **convert** = to change from one form to another

B | The Ladybug

Answers

| 1 Ⓑ | 2 Ⓐ | 3 ❷ | 4 ②, ③, ⑤ |

Answer Explanation

1　Ⓑ The sentence points out that there are seven spots on a ladybug's back and two more spots on its head. This thought is best expressed by the sentence in answer choice Ⓑ.

2　Ⓐ In writing, "While this helps the ladybug avoid attacks from some animals, other predators have become accustomed to the taste. Birds, frogs, spiders, and dragonflies are among these animals," the author implies that birds, frogs, spiders, and dragonflies hunt and eat ladybugs.

3　❷ The sentence before the second square reads, "The colored markings of the ladybug serve a purpose." The sentence to be added explains what the purpose is: to serve as a warning to predators. The two sentences therefore go well together.

4　②, ③, ⑤ The summary sentence points out that most ladybug species have colorful markings and hunt other animals. This thought is best reflected in answer choices ②, ③, and ⑤. Answer choice ① contains information that is not mentioned in the passage, so it is a wrong answer. And answer choice ④ is a minor point, so it is also incorrect.

Vocabulary

- **approximately** = around; about
- **be accustomed to** = to be used to
- **hibernate** = to sleep for a long period of time during winter
- **shed** = to lose one's skin, hair, or fur

iBT Practice Test　p. 148

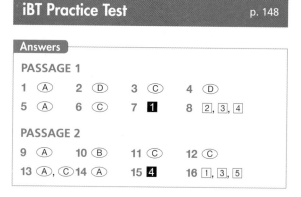

Answers

PASSAGE 1

| 1 Ⓐ | 2 Ⓓ | 3 Ⓒ | 4 Ⓓ |
| 5 Ⓐ | 6 Ⓒ | 7 ❶ | 8 ②, ③, ④ |

PASSAGE 2

| 9 Ⓐ | 10 Ⓑ | 11 Ⓒ | 12 Ⓒ |
| 13 Ⓐ, Ⓒ | 14 Ⓐ | 15 ❹ | 16 ①, ③, ⑤ |

PASSAGE 1

Answer Explanation

1　Factual Information Question

Ⓐ The passage reads, "New research suggests

that the Amazon was once a land of farms though. They supported millions of people and existed for thousands of years."

2 Vocabulary Question

Ⓓ When research centers on a specific topic, it focuses on that subject.

3 Sentence Simplification Question

Ⓒ The sentence points out that people learned that pre-Columbian societies learned how to use many plants but did not domesticate them. This thought is best expressed in the sentence in answer choice Ⓒ.

4 Negative Factual Information Question

Ⓓ It is not true that *terra preta* is found in a layer above the topsoil. Instead, the author notes that *terra preta* is beneath the topsoil in writing, "In many parts of the Amazon, there is dark nutrient-rich soil just beneath the surface topsoil. This was called *terra preta*, or black soil, by Portuguese colonists."

5 Reference Question

Ⓐ The "they" that saw people who looked healthy and well fed were these explorers.

6 Rhetorical Purpose Question

Ⓒ The author makes a comparison in writing, "Unlike the Aztecs and Mayans in Central America, the Amazonian people did not build with stone. Their main building material was wood."

7 Insert Text Question

🔳1 The sentence before the first square reads, "Their villages tended to be large, and their crops were plentiful." The sentence to be added points out that the people living in the villages had plenty of food for themselves. Both sentences are about food. So the two sentences go well together.

8 Prose Summary Question

2️⃣, 3️⃣, 4️⃣ The summary sentence points out that research has shown the pre-Columbian Amazonians farmed a lot of land in the region. This thought is best reflected in answer choices 2️⃣, 3️⃣, and 4️⃣. Answer choices 1️⃣ and 6️⃣ are minor points, so they are both incorrect. Answer choice 5️⃣ contains incorrect information, so it is also a wrong answer.

PASSAGE 2

Answer Explanation

9 Sentence Simplification Question

Ⓐ The sentence points out that farmers make sure their plants are identical by grafting apple trees onto rootstocks. This thought is best expressed by the sentence in answer choice Ⓐ.

10 Factual Information Question

Ⓑ It is written, "To produce fruit, apple tree blossoms must be pollinated. Many varieties of apple trees have male and female parts on the same flower. Nevertheless, apple tree blossoms are unable to self-pollinate. Bees assist in this process, so apple farmers often care for beehives."

11 Inference Question

Ⓒ The author writes, "Insects and diseases are controlled with chemical pesticides and insecticide sprays, but they cannot be used when trees are being pollinated since they may harm bees." Since the trees cannot be sprayed with pesticides or insecticides during some parts of the year, the author implies that apple trees are more vulnerable to diseases during these times.

12 Vocabulary Question

Ⓒ When traps are ingenious, they are clever.

13 Factual Information Question

Ⓐ, Ⓒ The author notes, "Strong fences are built around orchards to keep large animals out. Wire mesh wrapped around tree trunks stops smaller animals from climbing the trees."

14 Negative Factual Information Question

Ⓐ The author writes, "By using machines, the number of people needed to work on apple orchards has been reduced tremendously." It is therefore not true that the machines which farmers use in their apple orchards require more workers.

15 Insert Text Question

🔳4 The sentence before the fourth square reads, "Diseases that hurt apple trees include fire blight, apple scab, apple rust, and several molds and mildews." The sentence to be added points out that the diseases can be harmful to trees and even kill them. Thus the two sentences go well together.

16 Prose Summary Question

1️⃣, 3️⃣, 5️⃣ The summary sentence notes that apple farmers use science and technology to grow apples successfully. This thought is best described in answer choices 1️⃣, 3️⃣, and 5️⃣. Answer choices 2️⃣ and 6️⃣ are minor points, so they are incorrect answers. Answer choice 4️⃣ contains information not mentioned in the passage, so it is also incorrect.

Vocabulary Review

Answers

A
1 deposits 2 apparent
3 convert 4 immunity
5 vegetation

B
1 b 2 a 3 a 4 a 5 b
6 b 7 a 8 a 9 b

Chapter 09

Prose Summary

Basic Practice

Answers 1 ⓒ 2 Ⓐ

Practice with Short Passages

A | Star Carr

Answers ②, ④, ⑤

Answer Explanation

The summary sentence points out that Starr Carr is important to the archaeology of England. This thought is best reflected in answer choices ②, ④, and ⑤. Answer choices ② and ③ are both minor points, so they are incorrect answers.

B | Skyscraper Design

Answers ①, ④, ⑤

Answer Explanation

The summary sentence points out that skyscrapers could be made in the 1800s thanks to two developments. This thought is best reflected in answer choices ①, ④, and ⑤. Answer choices ② and ③ are both minor points, so they are incorrect answers.

Practice with Long Passages

A | The Amazon Reef

Answers

1 Ⓑ 2 Ⓐ 3 ❷ 4 ②, ④, ⑤

Answer Explanation

1 Ⓑ In writing, "Since the 1970s, scientists had hypothesized that a reef existed in the area. The outflow of muddy sediment from the Amazon River makes the nearby water very murky," the author implies that the coral reef is found in water which is difficult to see in since the water is very murky.

2 Ⓐ The "it" that another team found is the reef.

3 ❷ The sentence before the second square reads, "Coral does not grow well in these conditions." The conditions referred to are a low salt content and a high acid content. The sentence to be added notes that "a lack of salt in the water will cause coral to die." The two sentences therefore go well together.

4 ②, ④, ⑤ The summary sentence points out that a coral reef in the Atlantic Ocean near the Amazon River was discovered in recent times. This thought is best reflected in answer choices ②, ④, and ⑤. Answer choice ① contains information that is not found in the passage, so it is incorrect. And answer choice ③ is a minor point, so it is a wrong answer as well.

Vocabulary

- **hypothesize** = to believe; to theorize
- **choppy** = rough
- **suitable** = appropriate; acceptable
- **shallow** = not deep

B | Michael Faraday

Answers

1 Ⓓ 2 ⓒ 3 Ⓐ 4 ③, ④, ⑤

Answer Explanation

1 Ⓓ The passage notes, "As a result, he did not receive a proper education. He dropped out of school at the age of thirteen to work at a bookshop. There, he read science books in his free time."

2 ⓒ When Faraday worked as the apprentice of Sir Humphry Davy, he was a trainee.

3 Ⓐ The passage reads, "This became the principle upon which modern refrigeration is based," and, "Faraday did work in the field of electromagnetism as well. He started by doing basic experiments. They led him to find out that moving a magnet over

a wire could produce electricity in the wire. This is called electromagnetic induction. It is a form of kinetic energy. Modern electric motors rely on this method to make electricity." In addition, the author writes, "He learned that a magnetic field caused the plane of a light source to rotate. This is used to study remote sensing in magnetic fields. It also has applications for fiber optic systems used today." These all imply that many of Faraday's discoveries have uses in modern times.

4 ③, ④, ⑤ The summary sentence points out that Michael Faraday's discoveries helped advance scientific knowledge. This thought is best reflected in answer choices ③, ④, and ⑤. Answer choices ① and ② are minor points, so they are both incorrect answers.

Vocabulary

- **electromagnetism** = the science of electric and magnetic fields
- **liquefaction** = the act of making something a liquid
- **principle** = an accepted rule or belief
- **rotate** = to turn around in a circle

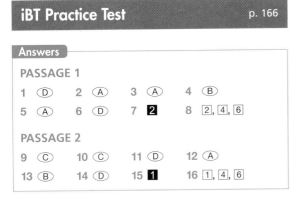

iBT Practice Test　　　　　p. 166

Answers

PASSAGE 1

| 1 | Ⓓ | 2 | Ⓐ | 3 | Ⓐ | 4 | Ⓑ |
| 5 | Ⓐ | 6 | Ⓓ | 7 | ❷ | 8 | ②, ④, ⑥ |

PASSAGE 2

| 9 | Ⓒ | 10 | Ⓒ | 11 | Ⓓ | 12 | Ⓐ |
| 13 | Ⓑ | 14 | Ⓓ | 15 | ❶ | 16 | ①, ④, ⑥ |

PASSAGE 1

Answer Explanation

1 **Factual Information Question**

　Ⓓ The author writes, "The woolly mammoth was an enormous elephantlike animal that once lived across the northern parts of Eurasia and North America."

2 **Rhetorical Purpose Question**

　Ⓐ In writing, "The mammoth flourished during the last ice age. It was much better adapted to cold climates than most other animals and humans were. When the last ice age ended, the glaciers retreated, and vegetation began growing again in many places. This could have been an advantage to the mammoth, an herbivore. But it also led to various animals encroaching on its territory, which resulted

in increasing competition for food sources. The more southerly mammoth herds died out first. Over time, the surviving mammoths migrated north to find better feeding grounds," the author points out how the end of the last ice age affected the woolly mammoth.

3 **Vocabulary Question**

　Ⓐ A remote island is one that is distant from other land.

4 **Factual Information Question**

　Ⓑ The passage reads, "Scientists believe some St. Paul mammoths died of thirst during a dry spell 5,600 years ago. Others also likely ate all the limited amount of vegetation on the island, making them starve to death."

5 **Reference Question**

　Ⓐ The "it" that could support a bigger woolly mammoth population was Wrangel Island.

6 **Negative Factual Information Question**

　Ⓓ There is no mention in the paragraph of how the woolly mammoths got to Wrangel Island.

7 **Insert Text Question**

　❷ The sentence before the second square reads, "It was much better adapted to cold climates than most other animals and humans were." The sentence to be added points out one of the adaptations—the long hair—that allowed it to survive in cold climates. The two sentences therefore go well together.

8 **Prose Summary Question**

　②, ④, ⑥ The summary sentence points out that there were multiple reasons why the woolly mammoth went extinct. This thought is best reflected in answer choices ②, ④, and ⑥. Answer choices ① and ③ are minor points, so they are both incorrect. Answer choice ⑤ contains information that is not in the passage, so it is a wrong answer as well.

PASSAGE 2

Answer Explanation

9 **Vocabulary Question**

　Ⓒ When the two sides clashed with one another, they fought against each other.

10 **Factual Information Question**

　Ⓒ The author notes, "Native Americans regarded land as being something that everyone in the community could use though. To them, all of nature was for everyone. Agreements between tribes often set boundaries. But within a tribal area, no person owned any land."

11 Negative Factual Information Question

Ⓓ There is no mention in the paragraph about why each of the two cultures was so different in its attitudes toward the roles of women.

12 Rhetorical Purpose Question

Ⓐ The author focuses on how Native Americans thought of trade in writing, "Natives considered trade more as a ceremonial activity. It was a way to build relationships with others. It often involved exchanging gifts. The giving and receiving of gifts was considered an integral part of tribal life. Acquiring gifts led to greater status while giving them showed generosity."

13 Factual Information Question

Ⓑ It is written, "The Europeans did not understand this importance. Thus they often unintentionally insulted Natives during trade talks."

14 Vocabulary Question

Ⓓ When there is an inevitable result, then the result is predictable.

15 Insert Text Question

■ The sentence before the first square reads, "So they wanted to get the best deal for the least amount." The sentence to be added follows up on this sentence by explaining that the Europeans were focused on making as much money as they could. Thus the two sentences go well together.

16 Prose Summary Question

1, 4, 6 The summary sentence notes that there were a lot of cultural differences between the Europeans and the Native Americans in the New World. This thought is best described in answer choices 1, 4, and 6. Answer choice 5 is a minor point, so it is an incorrect answer. Answer choices 2 and 3 contain information not mentioned in the passage, so they are also incorrect.

▌Vocabulary Review p. 174

> **Answers**
>
> A
> | | |
> |---|---|
> | 1 invention | 2 shallow |
> | 3 herbivore | 4 limitations |
> | 5 artifacts | |
>
> B
> | 1 b | 2 b | 3 a | 4 a | 5 b |
> |---|---|---|---|---|
> | 6 b | 7 a | 8 b | 9 b | |

Chapter 10

Fill in a Table

▌Basic Practice p. 177

> **Answers**
>
> Two well-known tribes of Native Americans are the Cherokee and the Apache. <u>The Cherokee were one of the major tribes in the southeastern part of the United States. They were among the first tribes to make contact with European settlers after they arrived in the New World.</u> As for the Apache, they lived in the central part of North America. They dwelled primarily on the Great Plains. The Apache were nomadic hunter-gatherers. The men hunted bison, deer, and other animals while the women gathered nuts and berries. <u>The Cherokee had permanent settlements. They lived an agrarian lifestyle in which they farmed the land.</u> While both tribes fought wars against the United States government, <u>the Cherokees ended their battles in the 1700s.</u> The Apaches fought during the 1800s and even had some battles with the U.S. government in the 1920s.
>
> | | Cherokee | Apache |
> |---|---|---|
> | Southeastern United States | ✓ | |
> | Great Plains | | ✓ |
> | Nomads | | ✓ |
> | Permanent Dwellings | ✓ | |
> | Wars in the Eighteenth Century | ✓ | |
> | Wars in the Nineteenth Century | | ✓ |

Practice with Short Passages p. 178

A▏ Telescopes

> **Answers** Refracting Telescope: 3, 6
> Reflecting Telescope: 4, 5

Answer Explanation

About refracting telescopes, the author writes, "Refracting telescopes use lenses whereas reflecting telescopes rely upon mirrors. In 1611, Galileo Galilei became the first person to use a telescope to look at the stars. The one he used was a refractor with two lenses, (3)" and adds, "This lens, called the eyepiece, magnified the object being viewed. (6)" As for reflecting telescopes, the passage reads, "Sir Isaac Newton invented the reflecting telescope in 1680 (5). His telescope contained two mirrors. The first gathered light and sent it to the second mirror. (4)"

B | Economic Downturns

Answer Explanation

About recessions, the author writes, "Most recessions last a few months, but others may last up to two years, (2)," and adds, "In the United States, recessions frequently occur when wars conclude. For instance, there were recessions in both 1945, when World War II ended, and in 1953, when the fighting in the Korean War ceased. (6)" As for depressions, the passage reads, "However, most state that it is an extended period of economic decline lasting at least two years. (5) A country's economy may decline more than ten percent during this period. And the unemployment rate may be twenty percent or higher. (1)"

Practice with Long Passages   p. 180

A | Sleeping Positions

Answers
1 C   2 D   3 **4**
4 On the Stomach: 5, 7 On the Side: 1
   On the Back: 2, 6

Answer Explanation

1 C The "them" that are positive are these positions.

2 D There is no mention in the passage regarding how serious the neck pain people who sleep on the their sides suffer.

3 **4** The sentence before the fourth square reads, "In addition, individuals are more likely to suffer from nightmares when sleeping in this position." The sentence to be added mentions that "they" are "vivid and more easily remembered." The "they" in this sentence are the nightmares mentioned in the previous sentence. The two sentences therefore go well together.

4 On the Stomach: 5, 7
   On the Side: 1
   On the Back: 2, 6
   Regarding sleeping on the stomach, the author writes, "Sleeping on the stomach is considered the worst of the three major sleeping methods. (5) The primary reason for this is that stomach sleepers

need to turn their heads in order to breathe. This can cause stress both on their necks and their lower backs. (7)" As for sleeping on the side, the passage reads, "In addition, individuals are more likely to suffer from nightmares when sleeping in this position. (1)" And concerning sleeping on the back, it is written, "Most experts believe that sleeping on the back is the ideal sleeping position, (2)" and, "This position could also result in a person suffering from sleep apnea, a condition in which a person stops breathing for a short period of time. (6)"

Vocabulary

- **negative** = bad; not positive
- **restlessness** = being unable to relax or rest
- **esophagus** = the passage connecting the mouth to the stomach
- **snore** = to make a loud sound while one is sleeping

B | Types of Precipitation

Answers
1 C   2 A   3 D
4 Liquid: 3, 6 Frozen: 2, 4

Answer Explanation

1 C The author notes, "When these clouds become too heavy, they release their water droplets, which fall to the Earth as precipitation."

2 A In writing, "Rain falls when the water droplets are 0.5 millimeters or larger in diameter. Droplets smaller than that are considered drizzle," the author implies that drizzle is smaller than raindrops.

3 D The core which could be dust or something similar is the center.

4 Liquid: 3, 6 Frozen: 2, 4
   About liquid precipitation, the author writes, "Rain falls when the water droplets are 0.5 millimeters or larger in diameter. Droplets smaller than that are considered drizzle, (3)" and adds, "In some situations, rain may begin to fall from clouds but evaporates before it reaches the ground. (6)" As for frozen precipitation, the passage reads, "Snow frequently falls when the temperature is below zero. (4) Snowflakes consist of water droplets that freeze around a core that could be dust or something similar. Hail is another type of frozen precipitation. Hailstones are chunks of ice which usually fall during thunderstorms. Sleet starts as snow but then melts as it is falling to the ground. Then, these raindrops freeze again on their way down and become pellets of ice. (2)"

Vocabulary

- **ascend** = to rise; to go up
- **droplet** = a small bit of a liquid shaped like a drop
- **assume** = to believe to be true
- **pellet** = something small, round, and hard

iBT Practice Test   p. 184

Answers

PASSAGE 1

1 Ⓑ   2 Ⓑ   3 Ⓓ   4 Ⓐ

5 Ⓐ   6 Ⓑ   7 Ⓒ

8 Modern Humans: ②, ④, ⑦   Disease: ①, ③

PASSAGE 2

9 Ⓒ   10 Ⓐ   11 Ⓑ   12 Ⓓ

13 Ⓓ   14 Ⓑ   15 Ⓓ

16 Using Memories: ②, ⑦, ⑨

   Using the Suns and Stars: ①, ⑥

   Using Genetic Coding: ④, ⑧

PASSAGE 1

Answer Explanation

1 Negative Factual Information Question

Ⓑ There is no mention in the paragraph of what caused the Neanderthals to go extinct.

2 Vocabulary Question

Ⓑ When the interaction between the two species was fatal to the Neanderthals, then interacting with humans was deadly for them.

3 Reference Question

Ⓓ The "ones" that were much better were the tools.

4 Factual Information Question

Ⓐ The author writes, "Modern humans are thought to have arrived in Europe and Western Asia from Africa around 45,000 years ago. Within the next 5,000 years, the Neanderthals were gone."

5 Rhetorical Purpose Question

Ⓐ The author focuses on showing the humans and Neanderthals bred with each other in writing, "The DNA evidence shows that humans and Neanderthals interacted as the two bred with each other. A small percentage—less than four percent—of human DNA comes from Neanderthals."

6 Vocabulary Question

Ⓑ When a theory is intriguing, it is fascinating.

7 Inference Question

Ⓒ The passage reads, "When the Neanderthals disappeared, for some reason, forests began to vanish. They were then replaced by plains. This may have happened because ash from a massive volcanic eruption changed the temperatures and growing periods in the region. This would have hurt the Neanderthals' ability to get food. They hunted animals by ambushing them in forests. Their short, squat bodies were suitable for living in cold weather and for running short distances. Their bodies were not suitable for stalking game in warm climates over long distances on plains. So the change in the climate might have caused the Neanderthals to disappear." In discussing the possibility of a huge volcanic eruption killing the Neanderthals, the author implies that they may have died out due to a natural disaster.

8 Fill in a Table Question

Modern Humans: ②, ④, ⑦   Disease: ①, ③

About modern humans, the author writes, "Modern humans are thought to have arrived in Europe and Western Asia from Africa around 45,000 years ago. Within the next 5,000 years, the Neanderthals were gone. This suggests that the interaction between the two species was fatal for the Neanderthals. (④) Some experts believe they fought wars against each other. Modern humans then proved superior at making weapons and at coming up with battle tactics. The evidence for this is that modern humans had bows and arrows, which their opponents lacked. (②) While this theory appeals to many, there is no real evidence of wars between the two species. It may be true, however, that humans were better hunters and thus outcompeted the Neanderthals for limited food resources. A comparison of the tools that each used in the past shows that human ones were much better. (⑦)" Regarding disease, the passage reads, "It is possible that the close interaction between the two groups led to the rapid spread of diseases and then death. (③) Some speculate that humans carried diseases which the Neanderthals had no defense against. (①) The Neanderthals then got sick and could not recover."

PASSAGE 2

Answer Explanation

9 Vocabulary Question

Ⓒ When animals retain memories, they keep those memories.

10 Negative Factual Information Question

(A) There is no mention in the paragraph of the destination that butterflies go to on their migrations with regard to mental maps that animals may have.

11 Rhetorical Purpose Question

(B) In writing, "Biologists believe the monarch butterfly navigates by using the sun as it travels from Canada to Mexico," the author focuses on the fact that the monarch butterfly uses the sun to navigate.

12 Vocabulary Question

(D) When animals innately know where to go the first time they migrate, they naturally know where their destination is.

13 Sentence Simplification Question

(D) The sentence points out that another idea is that animals can smell the route that others of the same species followed before. This thought is best expressed by the sentence in answer choice (D).

14 Factual Information Question

(B) The passage reads, "Sea turtles also return to the same beach where they hatched to breed and to lay eggs."

15 Factual Information Question

(D) The author points out, "Homing pigeons appear to have the ability to sense the magnetic field and can use it to find their way. In some experiments, magnets were strapped to their backs. The pigeons' navigational skills were then disrupted."

16 Fill in a Table Question

Using Memories: ②, ⑦, ⑨
Using the Suns and Stars: ①, ⑥
Using Genetic Coding: ④, ⑧
About animals using memories to guide them, the author writes, "By following landmarks which they remember, they can navigate long distances. Basically, they form a mental map of their course by following these landmarks." (②)The author also mentions, "Migratory birds, for example, visit the same trees and ponds year after year on their journeys north and south," (⑦) and, "And gray whales swim along the Pacific coast of North America when they migrate between Alaskan and Mexican waters." (⑨) As for animals using the suns and stars to navigate, the author points out, "Experiments with the bird called the indigo bunting proved it uses the stars to navigate," (①) and, "The positions of the sun and the stars help other animals migrate. The angle of the sun above the horizon changes as one moves north and south. The sun also rises in the east and sets in the west,

making it a natural navigation tool . . . Other species that travel at night use the positions of the stars to assist them." (⑥) With regard to animals having genetic coding that helps them migrate, the author notes, "For example, salmon always return to the same stream where they hatched. It is as if the way there was encoded when they hatched from eggs," (④) and, "Some species of birds and insects seem to innately know where to go the first time they migrate. Biologists are unsure whether this is a genetic trait or if some other factor is at work." (⑧)

Vocabulary Review   p. 192

Answers

A
1 magnify   2 droplets
3 ascend   4 unemployment
5 lack
B
1 a   2 a   3 b   4 a   5 b
6 a   7 a   8 b   9 a

Actual Test

Answers

PASSAGE 1

1 (B)	2 (C)	3 (D)	4 (B)	5 (B)
6 (A)	7 (A)	8 (B)	9 ❸	
10 ①, ③, ⑥				

PASSAGE 2

11 (B)	12 (A)	13 (C)	14 (D)	15 (D)
16 (A)	17 (A)	18 (B)	19 ❶	
20 Honeybee: ④, ⑥, ⑦ Bumblebee: ②, ③				

PASSAGE 3

21 (C)	22 (A)	23 (B)	24 (A)	25 (D)
26 (C)	27 (D)	28 (B)	29 ❷	
30 ②, ③, ⑤				

1 Negative Factual Information Question

Ⓑ There is no mention in the passage about there being any oceans on Mars.

2 Sentence Simplification Question

Ⓒ The sentence points out that life might have existed on Mars, but nobody knows for sure. This thought is best expressed by the sentence in answer choice Ⓒ.

3 Factual Information Question

Ⓓ The passage reads, "Mars is smaller than Earth and also has less gravity and a thinner atmosphere. In addition, it has low temperatures and low atmospheric pressure. These conditions combined to allow evaporated water to escape into space."

4 Vocabulary Question

Ⓑ When carbon dioxide transforms from a solid state to a gaseous one, it changes its form.

5 Rhetorical Purpose Question

Ⓑ Most of the paragraph focuses on the role that the *Mars Reconnaissance Orbiter* played in finding water on Mars.

6 Inference Question

Ⓐ About the water on Mars, the author notes, "Other smaller patches of underground water have also been found, and more may be discovered in the future." Since "more may be discovered in the future," it can be inferred that nobody is sure how much water there is on Mars.

7 Factual Information Question

Ⓐ About hydrated salts, the passage reads, "If a layer of frozen ice is located just below the surface, the hydrated salts could melt it in warm conditions. Then, the water flows downhill."

8 Vocabulary Question

Ⓑ When a planet is not completely sterile, it means that the planet is not dead but that it has some life on it.

9 Insert Text Question

❸ The sentence before the third square reads, "The carbon dioxide undergoes sublimation and transforms from a solid state to a gaseous one." The sentence to be added explains why the carbon dioxide goes from a solid state to a gaseous one without becoming a liquid first. Since the sentence to be added explains the process of sublimation, the two sentences therefore go well together.

10 Prose Summary Question

⒈, ⒊, ⒍ The summary sentence points out that liquid, solid, and gaseous forms of water exist on Mars. This thought is best reflected in answer choices ⒈, ⒊, and ⒍. Answer choices ⒉ and ⒋ are minor points, so they are both incorrect. Answer choice ⒌ contains information that is not mentioned in the passage, so it is a wrong answer as well.

11 Factual Information Question

Ⓑ The author writes, "Honeybees and bumblebees are two insects that many people confuse with each other. While they share a few similarities, they also have a large number of differences."

12 Inference Question

Ⓐ In writing, "The three types are the solitary queen, a few male drones, and the numerous female worker bees," the author implies that there are more female bees than male ones.

13 Reference Question

Ⓒ The "ones" that bumblebees have that are more rounded are abdomen tips.

14 Vocabulary Question

Ⓓ When honeybees build nests in sheltered places, they are protected from enemies and other dangers.

15 Factual Information Question

Ⓓ About the bumblebee queen, the author writes, "In the spring, she starts a new colony and dies once the new queen hatches."

16 Negative Factual Information Question

Ⓐ There is no mention in the passage regarding how long it takes honeybees to make honey.

17 Vocabulary Question

Ⓐ When bumblebees sting because they are aggravated, they are annoyed with the animal that they are stinging.

18 Factual Information Question

Ⓑ About the waggle dance, the author notes, "They fly in circles and make various movements that appear as though the bees are dancing. However, they are simply informing other bees where food sources are, what they are, and how far away they are."

19 Insert Text Question

1 The sentence before the first square reads, "When the honeybee moves away, the stinger rips off. The damage this does to the bee's body results in its death." The sentence to be added points out that in dying, the bees sacrifice their lives to protect the hive. The two sentences therefore go well together.

20 Fill in a Table Question

Honeybee: ④, ⑥, ⑦ Bumblebee: ②, ③

About the honeybee, the author writes, "Honeybees collect nectar and pollen and return to their hives. There, they pass on the food to receiver workers, which then store it in cells, (④)" and adds, "Honeybees also have short tongues, so they lap up nectar from open flowers. (⑥)" The author also writes, "Honeybees also live in enormous colonies with more than 20,000 bees per hive. (⑦)" As for the bumblebee, the passage reads, "Bumblebees construct their nests close to or on the ground, (②)" and also notes, "Bumblebees rarely sting and only do so if they are aggravated. However, they are capable of stinging many times in a row. (③)"

PASSAGE 3
p. 210

Answer Explanations

21 Vocabulary Question

Ⓒ When people provided illumination in their homes, they put light in them.

22 Sentence Simplification Question

Ⓐ The sentence points out that the first practical use of electricity came with the invention of the light bulb. This thought is best expressed by the sentence in answer choice Ⓐ.

23 Rhetorical Purpose Question

Ⓑ The author focuses on the differences between AC and DC power in writing, "At the same time, inventor Nikola Tesla was developing alternating current, or AC, electrical power. The first AC power station in the United States was built near Niagara Falls in 1895. It sent electricity to nearby Buffalo, New York. A power war between Edison and Tesla over which system was better began. In the end, Tesla's AC power proved that it was better able to send electricity over long distances and that it was safer than DC power."

24 Inference Question

Ⓐ In writing, "In the end, Tesla's AC power proved that it was better able to send electricity over long distances and that it was safer than DC power," the author implies that AC power is more commonly used than DC power.

25 Vocabulary Question

Ⓓ When people had to make modifications in their homes, they had to make alterations in them.

26 Factual Information Question

Ⓒ The passage reads, "In many cases, the wires for new electrical systems used the same pathways as plumbing pipes. This was necessary in old brick and stone homes that lacked easy access for the new system."

27 Negative Factual Information Question

Ⓓ There is no mention in the passage of how much the electrical devices cost to purchase.

28 Factual Information Question

Ⓑ The passage reads, "Fireplaces were not needed, so they were no longer made in new homes. In places that had them, they became status symbols rather than practical devices for heating and cooking."

29 Insert Text Question

2 The sentence before the second square reads, "A power war between Edison and Tesla over which system was better began." The sentence to be added mentions both the battle that they fought and that it was later called "the War of the Currents." The two sentences therefore go well together.

30 Prose Summary Question

②, ③, ⑤ The summary sentence points out that developments in electricity changed both modern homes and lives. This thought is best reflected in answer choices ②, ③, and ⑤. Answer choices ①, ④, and ⑥ are all minor points, so they are incorrect answers.

Memo

Decoding the TOEFL® iBT

Basic

INTRODUCTION

For many learners of English, the TOEFL® iBT will be the most important standardized test they ever take. Unfortunately for a large number of these individuals, the material covered on the TOEFL® iBT remains a mystery to them, so they are unable to do well on the test. We hope that by using the *Decoding the TOEFL® iBT* series, individuals who take the TOEFL® iBT will be able to excel on the test and, in the process of using the book, may unravel the mysteries of the test and therefore make the material covered on the TOEFL® iBT more familiar to themselves.

The TOEFL® iBT covers the four main skills that a person must learn when studying any foreign language: reading, listening, speaking, and writing. The *Decoding the TOEFL® iBT* series contains books that cover all four of these skills. The *Decoding the TOEFL® iBT* series contains books with three separate levels for all four of the topics as well as the *Decoding the TOEFL® iBT Actual Test* books. These books are all designed to enable learners to utilize them to become better prepared to take the TOEFL® iBT. This book, *Decoding the TOEFL® iBT Reading Basic,* covers the reading aspect of the test. It is designed to help learners prepare for the Reading section of the TOEFL® iBT. Finally, the TOEFL® iBT underwent a number of changes in August 2019. This book—and the others in the series—takes those changes into account and incorporates them in the texts and questions, so readers of this second edition can be assured that they have up-to-date knowledge of the test.

Decoding the TOEFL® iBT Reading Basic can be used by learners who are taking classes and also by individuals who are studying by themselves. It contains ten chapters, each of which focuses on a different reading question, and one actual test at the end of the book. Each chapter contains explanations of the questions and how to answer them correctly. It also contains passages of varying lengths, and it focuses on the types of questions that are covered in the chapter. The passages and question types in *Decoding the TOEFL® iBT Reading Basic* are less difficult levels than those found on the TOEFL® iBT. Individuals who use *Decoding the TOEFL® iBT Reading Basic* will therefore be able to prepare themselves not only to take the TOEFL® iBT but also to perform well on the test.

We hope that everyone who uses *Decoding the TOEFL® iBT Reading Basic* will be able to become more familiar with the TOEFL® iBT and will additionally improve his or her score on the test. As the title of the book implies, we hope that learners can use it to crack the code on the TOEFL® iBT, to make the test itself less mysterious and confusing, and to get the highest grade possible. Finally, we hope that both learners and instructors can use this book to its full potential. We wish all of you the best of luck as you study English and prepare for the TOEFL® iBT, and we hope that *Decoding the TOEFL® iBT Reading Basic* can provide you with assistance during the course of your studies.

Michael A. Putlack
Stephen Poirier
Allen C. Jacobs

TABLE
OF
CONTENTS

ABOUT THE TOEFL® iBT READING SECTION

Changes in the Reading Section

TOEFL® underwent many changes in August of 2019. The following is an explanation of the changes that have been made to the Reading section.

Format

The number of passages that appear in the Reading section is either 3 or 4. The time given for the Reading section is either 54 (3 passages) or 72 (4 passages) minutes.

Passages

The length of each passage has been slightly shortened. A typical Reading passage is between 690 and 710 words. However, there are some passages with as few as 670 words.

In addition, there is a heavier emphasis on science topics. This includes topics such as biology, zoology, and astronomy.

There are sometimes pictures accompanying the text. They are used to provide visual evidence of various objects discussed in the passage. On occasion, there are also pictures used for glossary words.

The glossary typically defines 0-2 words or phrases.

Questions

There are only 10 questions per Reading passage now. This is a decrease from the 12-14 questions that were asked on previous tests.

Question Types

TYPE 1 Vocabulary Questions

Vocabulary questions require the test taker to understand specific words and phrases that are used in the passage. Each of these questions asks the test taker to select another word or phrase that is the most similar in meaning to a word or phrase that is highlighted. The vocabulary words that are highlighted are often important words, so knowing what these words mean can be critical for understanding the entire passage. The highlighted words typically have several different meanings, so test takers need to be careful to avoid selecting an answer choice simply because it is the most common meaning of the word or phrase.

- There are 1-3 Vocabulary questions per passage.
- Passages typically have 2 Vocabulary questions.

TYPE 2 Reference Questions

Reference questions require the test taker to understand the relationships between words and their referents in the passage. These questions most frequently ask the test taker to identify the antecedent of a pronoun. In many instances, the pronouns are words such as *he, she,* or *they* or *its, his, hers,* or *theirs.* However, in other instances, relative pronouns such as *which* or demonstrative pronouns such as *this* or *that* may be asked about instead.

- There are 0-1 Reference questions per passage. However, these questions rarely appear anymore.

TYPE 3 Factual Information Questions

Factual Information questions require the test taker to understand and be able to recognize facts that are mentioned in the passage. These questions may be about any facts or information that is explicitly covered in the passage. They may appear in the form of details, definitions, explanations, or other kinds of data. The facts which the questions ask about are typically found only in one part of the passage—often just in a sentence or two in one paragraph—and do not require a comprehensive understanding of the passage as a whole.

- There are 1-3 Factual Information questions per passage. There is an average of 2 of these questions per passage.
- Some Factual Information questions require test takers to understand the entire paragraph, not just one part of it, to find the correct answer.

TYPE 4 Negative Factual Information Questions

Negative Factual Information questions require the test taker to understand and be able to recognize facts that are mentioned in the passage. These questions may be about any facts or information that is explicitly covered in the passage. However, these questions ask the test taker to identify the incorrect information in the answer choices. Three of the four answer choices therefore contain correct information that is found in the passage. The answer the test taker must choose therefore either has incorrect information or information that is not mentioned in the passage.

- There are 0-2 Negative Factual Information questions per passage.

TYPE 5 Sentence Simplification Questions

Sentence Simplification questions require the test taker to select a sentence that best restates one that has been highlighted in the passage. These questions ask the test taker to recognize the main points in the sentence and to make sure that they are mentioned in the rewritten sentence. These rewritten sentences use words, phrases, and grammar that are different from the highlighted sentence. Sentence Simplification questions do not always appear in a passage. When they are asked, there is only one Sentence Simplification question per passage.

- There are 0-1 Sentence Simplification questions per passage.
- The answer choices for these questions are approximately half the length of the sentences being asked about.

TYPE 6 Inference Questions

Inference questions require the test taker to understand the argument that the passage is attempting to make. These questions ask the test taker to consider the information that is presented and then to come to a logical conclusion about it. The answers to these questions are never explicitly stated in the passage. Instead, the test taker must infer what the author means. These questions often deal with cause and effect or comparisons between two different things, ideas, events, or people.

- There are 0-2 Inference questions per passage. Most passages have at least 1 Inference question though.
- The difficulty level of these questions has increased. In some cases, test takers must be able to understand an entire paragraph rather than only a part of it.

TYPE 7 Rhetorical Purpose Questions

Rhetorical Purpose questions require the test taker to understand why the author mentioned or wrote about something in the passage. These questions ask the test taker to consider the reasoning behind the information being presented in the passage. For these questions, the function—not the meaning—of the material is the most important aspect for the test taker to be aware of. The questions often focus on the relationship between the information mentioned or covered either in paragraphs or individual sentences in the passage and the purpose or intention of the information that is given.

- There are 1-2 Rhetorical Purpose questions per passage.
- There is a special emphasis on these questions. Some questions ask about entire sentences, not just words or phrases.

TYPE 8 Insert Text Questions

Insert Text questions require the test taker to determine where in the passage another sentence should be placed. These questions ask the test taker to consider various aspects, including grammar, logic, connecting words, and flow, when deciding where the new sentence best belongs. Insert Text questions do not always appear in a passage. When they are asked, there is only one Insert Text question per passage. This question always appears right before the last question.

- There are 0-1 Insert Text questions per passage.
- There is a special emphasis on these questions. Almost every passage now has 1 Insert Text question.

TYPE 9 Prose Summary Questions

Prose Summary questions require the test taker to understand the main point of the passage and then to select sentences which emphasize the main point. These questions present a sentence which is essentially a thesis statement for the entire passage. The sentence synthesizes the main points of the passage. The test taker must then choose three out of six sentences that most closely describe points mentioned in the introductory sentence. As for the other three choices, they describe minor points, have incorrect information, or contain information that does not appear in the passage, so they are all therefore incorrect. This is always the last question asked about a Reading passage, but it does not always appear. Instead, a Fill in a Table question may appear in its place.

- There are 0-1 Prose Summary questions per passage.
- There is a special emphasis on these questions. Almost every passage now has 1 Prose Summary question.

TYPE 10 Fill in a Table Questions

Fill in a Table questions require the test taker to have a comprehensive understanding of the entire passage. These questions typically break the passage down into two—or sometimes three—main points or themes. The test taker must then read a number of sentences or phrases and determine which of the points or themes the sentences or phrases refer to. These questions may ask the test taker to consider cause and effect, to compare and contrast, or to understand various theories or ideas covered. This is always the last question asked about a Reading passage, but it does not always appear. Instead, a Prose Summary question may appear in its place.

- There are 0-1 Fill in a Table questions per passage.
- These questions rarely appear anymore. Prose Summary questions are much more common than Fill in a Table questions.

HOW TO USE THIS BOOK

Decoding the TOEFL® iBT Reading Basic is designed to be used either as a textbook in a classroom environment or as a study guide for individual learners. There are 10 chapters in this book. Each chapter provides comprehensive information about one type of reading question. There are 6 sections in each chapter, which enable you to build up your skills on a particular reading question. At the end of the book, there is one actual test of the Reading section of the TOEFL® iBT.

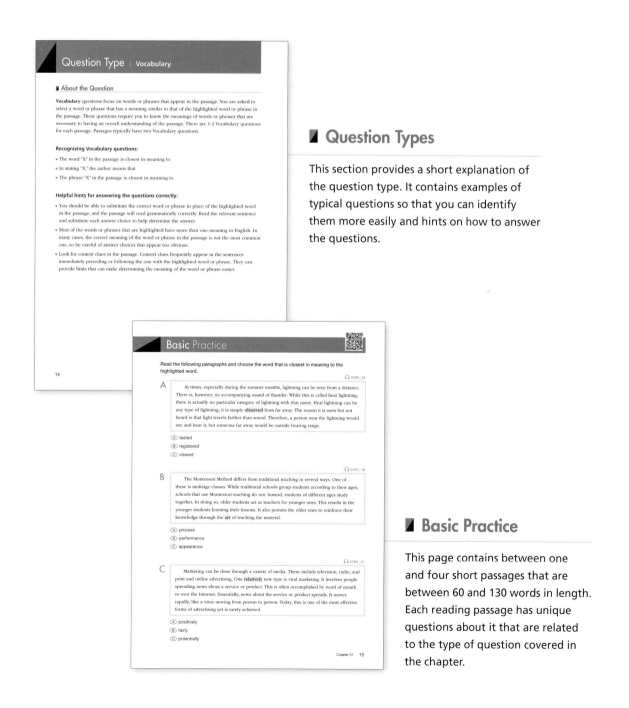

◼ Question Types

This section provides a short explanation of the question type. It contains examples of typical questions so that you can identify them more easily and hints on how to answer the questions.

◼ Basic Practice

This page contains between one and four short passages that are between 60 and 130 words in length. Each reading passage has unique questions about it that are related to the type of question covered in the chapter.

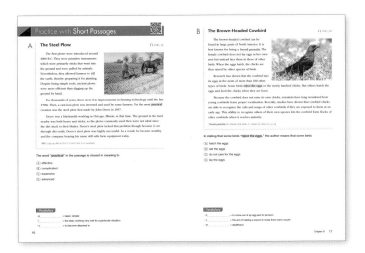

■ Practice with Short Passages

....

This part contains two reading passages that are between 125 and 175 words long. Each reading passage contains one question of the type covered in the chapter and has a short vocabulary section.

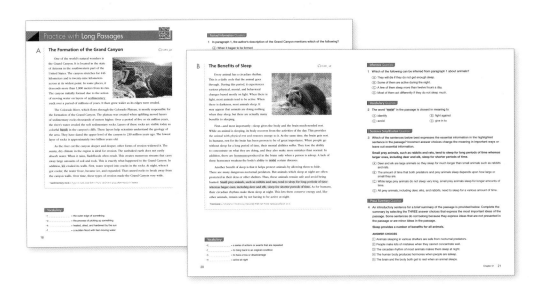

■ Practice with Long Passages

....

This section has two reading passages that are between 250 and 300 words long. Each reading passage contains four questions. There is one question about the type of question covered in the chapter. The other three questions are of various types. There is also a short vocabulary section after each passage to test your knowledge.

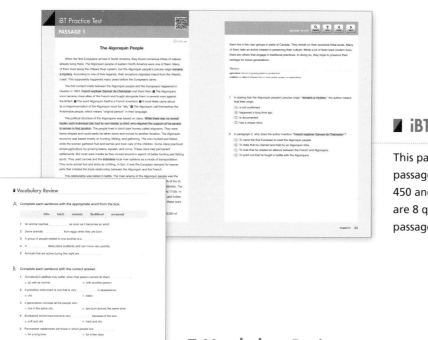

iBT Practice Test

This part has two reading passages that are between 450 and 500 words, and there are 8 questions for each passage.

Vocabulary Review

This section has two vocabulary exercises using words that appear in the passages in the chapter.

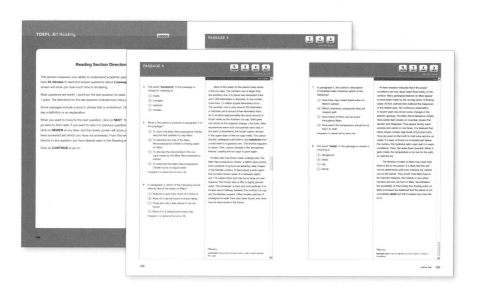

Actual Test (at the end of the book)

This section has three full-length reading passages with 10 questions each.

Chapter **01**

Vocabulary

Question Type | Vocabulary

◢ About the Question

Vocabulary questions focus on words or phrases that appear in the passage. You are asked to select a word or phrase that has a meaning similar to that of the highlighted word or phrase in the passage. These questions require you to know the meanings of words or phrases that are necessary to having an overall understanding of the passage. There are 1-3 Vocabulary questions for each passage. Passages typically have two Vocabulary questions.

Recognizing Vocabulary questions:

- The word "X" in the passage is closest in meaning to

- In stating "X," the author means that

- The phrase "X" in the passage is closest in meaning to

Helpful hints for answering the questions correctly:

- You should be able to substitute the correct word or phrase in place of the highlighted word in the passage, and the passage will read grammatically correctly. Read the relevant sentence and substitute each answer choice to help determine the answer.

- Most of the words or phrases that are highlighted have more than one meaning in English. In many cases, the correct meaning of the word or phrase in the passage is not the most common one, so be careful of answer choices that appear too obvious.

- Look for context clues in the passage. Context clues frequently appear in the sentences immediately preceding or following the one with the highlighted word or phrase. They can provide hints that can make determining the meaning of the word or phrase easier.

Read the following paragraphs and choose the word that is closest in meaning to the highlighted word.

CH01_1A

A

At times, especially during the summer months, lightning can be seen from a distance. There is, however, no accompanying sound of thunder. While this is called heat lightning, there is actually no particular category of lightning with that name. Heat lightning can be any type of lightning; it is simply observed from far away. The reason it is seen but not heard is that light travels farther than sound. Therefore, a person near the lightning would see and hear it, but someone far away would be outside hearing range.

(A) tested

(B) registered

(C) viewed

CH01_1B

B

The Montessori Method differs from traditional teaching in several ways. One of these is multiage classes. While traditional schools group students according to their ages, schools that use Montessori teaching do not. Instead, students of different ages study together. In doing so, older students act as teachers for younger ones. This results in the younger students learning their lessons. It also permits the older ones to reinforce their knowledge through the act of teaching the material.

(A) process

(B) performance

(C) appearance

CH01_1C

C

Marketing can be done through a variety of media. These include television, radio, and print and online advertising. One relatively new type is viral marketing. It involves people spreading news about a service or product. This is often accomplished by word of mouth or over the Internet. Essentially, news about the service or product spreads. It moves rapidly, like a virus moving from person to person. Today, this is one of the most effective forms of advertising yet is rarely achieved.

(A) positively

(B) fairly

(C) potentially

A | **The Steel Plow**

🎧 CH01_2A

The first plows were introduced around 4000 B.C. They were primitive instruments which were primarily sticks that went into the ground and were pulled by animals. Nevertheless, they allowed farmers to **till** the earth, thereby preparing it for planting. Despite being simple tools, ancient plows were more efficient than digging up the ground by hand.

For thousands of years, there were few improvements in farming technology until the late 1700s. Then, a cast-iron plow was invented and used by some farmers. Yet the most practical creation was the steel plow first made by John Deere in 1837.

Deere was a blacksmith working in Chicago, Illinois, at that time. The ground in the land nearby was both heavy and sticky, so the plows commonly used then were not ideal since the dirt stuck to their blades. Deere's steel plow lacked that problem though because it cut through dirt easily. Deere's steel plow was highly successful. As a result, he became wealthy, and the company bearing his name still sells farm equipment today.

*till: to dig up dirt so that it is not hard and compact

The word "practical" in the passage is closest in meaning to

Ⓐ effective

Ⓑ complicated

Ⓒ expensive

Ⓓ advanced

Vocabulary

• p_____ = basic; simple

• i_____ = the best; working very well for a particular situation

• s_____ = to become attached to

B The Brown-Headed Cowbird

The brown-headed cowbird can be found in large parts of North America. It is best known for being a **brood parasite**. The female cowbird does not lay eggs in her own nest but instead lays them in those of other birds. When the eggs hatch, the chicks are then raised by other species of birds.

Research has shown that the cowbird lays its eggs in the nests of more than 100 other types of birds. Some birds reject the eggs or the newly hatched chicks. But others hatch the eggs and feed the chicks when they are born.

Because the cowbird does not raise its own chicks, scientists have long wondered how young cowbirds learn proper vocalization. Recently, studies have shown that cowbird chicks are able to recognize the calls and songs of other cowbirds if they are exposed to them at an early age. This ability to recognize others of their own species lets the cowbird form flocks of other cowbirds when it reaches maturity.

*brood parasite: an animal that relies on others to raise its young

---

In stating that some birds "reject the eggs," the author means that some birds

Ⓐ hatch the eggs

Ⓑ eat the eggs

Ⓒ do not care for the eggs

Ⓓ lay the eggs

Vocabulary

- h_____ = to come out of an egg and to be born
- v_____ = the act of making a sound or noise from one's mouth
- m_____ = adulthood

A The Formation of the Grand Canyon

🎧 CH01_3A

One of the world's natural wonders is the Grand Canyon. It is located in the state of Arizona in the southwestern part of the United States. The canyon stretches for 446 kilometers and is twenty-nine kilometers across at its widest point. In some places, it descends more than 1,800 meters from its rim. The canyon initially formed due to the action of moving water on layers of **sedimentary rock** over a period of millions of years. It then grew wider as its edges were eroded.

The Colorado River, which flows through the Colorado Plateau, is mostly responsible for the formation of the Grand Canyon. The plateau was created when uplifting moved layers of sedimentary rocks thousands of meters higher. Over a period of five or six million years, the river's water eroded the soft sedimentary rocks. Layers of these rocks are visible today as colorful bands in the canyon's cliffs. These layers help scientists understand the geology of the area. They have dated the upper level of the canyon to 230 million years ago. The lowest layer of rocks is approximately two billion years old.

As the river cut the canyon deeper and deeper, other forms of erosion widened it. The sunny, dry climate in the region is ideal for erosion. The sunbaked earth does not easily absorb water. When it rains, flashfloods often result. This creates numerous streams that carry away large amounts of soil and rock. This is exactly what happened to the Grand Canyon. In addition, ice eroded its walls. First, water seeped into cracks in the rocks. At night, when it got cooler, the water froze, became ice, and expanded. That caused rocks to break away from the canyon walls. Over time, these types of erosion made the Grand Canyon very wide.

*sedimentary rock: a type of rock that forms from sediment and often exists in layers

Vocabulary

- r_____ = the outer edge of something
- u_____ = the process of picking up something
- s_____ = heated, dried, and hardened by the sun
- f_____ = a sudden flood with fast-moving water

1   In paragraph 1, the author's description of the Grand Canyon mentions which of the following?

   (A) When it began to be formed

   (B) How high above sea level it is

   (C) How many people visit it each year

   (D) What its dimensions are

2   The word "**bands**" in the passage is closest in meaning to

   (A) groups

   (B) designs

   (C) sets

   (D) strips

3   In paragraph 3, the author uses "**ice**" as an example of

   (A) a type of erosion that widened the Grand Canyon

   (B) something that rarely eroded the Grand Canyon

   (C) a method of erosion that made the Grand Canyon deeper

   (D) something accompanying flashfloods in the Grand Canyon

4   Select the appropriate statements from the answer choices and match them to the period of the Grand Canyon's formation to which they relate. TWO of the answer choices will NOT be used.

Initial Formation	Widening of the Canyon
•	•
•	•

STATEMENTS

☐1 Resulted in visible layers of rocks
☐2 Had rocks broken by ice
☐3 Were rocks carried away by flashfloods

☐4 Was caused by the Colorado River
☐5 Had sand blown away by the wind
☐6 Started happening two billion years ago

The Benefits of Sleep

Every animal has a circadian rhythm. This is a daily cycle that the animal goes through. During this period, it experiences various physical, mental, and behavioral changes based mostly on light. When there is light, most animals tend to be active. When there is darkness, most animals sleep. It may appear that animals are doing nothing when they sleep, but there are actually many benefits to sleeping.

First—and most importantly—sleep gives the body and the brain much-needed rest. While an animal is sleeping, its body recovers from the activities of the day. This provides the animal with physical rest and restores energy to it. At the same time, the brain gets rest. In humans, rest for the brain has been proven to be of great importance. When people go without sleep for a long period of time, their mental abilities suffer. They lose the ability to concentrate on what they are doing, and they also make more mistakes than normal. In addition, there are **hormones** produced in the brain only when a person is asleep. A lack of these hormones weakens the body's ability to resist certain diseases.

Another benefit of sleep is that it helps protect animals by allowing them to hide. There are many dangerous nocturnal predators. But animals which sleep at night are often protected in their dens or other shelters. Thus, these animals remain safe and avoid being hunted. Small prey animals, such as rabbits and rats, tend to sleep for long periods of time whereas larger ones, including deer and elk, sleep for shorter periods of time. As for humans, their circadian rhythms make them sleep at night. This lets them conserve energy and, like other animals, remain safe by not having to be active at night.

*hormone: a substance created by the body that can have various effects on it

Vocabulary

- c _____ = a series of actions or events that are repeated
- r _____ = to bring back to an original condition
- s _____ = to have a loss or disadvantage
- n _____ = active at night

1   Which of the following can be inferred from paragraph 1 about animals?

    Ⓐ They will die if they do not get enough sleep.

    Ⓑ Some of them are active during the night.

    Ⓒ A few of them sleep more than twelve hours a day.

    Ⓓ Most of them act differently if they do not sleep much.

Vocabulary Question

2   The word "**resist**" in the passage is closest in meaning to

    Ⓐ identify   Ⓑ fight against

    Ⓒ avoid   Ⓓ give in to

Sentence Simplification Question

3   Which of the sentences below best expresses the essential information in the highlighted sentence in the passage? Incorrect answer choices change the meaning in important ways or leave out essential information.

    Small prey animals, such as rabbits and rats, tend to sleep for long periods of time whereas larger ones, including deer and elk, sleep for shorter periods of time.

    Ⓐ Deer and elk are large animals so they sleep for much longer than small animals such as rabbits and rats.

    Ⓑ The amount of time that both predators and prey animals sleep depends upon how large or small they are.

    Ⓒ While large prey animals do not sleep very long, small prey animals sleep for longer amounts of time.

    Ⓓ All prey animals, including deer, elks, and rabbits, need to sleep for a various amount of time.

Prose Summary Question

4   An introductory sentence for a brief summary of the passage is provided below. Complete the summary by selecting the **THREE** answer choices that express the most important ideas of the passage. Some sentences do not belong because they express ideas that are not presented in the passage or are minor ideas in the passage.

    Sleep provides a number of benefits for all animals.

    ANSWER CHOICES

    1 Animals sleeping in various shelters are safe from nocturnal predators.

    2 People make lots of mistakes when they cannot concentrate well.

    3 The circadian rhythm of most animals makes them sleep at night.

    4 The human body produces hormones when people are asleep.

    5 The brain and the body both get to rest when an animal sleeps.

The Algonquin People

When the first Europeans arrived in North America, they found numerous tribes of natives already living there. The Algonquin people of eastern North America were one of them. Many of them lived along the Ottawa River system, but the Algonquin people's precise origin remains a mystery. According to one of their legends, their ancestors migrated inland from the Atlantic coast. This supposedly happened many years before the Europeans came.

The first contact made between the Algonquin people and the Europeans happened in Quebec in 1603. French explorer Samuel de Champlain met them then. ∎ The Algonquins soon became close allies of the French and fought alongside them in several wars against the British. ❷ The word Algonquin itself is a French invention. ❸ It most likely came about as a mispronunciation of the Algonquin word for "ally." ❹ The Algonquin call themselves the Anishinabe people, which means "original person" in their language.

The political structure of the Algonquins was based on clans. While there was no overall leader, each individual clan had its own leader, a chief, who required the support of his people to remain in that position. The people lived in birch bark homes called wigwams. They were dome shaped and could easily be taken down and moved to another location. The Algonquin economy was based mostly on hunting, fishing, and gathering. The men hunted and fished while the women gathered fruit and berries and took care of the children. Some clans practiced simple agriculture by growing beans, squash, and corn. These clans had permanent settlements. But most were mobile as they moved around in search of better hunting and fishing spots. They used canoes and the extensive local river systems as a mode of transportation. They wore animal furs and skins as clothing. In fact, it was the European demand for beaver pelts that initiated the trade relationship between the Algonquin and the French.

This relationship was tested in battle. The main enemy of the Algonquin people was the Iroquois Confederacy. This was a strong coalition of tribes that mostly resided south of the St. Lawrence River and Lake Ontario. The Iroquois allied themselves with the British colonists. The French and British fought several wars for control of North America in the 1600s and 1700s. In the end, the British and Iroquois defeated the French and Algonquins in the French and Indian War, which was fought from 1744 to 1763. The Algonquins suffered many losses in these wars and were also weakened by diseases carried by the Europeans.

Despite these setbacks, the Algonquin people did not die out. Today, around 15,000 of them live in ten clan groups in parts of Canada. They reside on their ancestral tribal lands. Many of them take an active interest in preserving their culture. While a lot of them lead modern lives, there are others that engage in traditional practices. In doing so, they hope to preserve their heritage for future generations.

*Glossary

agriculture: the act of growing plants to provide food

coalition: an alliance between two or more people, groups, or organizations

1   In stating that the Algonquin people's precise origin "remains a mystery," the author means that their origin

    (A) is not confirmed

    (B) happened a long time ago

    (C) is documented

    (D) has a unique story

2   In paragraph 2, why does the author mention "French explorer Samuel de Champlain"?

    (A) To name the first European to meet the Algonquin people

    (B) To state that he claimed land held by an Algonquin tribe

    (C) To note that he created an alliance between the French and Algonquins

    (D) To point out that he fought in battle with the Algonquins

3 Which of the sentences below best expresses the essential information in the highlighted sentence in the passage? Incorrect answer choices change the meaning in important ways or leave out essential information.

While there was no overall leader, each individual clan had its own leader, a chief, who required the support of his people to remain in that position.

  Ⓐ The clans got support for their own leaders, who then competed for the role of overall leader.

  Ⓑ Each of the chiefs in the clans had to be supported by the members, or they would lose their positions.

  Ⓒ Every clan had a leader who needed backing from the people, but no single leader existed.

  Ⓓ Most of the people did not want an overall leader, so there were just clan leaders instead.

4 The word "extensive" in the passage is closest in meaning to

  Ⓐ complicated   Ⓑ diverse

  Ⓒ broad   Ⓓ fertile

5 In paragraph 4, the author's description of the Iroquois Confederacy mentions all of the following EXCEPT:

  Ⓐ who its members fought wars with

  Ⓑ how many tribes were a part of it

  Ⓒ where its member tribes lived

  Ⓓ which war it fought against the Algonquins

6 According to paragraph 5, many Algonquins today lead traditional lives because

  Ⓐ they want their offspring to learn their customs

  Ⓑ they have no interest in modern-day culture

  Ⓒ there are no modern conveniences on tribal lands

  Ⓓ they cannot afford to live modern lives

7 Look at the four squares [■] that indicate where the following sentence could be added to the passage.

This relationship lasted for 150 years until the French were driven away from North America.

Where would the sentence best fit?

Click on a square [■] to add the sentence to the passage.

8 **Directions:** An introductory sentence for a brief summary of the passage is provided below. Complete the summary by selecting the THREE answer choices that express the most important ideas of the passage. Some sentences do not belong because they express ideas that are not presented in the passage or are minor ideas in the passage. **This question is worth 2 points.**

The Algonquin people have had relationships with Europeans ever since they met in North America.

-
-
-

ANSWER CHOICES

1 Many Algonquin people live on tribal lands but practice modern ways there these days.

2 The Algonquins and their French allies were defeated by England in the French and Indian War.

3 The Algonquin tribes may have lived near the Atlantic Ocean before moving inland.

4 Europeans engaged in trade for animal furs with the Algonquin people.

5 The Algonquin people mostly hunted and gathered, but they did some farming, too.

6 The French allied themselves with the Algonquins soon after they met in 1603.

The Effects of Glaciers on Land Formation

Glaciers are giant masses of ice that move slowly across the land. They normally form in the Arctic and Antarctic regions but may also be created in mountain ranges at high altitudes. Most glaciers move only a few centimeters each year. Over an extensive period of time, they can travel great distances. As they move forward and backward, they carve up the land beneath them. They also transport a large amount of soil and rock debris, which is pushed ahead of them and to their sides.

The most notable effect of glaciers is how they depress the land under them. Depending upon the composition of the soil and the rock, the land may retain its former shape. However, the passing of a glacier typically leaves large depressions in the soil. These fill with water and form lakes. The northern regions of Canada, Scandinavia, and Russia are dotted with many lakes created during the last ice age.

The passing of a glacier often leaves behind a trough-shaped valley. This is most notable in mountain ranges where glaciers form. The sides of these valleys are steep with near-vertical walls of rock. The famous long fjords of Scandinavia were created in this manner during the last ice age thousands of years ago. When the glaciers retreated, new valleys were opened to the ocean, whose waters flooded in to create deep-water fjords.

Three other major types of land formations occur due to glacial erosion. They are cirques, arêtes, and horns. A cirque forms when a glacier erodes a mountainside. It is a bowl-shaped depression which has a steeper side facing uphill, giving it a tilted appearance. Cirques are especially common in the Alps Mountains of Europe. An arête is a sharp ridge of rock that forms when two glaciers meet as they move. The glaciers erode the land partially, not entirely, and they leave behind a sharp, steep, narrow ridge of rock. A horn forms when several glaciers erode all of the rock around a mountain and leave a tall, narrow peak. There are often several arêtes created around its base.

When a glacier halts its movement, the soil and the rock debris it carries form ridges called moraines. These are narrow ridges that form in front of and on the sides of glaciers. When the ice begins melting and the glacier retreats, it leaves behind these ridges. Geologists use moraines to locate the historic progress of glaciers. Another land formation, called a kame, is a small mound with an irregular shape that is formed by water carrying debris from under a glacier.

Water flowing on or beneath a glacier also creates beds of gravel. When the ice retreats, these leave behind long, thin gravel beds called eskers. Another formation is called the drumlin. A drumlin is a long, teardrop-shaped hill of soil and rock that most likely forms when ice carves it out of the soil as a glacier moves across the land.

*Glossary

depress: to put into a lower position

fjord: a long, narrow part of the ocean with steep sides and which is often formed by glacial action

9 The phrase "carve up" in the passage is closest in meaning to

   Ⓐ move

   Ⓑ rearrange

   Ⓒ erode

   Ⓓ cut

10 According to paragraph 1, which of the following is true about glaciers?

   Ⓐ They may move a few centimeters or many meters each year.

   Ⓑ They contain not only ice and snow but also soil and rock debris.

   Ⓒ They can form on mountains that are high above the ground.

   Ⓓ They are both small and large masses of ice and snow.

11 According to paragraph 2, glaciers create land that will become lakes by

   Ⓐ pushing down on the land below them as they move

   Ⓑ moving soil and rock debris to levels higher than the land around them

   Ⓒ carving out large sections of rock from the ground

   Ⓓ melting partially and causing the water to fill places on the ground

12 According to paragraph 3, which of the following is NOT true about fjords?

Ⓐ They are filled with water and connected to the ocean.

Ⓑ There are some that are several million years old.

Ⓒ There are long ones found in the region called Scandinavia.

Ⓓ They have an appearance that makes them look like valleys.

13 In paragraph 4, which of the following can be inferred about the Alps Mountains?

Ⓐ Cirques can be found nowhere in the world but in them.

Ⓑ It is possible to see cirques, arêtes, and horns in them.

Ⓒ They do not have any bowl-shaped depressions.

Ⓓ Many of them were eroded by the actions of glaciers.

14 The word "halts" in the passage is closest in meaning to

Ⓐ reduces

Ⓑ stops

Ⓒ accelerates

Ⓓ changes

15 Which of the sentences below best expresses the essential information in the highlighted sentence in the passage? Incorrect answer choices change the meaning in important ways or leave out essential information.

A drumlin is a long, teardrop-shaped hill of soil and rock that most likely forms when ice carves it out of the soil as a glacier moves across the land.

Ⓐ A drumlin is a hill that is formed of soil, rock, and ice due to the movement of a glacier across the land.

Ⓑ When a drumlin forms, ice in a glacier is responsible for carving it out as the glacier moves forward or backward.

Ⓒ A drumlin is formed by the movement of a glacier and looks like a long hill of soil or rock in the shape of a teardrop.

Ⓓ The appearance of a drumlin is that of a long hill in the shape of a teardrop, and there is often ice on top of it.

16 Directions: An introductory sentence for a brief summary of the passage is provided below. Complete the summary by selecting the THREE answer choices that express the most important ideas of the passage. Some sentences do not belong because they express ideas that are not presented in the passage or are minor ideas in the passage. **This question is worth 2 points.**

The movement of glaciers causes a wide variety of changes to the land beneath them.

-

-

-

ANSWER CHOICES

1. The majority of glaciers move a tiny amount each year, but some can move more quickly.

2. Glaciers that move in mountain ranges are known to create cirques, arêtes, and horns.

3. Some glaciers create lakes when they move and depress the land over which they travel.

4. Moraines are formed when glaciers stop moving and soil and rock debris pile up.

5. The fjords that glaciers formed years ago were filled with water coming from rivers.

6. Some glaciers form in mountains while others are found in the Arctic and Antarctic regions.

◼ Vocabulary Review

A Complete each sentence with the appropriate word from the box.

tribe	hatch	maturity	flashflood	nocturnal

1 An animal reaches _____ as soon as it becomes an adult.

2 Some animals _____ from eggs when they are born.

3 A group of people related to one another is a _____.

4 A _____ takes place suddenly and can move very quickly.

5 Animals that are active during the night are _____.

B Complete each sentence with the correct answer.

1 Somebody's abilities may **suffer** when that person cannot do them _____.

   a. as well as normal   b. with another person

2 A **primitive** instrument is one that is very _____ in appearance.

   a. old   b. basic

3 A **generation** includes all the people who _____.

   a. live in the same city   b. are born around the same time

4 **Sunbaked** bricks have become very _____ because of the sun.

   a. soft and old   b. hard and dry

5 **Permanent** settlements are those in which people live _____.

   a. for a long time   b. for a few days

6 People at the **rim** of the Grand Canyon are standing at its _____.

   a. bottom   b. edge

7 When trade is **initiated**, one person _____ with another one.

   a. hopes to do business   b. begins doing business

8 Physical rest can **restore** energy to people by _____.

   a. giving them more of it   b. taking it from them

9 **Uplifting** is the process through which rock becomes _____ it once was.

   a. harder than   b. higher than

Chapter **02**

Reference

Question Type | Reference

◢ About the Question

Reference questions focus on the relationships between words and their referents in the passage. You are asked to identify what the antecedent of a pronoun is. There are often questions with subject pronouns such as *he, she, it,* and *they* and object pronouns such as *him, her,* and *them.* There are also questions with relative pronouns such as *which* and demonstrative pronouns such as *this, that, these,* and *those.* There are 0-1 Reference questions for each passage. However, these questions rarely appear anymore. There may be 1 Reference question in an entire Reading section, or there may be none.

Recognizing Reference questions:

• The word "X" in the passage refers to

Helpful hints for answering the questions correctly:

• The correct answer choice can always fit into the sentence. So try inserting each answer choice into the sentence to see which one reads the best.

• All four of the answer choices always appear in the same order as they are written in the passage. They are also the exact words or phrases that appear in the passage.

• On rare occasions, the correct answer appears in the passage after the highlighted word. Most of the time, however, it can be found before the highlighted word.

Basic Practice

Read the following paragraphs and choose what each highlighted word refers to.

🎧 CH02_1A

A

Among the largest of all the body's organs is the liver. One of its primary functions is to clean the blood in the body. After a person consumes food, vitamins, minerals, and other nutrients get into the blood. Before the blood travels to the rest of the body, it stops at the liver. There, the liver processes the blood so that anything harmful is removed from it. The waste is taken to the intestines or the kidneys while the rest can then be brought to other parts of the body.

Ⓐ the liver

Ⓑ the blood

Ⓒ anything harmful

🎧 CH02_1B

B

A tsunami is a fast-moving wave which does not become very high until it nears land. There are several ways a tsunami can form. The vast majority of tsunamis are caused by earthquakes that take place underwater. Volcanic eruptions, landslides, and meteorite impacts can also create them. If a tsunami is powerful enough, it can travel far inland. In the process, it may devastate the coast, which could result in a great amount of property damage and deaths.

Ⓐ tsunamis

Ⓑ earthquakes

Ⓒ volcanic eruptions, landslides, and meteorite impacts

🎧 CH02_1C

C

The Great Auk was an enormous seabird that went extinct in 1844. It once existed in large numbers in the North Atlantic Ocean. In the decades before it went extinct, there were several efforts made to save the species. For instance, in 1775, people in Great Britain were punished for hunting it for its eggs or feather. Decades later, killing the Great Auk for its feathers was banned in Great Britain. These ultimately failed though as too many fishermen and others killed the bird for its feathers and meat.

Ⓐ Several efforts

Ⓑ People in Great Britain

Ⓒ Its feathers

A The Life Cycle of the Grasshopper

🎧 CH02_2A

There are approximately 11,000 species of grasshoppers that live throughout the Earth. These insects have a lifespan of roughly a year. During that time, they go through three stages in their lives.

The egg is the first stage in a grasshopper's life cycle. Most grasshoppers lay their eggs in the summer months, and they remain underground for around ten months. Grasshoppers hatch in late spring or early summer.

Once the grasshoppers emerge from their eggs, the nymph stage follows. Young grasshoppers in this stage lack wings and **reproductive organs.** Grasshoppers eat constantly and become larger during this stage. They molt by shedding their outer shell, called an exoskeleton, several times.

When grasshoppers become adults, they develop wings. They can move faster as adults, so they can avoid predators better. During this stage, female grasshoppers lay eggs while males fertilize them. After about two months of the adult stage, the grasshoppers die.

*reproductive organ: the part of the body which allows an animal to create young

The word "they" in the passage refers to

Ⓐ most grasshoppers

Ⓑ their eggs

Ⓒ the summer months

Ⓓ ten months

Vocabulary

• l_____ = the length of time an organism lives

• s_____ = a level

• s_____ = to get rid of

B | Crowd Psychology

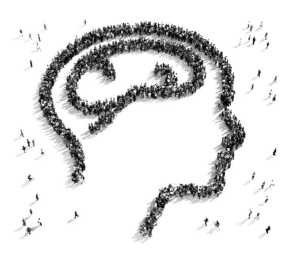

When alone, a person behaves in a particular manner according to his or her characteristics. However, when that same person joins a group, his or her behavior, personality, and characteristics may change. This is known as crowd psychology.

The basic idea behind crowd psychology is that people's behavior and thought patterns change when they join groups. Rather than doing what they want or believe, the members go along with the beliefs and actions of the group to which they belong. This allows them to remain in a **harmonious** state with the group. This also accounts for mob behavior. When normally calm people become violent and destroy property or harm others while in a large group, it takes place.

Charles Mackay was one of the first individuals to write about crowd psychology. He did so in his book *Extraordinary Popular Delusions and the Madness of Crowds*. It was first published in 1841. Since then, a large number of works on crowd psychology have been written.

*harmonious: peaceful; agreeable

The word "it" in the passage refers to

Ⓐ the group

Ⓑ mob behavior

Ⓒ property

Ⓓ a large group

Vocabulary

• a _____ f _____ = to explain; to be responsible for

• m _____ = a large group of people who behave badly and are often violent

• d _____ = a false belief or opinion

A | Orca Hunting Methods

CH02_3A

The orca, commonly called the killer whale, is a carnivorous toothed whale which is an excellent hunter. It is considered an <u>apex predator</u> since no animals hunt the orca, and it feeds on fish, seals, and dolphins as well as sharks and small whales. A highly social animal, the orca often hunts prey in groups.

Fish are the orca's primary food source as it consumes more than 200 kilograms of it every day. Off the coast of Norway, where many orcas can be found, it hunts herring, a small fish that swims in large schools. The orca utilizes a method called the carousel to hunt herring. Hunting in groups, several orcas surround the herring, move their bodies rapidly, and create air bubbles in the water. These actions herd the herring into a tightly rotating ball like a carousel. The orcas then slap the ball with their tails to stun large numbers of herring, making it easy for the orcas to eat them. The orca also employs the tail slap when hunting sharks. It slaps the shark on the head to stun it, and then the orca flips the shark upside down. This makes the shark defenseless, so the orca can easily kill and eat it.

Another hunting method is used in cold waters. Sometimes seals climb onto an ice sheet to escape from a group of orcas. The orcas then swim together toward the ice sheet, which creates a wave of water as they move. Occasionally, the wave rocks the ice sheet enough so that it knocks the seals into the water. In other instances, the water washes over the ice and throws the seals into the water. The orcas then attack the seals and kill them.

*apex predator: a predator at the top of the food chain since it has no natural enemies

Vocabulary

- f_____ o_____ = to eat
- p_____ = to hunt other animals
- d_____ = unable to protect oneself
- r_____ = to move from side to side

1   In paragraph 1, the author's description of the orca mentions all of the following EXCEPT:

    (A) why it may not hunt by itself

    (B) which types of animals it often eats

    (C) where it prefers to hunt animals

    (D) how its hunting skills are considered

2   The word "it" in the passage refers to

    (A) the orca

    (B) the tail slap

    (C) the shark

    (D) the head

3   According to paragraph 2, the orca uses the tail slap to hunt sharks because

    (A) its tail is the hardest and strongest part of its body

    (B) it needs to avoid the sharp teeth that most sharks have

    (C) the air bubbles that it creates help stun the sharks

    (D) the sharks cannot move after they are hit by the tail

4   Select the appropriate statements from the answer choices and match them to the animal hunted by orcas to which they relate. TWO of the answer choices will NOT be used.

Herring	Seal
•	•
•	•

STATEMENTS

1 Is unable to swim fast enough to escape

2 Is attacked while it is hiding on floating ice

3 Is turned over in the water so that it is upside down

4 Is surrounded by a large number of orcas

5 Is herded into a circle by air bubbles

6 Gets knocked into the water by a wave

B | The Evolution of the Romance Languages

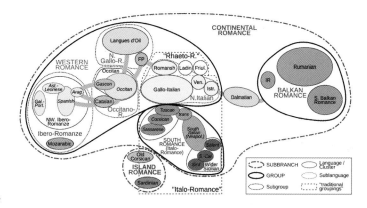

The Romance languages are a group of thirty-five languages that are used on the European continent. They evolved from Latin during the centuries after the fall of the Roman Empire. French, Italian, Spanish, Portuguese, and Romanian are the five major Romance languages. Most of the other ones are related to these five languages in some way. Today, there are about 800 million people around the world who speak a Romance language.

Latin, the language of the Roman Empire, was the <u>root</u> of these languages. The empire collapsed in the late fifth century. At that time, there were still many Romans living throughout the lands Rome had once controlled. They spoke a version of Latin that is known today as Vulgar Latin. The word vulgar comes from the Latin *vulgaris*. It means "of the common people." Vulgar Latin was the language of common people, soldiers, and merchants. Classical Latin, on the other hand, was the language of upper-class Romans. There were distinct differences between these two types of Latin.

When the Roman Empire fell, there was no central governing authority throughout the empire's former lands. As a result, the people living in certain regions often found themselves isolated from those who were living in other lands. This resulted in the Vulgar Latin that the people in each region spoke evolving into different languages. Basically, regional dialects were created in a large number of areas. As time passed, these changed into individual languages such as French and Spanish. While these Romance languages were different, they often retained some similarities. For instance, most of them use the same sentence order while many words have similar spellings, pronunciations, and meanings.

*root: a source; a base

Vocabulary

- c_____ = to fall apart
- m_____ = a person who sells things to others
- d_____ = unique; individual
- d_____ = a local variation of a language

1 The author discusses "Classical Latin" in paragraph 2 in order to

   (A) show how it evolved from another type of Latin

   (B) claim that more people spoke it than Vulgar Latin

   (C) argue that it was the source of many Romance languages

   (D) point out how it differed from Vulgar Latin

Reference Question

2 The word "these" in the passage refers to

   (A) the people in each region

   (B) regional dialects

   (C) a large number of areas

   (D) individual languages

Vocabulary Question

3 The word "retained" in the passage is closest in meaning to

   (A) kept

   (B) stressed

   (C) experienced

   (D) provided

Prose Summary Question

4 An introductory sentence for a brief summary of the passage is provided below. Complete the summary by selecting the THREE answer choices that express the most important ideas of the passage. Some sentences do not belong because they express ideas that are not presented in the passage or are minor ideas in the passage.

The Romance languages evolved from the Latin language over a long period of time.

ANSWER CHOICES

   [1] There are numerous Romance languages that developed in places all throughout Europe.

   [2] The Romance languages are dialects of Latin that were created over centuries.

   [3] People quit speaking the Latin language as soon as the Roman Empire fell.

   [4] Most of the Romance languages still contain similarities to the Latin language.

   [5] Vulgar Latin was the basis for the Romance languages that later developed.

🎧 CH02_4A

The Ecology of Lake Victoria

Lake Victoria, the largest lake in Africa, covers an area of around 68,000 square kilometers. It is located on the borders of three countries: Kenya, Uganda, and Tanzania. The lake is shallow, averaging about forty meters in depth. While it is fed by many small streams and a few large rivers, Lake Victoria is drained almost exclusively by the Nile River. There are nearly 3,000 islands in the lake, many of which are inhabited.

The lake is home to a wide variety of flora and fauna. All kinds of mammals, reptiles, birds, and fish live in and around its shores. Among them are the Nile crocodile, otter, hippo, and mongoose. For much of the lake's history, the main species of fish was the native haplochromine cichlid. There were once 500 species of it in the lake. This large number of species was the result of adaptive radiation. This is an evolutionary process in which many new species develop from a single species in the past. Scientists are unsure why the cichlid evolved in this way and why it did so in Lake Victoria.

If they do not discover the answer soon, they might never be able to do so. The reason is that the cichlid population is dying out. Two invasive species are to blame. In an effort to improve the lake's fisheries, new species were introduced to Lake Victoria in the 1950s and 1960s. However, rather than helping, they have had a devastating impact on the ecosystem of the lake. The first fish introduced was the Nile perch. This giant fish can grow up to two meters long and weigh around 200 kilograms. It has an enormous appetite and devours numerous small fish. In addition, several species of Nile tilapia were put in Lake Victoria. While tilapia is much smaller than the Nile perch, it has had a negative impact on the lake's smaller fish.

As the Nile perch and tilapia consume the native species, they are changing the lake's ecology. Since many small fish species are disappearing, the growth of algae in the lake has exploded. Small fish like the cichlid eat the algae, but now these plants are widespread around the lake and absorb oxygen required by fish. Hundreds of cichlid species have disappeared from the lake, and so have many other species of fish.

Pollution has had a negative effect on fish stocks, too. Much of it comes from chemical runoff and erosion. The shores of Lake Victoria are heavily populated. Many of these people clear trees to create farmland. Fewer trees mean that more soil erodes into the lake. Farms use chemical fertilizers, which get into the lake's waters. They increase the nitrogen level in the lake. The results are more algae, less oxygen, and more dead fish. The increased amount of nitrogen has also led to the unchecked growth of the water hyacinth, an invasive species. The plant absorbs large amounts of oxygen, which is further causing changes in the lake's ecosystem.

*Glossary

fishery: a place where fish are born and raised

runoff: something that flows from the land into bodies of water

1 In paragraph 1, the author's description of Lake Victoria mentions all of the following EXCEPT:

    (A) how deep the lake is

    (B) which nations the lake is in

    (C) how it gets much of its water

    (D) how many people live on its islands

2 According to paragraph 2, there were hundreds of species of haplochromine cichlid because

    (A) many fish developed from one species

    (B) the lake's waters helped the fish survive

    (C) adaptive radiation did not take place

    (D) Lake Victoria has few predators in it

3 The word "it" in the passage refers to

    (A) a single species

    (B) the past

    (C) the cichlid

    (D) this way

4 In stating that new species "were introduced" to Lake Victoria, the author means that new species

    (A) were caught in the lake

    (B) met in the lake

    (C) evolved in the lake

    (D) were put in the lake

5 In paragraph 3, the author uses "the Nile perch" as an example of

    Ⓐ an animal causing harm in Lake Victoria

    Ⓑ one of the largest fish in Lake Victoria

    Ⓒ a natural enemy of the tilapia

    Ⓓ an animal that lives well with the cichlid

6 Which of the sentences below best expresses the essential information in the highlighted sentence in the passage? Incorrect answer choices change the meaning in important ways or leave out essential information.

Hundreds of cichlid species have disappeared from the lake, and so have many other species of fish.

    Ⓐ The cichlid has caused many other species of fish in the lake to die out.

    Ⓑ The lake no longer has any species of cichlid living in its waters.

    Ⓒ Numerous species of fish, including the cichlid, no longer live in the lake.

    Ⓓ Several species of fish, such as the cichlid, have moved to other parts of the lake.

7 The word "They" in the passage refers to

    Ⓐ The shores of Lake Victoria

    Ⓑ Fewer trees

    Ⓒ Chemical fertilizers

    Ⓓ The lake's waters

8 **Directions:** An introductory sentence for a brief summary of the passage is provided below. Complete the summary by selecting the THREE answer choices that express the most important ideas of the passage. Some sentences do not belong because they express ideas that are not presented in the passage or are minor ideas in the passage. **This question is worth 2 points.**

Many fish are disappearing from Lake Victoria for a variety of reasons.

-
-
-

ANSWER CHOICES

1 People have introduced invasive species such as the Nile perch to Lake Victoria.

2 Large numbers of mammals and reptiles no longer make the lake their home.

3 There were once more than 500 species of cichlid living in the waters of the lake.

4 The waters of the lake are being polluted by chemical runoff and other human actions.

5 Too many of the roughly 3,000 islands found in the lake are inhabited by people.

6 The extreme growth of algae in parts of the lake is removing oxygen from the water.

The Archaeopteryx

One of the most unusual prehistoric animals was the archaeopteryx. The name is Greek for ancient feather or ancient wing. Fossilized remains of this animal were first discovered in Germany in 1861. The scientists who first examined them thought the remains were those of a bird. While it looked like a bird and was long thought to be one, many paleontologists now consider it a transitional species between dinosaurs and birds. There is also a debate on whether it could fly or not.

The archaeopteryx lived about 150 million years ago during the Late Jurassic Period. It was not a large animal, being less than half a meter in length and weighing less than one kilogram. Much of its length came from its long, bony tail. It had rounded wings with feathers, small teeth, claws at its wingtips, and strong legs with three-fingered claws. Experts believe it was a carnivore which used its claws and teeth to attack and eat other animals.

Every archaeopteryx fossil found as of today has been dug up in Germany in limestone formations. So far, only eleven specimens have been unearthed. Some of them clearly show that the species had feathers on its wings and body. Its neck and head, however, had no feathers. However, it is possible that they had smaller feathers which easily decomposed after death and prior to fossilization. The archaeopteryx's feathers had the same appearance and structure as modern bird feathers. Other hints from the fossils show certain birdlike features. These include a similar bone structure with modern birds.

Despite the archaeopteryx looking like a bird and having wings, there is some debate on whether it could fly or not. Its feathers appear to be designed for flight. Yet a close examination of the structure of its shoulder bones suggests that it could not lift its wings high above its body. It could therefore not flap its wings rapidly like modern birds do to achieve flight. It is possible that the animal used its wings and feathers to glide from a high position to a lower one. Perhaps it climbed to high places and then did controlled glides to attack prey beneath it.

An even bigger question is whether it was a bird. Paleontologists believe that it evolved from a small dinosaur species and long thought it was one of the first species of birds. Yet recent discoveries in China of a new birdlike animal appear to dispute this finding. The new species, named the xiaotingia, lived five million years before the archaeopteryx. Whether it and other birdlike dinosaurs evolved from the xiaotingia is disputed. The debate continues as some experts call these species the first examples of birds while others believe they can be classified as dinosaurs that developed birdlike features. Others say that they are a transitional set of species and mark the time when a branch family of dinosaurs began evolving into birds.

*Glossary

transitional species: a creature that has similarities to an ancestral group and a descendant group

flap: to move up and down, like wings when a bird is flying

9 The word "them" in the passage refers to

   Ⓐ the most unusual prehistoric animals

   Ⓑ fossilized remains

   Ⓒ the scientists

   Ⓓ many paleontologists

10 According to paragraph 2, which of the following is NOT true about the archaeopteryx?

   Ⓐ It had feathers as well as claws on its wings.

   Ⓑ It survived by eating the meat of animals.

   Ⓒ It lived for more than 150 million years.

   Ⓓ Its tail comprised most of its length.

11 The word "decomposed" in the passage is closest in meaning to

   Ⓐ absorbed

   Ⓑ rotted

   Ⓒ vanished

   Ⓓ removed

12 In paragraph 3, the author implies that the archaeopteryx

   Ⓐ was probably a relative of modern-day birds

   Ⓑ preferred to hunt fish rather than land animals

   Ⓒ left few fossils because its bones were too fragile

   Ⓓ was able to run on the ground at great speeds

13 According to paragraph 4, which of the following is true about the archaeopteryx?

Ⓐ It might have glided instead of actually flown.

Ⓑ It could lift its wings high above its body.

Ⓒ It built nests in high places such as tall trees.

Ⓓ It had several types of feathers which let it fly.

14 The author discusses "the xiaotingia" in paragraph 5 in order to

Ⓐ compare its primary features with those of the archaeopteryx

Ⓑ prove that it was the first bird to have lived on the Earth

Ⓒ describe another animal similar to the archaeopteryx

Ⓓ explain what caused it to go extinct millions of years ago

15 Which of the sentences below best expresses the essential information in the highlighted sentence in the passage? Incorrect answer choices change the meaning in important ways or leave out essential information.

The debate continues as some experts call these species the first examples of birds while others believe they can be classified as dinosaurs that developed birdlike features.

Ⓐ Most experts agree that these species were birds and not just dinosaurs that looked like birds.

Ⓑ More research needs to be conducted to conclude the debate on exactly what kinds of animals these species were.

Ⓒ It is known that these animals were merely dinosaurs that were similar to birds and were not the first birds.

Ⓓ There is a debate between people who believe these species were birds and others who think they only resembled birds.

16 Directions: An introductory sentence for a brief summary of the passage is provided below. Complete the summary by selecting the THREE answer choices that express the most important ideas of the passage. Some sentences do not belong because they express ideas that are not presented in the passage or are minor ideas in the passage. **This question is worth 2 points.**

The archaeopteryx was a prehistoric animal with birdlike characteristics that may have been a species which modern birds evolved from.

-
-
-

ANSWER CHOICES

1. All of the archaeopteryx fossils that have been found were located in Germany.

2. The xiaotingia is a dinosaur whose fossils were unearthed in China in recent times.

3. Scientists are not yet sure if the archaeopteryx was able to fly or not.

4. The archaeopteryx was a small animal that had wings and feathers and looked like a bird.

5. Scientists are currently engaged in a debate over how the archaeopteryx should be classified.

6. Paleontologists have determined that the archaeopteryx was the first bird ever to live.

■ Vocabulary Review

A Complete each sentence with the appropriate word from the box.

lifespan	mob	merchants	erosion	impact

1 A _____ is typically a large group of people who may be violent.

2 When _____ occurs, an area of land is destroyed.

3 The people trying to sell goods to the tourists are _____.

4 The _____ of an animal refers to around how long it will live.

5 When something has a great effect on another thing, it has an _____ on it.

B Complete each sentence with the correct answer.

1 Because the sharks cannot _____, they are **defenseless** and can be attacked.
   a. protect themselves   b. swim well

2 When people speak _____, they are speaking a **dialect** of that language.
   a. a dead language   b. a version of a language

3 The different **stages** of an animal's life are the various _____ it goes through.
   a. sizes   b. phases

4 An island that is **inhabited** has people _____ it.
   a. living on   b. visiting

5 They _____ the answer because they are **unsure** of it.
   a. do not know   b. cannot remember

6 His **delusions** were basically various _____ that he had.
   a. opinions   b. misbeliefs

7 Some animals **devour** their food by _____ quickly.
   a. eating it   b. killing it

8 A **distinct** difference is one that is very _____.
   a. clear   b. well known

9 Animals that are _____ are known as **prey**.
   a. hunters of others   b. hunted by others

Chapter 03

Factual Information

◣ About the Question

Factual Information questions focus on the facts that are included in the passage. You are asked to answer a question asking about the facts or information that are covered in the passage. These questions may ask about details, definitions, explanations, or other kinds of information. The information asked about in these questions is always included in a small section of the passage. There are 1-3 Factual Information questions for each passage. There is an average of 2 of these questions per passage.

Recognizing Factual Information questions:

- According to paragraph 1, which of the following is true about X?
- The author's description of X mentions which of the following? (much less common than before)
- According to paragraph 1, X occurred because . . .
- According to paragraph 1, X did Y because . . .
- According to paragraph 1, why did X do Y?
- Select the TWO answer choices from paragraph 1 that identify X. *To receive credit, you must select TWO answers.* (seldom asked)

Helpful hints for answering the questions correctly:

- Most of these questions indicate the paragraph in which the correct answer is found. When trying to answer one of these questions, only look for the information in the paragraph mentioned in the question itself.
- Read carefully so that you understand what the facts are and what the author's opinions or thoughts are.
- Make sure that the entire answer choice is accurate. Be especially careful of absolute words such as *always* and *never*.
- Some answer choices may contain accurate information that does not appear in the passage. Do not select these answer choices. Make sure the answer choice you select has information that appears in the passage.
- Some of these questions require test takers to understand the entire paragraph, not just one part of it, to find the correct answer.

Basic Practice

Check T if the statement is true and F if the statement is false according to each paragraph.

CH03_1A

A

    One common type of erosion is caused by the wind. For the most part, wind erosion takes place in flat areas with few trees as well as in areas which have loose soil. When the wind blows in these regions, it often picks up part of the soil and carries it away. This may result in the desertification of places as valuable topsoil gets taken away. Fertile land can suddenly become barren, unproductive land due solely to the action of the wind.

1 The wind can erode places that do not have many trees.   T ☐ F ☐

2 Desertification may occur when topsoil is blown away.   T ☐ F ☐

3 The wind can combine with water to make land barren.   T ☐ F ☐

CH03_1B

B

    Most cultures have their own traditional songs and music. These tend to be passed on from generation to generation. Folk music, as it is often called, comes in a variety of genres. But it is almost always unique to the people who play it. In many instances, traditional instruments are used to play the music. For instance, in the United States, the fiddle and banjo are two instruments used to play folk music. In Italy, the mandolin is used to perform folk music.

1 People normally learn folk music from previous generations.   T ☐ F ☐

2 There are not many different kinds of folk music.   T ☐ F ☐

3 The mandolin and banjo are used in American folk music.   T ☐ F ☐

CH03_1C

C

    In ancient times, traveling to distant places involved long, difficult trips. Nevertheless, some individuals, especially merchants, made journeys covering great distances. They would travel hundreds or thousands of kilometers to sell their goods. They typically used trade routes to get to their destinations. One of these trade routes was the Silk Road, which originated in China and went to Rome. It was not a single road though. Instead, it was a number of paths and trails, some of which required people to travel by ship.

1 Only merchants went on long trips in ancient times.   T ☐ F ☐

2 The Silk Road was the name of a trade route.   T ☐ F ☐

3 People on the Silk Road traveled by land and sea.   T ☐ F ☐

A | Taylorism

CH03_2A

In the early twentieth century, the **mass production** of goods started to take place in the United States. This happened in the automobile industry. Henry Ford, the owner of the Ford Motor Company, introduced the assembly line to his factories. This enabled workers to make cars faster than ever before.

Frederick Winslow Taylor studied these mass-production methods. He was interested in finding the most efficient way to make products. In 1911, he published the book *Principles of Scientific Management*. In it, he explained the best ways to engage in large-scale manufacturing in factories.

Scientific management, or Taylorism, stressed efficiency. Taylor wanted to create as many steps as possible in the manufacturing process. This would result in workers needing less training to do work. It would also make them more productive. Taylorism had many critics. They disliked the way that it treated workers. However, it was very influential in the first half of the 1900s.

*mass production: the making of many goods at the same time

In paragraph 3, the author's description of Taylorism mentions which of the following?

Ⓐ Which companies used it

Ⓑ Why some people were opposed to it

Ⓒ How workers were trained in it

Ⓓ What products it was used to make

Vocabulary

- e _____ = making the best use of time, money, or other resources
- s _____ = to emphasize
- c _____ = a person who comments on something, often in a negative way

B   Mosaics

Mosaics are an old type of art form made more than 4,000 years ago. To create a mosaic, an artist used small pieces of glass, stone, or other items that were different colors. The pieces were glued together to create an image.

In the ancient world, mosaics were created by the Mesopotamians, Greeks, and Romans. They often decorated walls in temples or made mosaic floors on tiles in villas. Stones, shells, and ivory were common items used to create mosaics. The Greeks and Romans made mosaics that had scenes from **mythology** on them. Gods, humans, and animals were featured on these mosaics. Geometrical figures and scenes from daily life were also used.

During Christian times, the Byzantine Empire took the lead in making mosaics. Its artists created extravagant works on walls and ceilings. Scenes from the Bible and images of Christian saints were the most popular topics. In other instances, mosaics of Byzantine emperors and empresses were made.

*mythology: a collection of stories from the past that may or may not be true

According to paragraph 2, which of the following is true about mosaics?

Ⓐ The Mesopotamians preferred to use colorful shells.

Ⓑ They were rarely made by the ancient Greeks.

Ⓒ The Romans made mosaics of their emperors.

Ⓓ They were sometimes made in people's homes.

Vocabulary

• g＿＿＿＿＿＿ = to connect two things together by using a sticky substance

• f＿＿＿＿＿＿ = to be a main part of

• e＿＿＿＿＿＿ = wild; flashy

A | **The Rings of Saturn**

🎧 CH03_3A

Saturn is the second largest planet in the solar system in addition to being the sixth closest to the sun. The most prominent feature of the planet is its rings. These are wide regions comprised of billions of ice and rock particles which form ring-shaped bands around the planet. They are not visible to the <u>naked eye</u> from the Earth. The first person to see them was Italian astronomer Galileo

Galilei. He used a telescope to observe them in 1601 but was not certain what they were. Decades later in 1655, Dutch astronomer Christiaan Huygens declared it was possible there were rings surrounding Saturn.

While other planets have rings, Saturn's are the most extensive. There are seven main rings and several smaller ones both between and beyond the main rings. The main rings have letters for names. From closest to farthest from the planet, they are called D, C, B, A, F, G, and E. They extend from 67,000 kilometers to 450,000 kilometers from the planet's center. The rings have several major gaps. The largest is the Cassini Division between the B and A rings. The thickness of the rings varies as they range from being a few meters to around a kilometer thick. In addition, the particles making up the rings are different sizes. Some are tiny grains of sand while others are massive rock and ice formations.

Astronomers are not sure how the rings formed, but there are two primary theories. They are the remains of a moon according to some. Saturn's strong gravity destroyed the moon, and its particles then formed the rings. The second theory states that the rings formed at the same time as Saturn. The rings are thus leftover material from the original mass that became Saturn.

*naked eye: sight without using equipment like a telescope

Vocabulary

- p_____ = obvious; apparent
- b_____ = a thin, flat strip
- e_____ = widespread
- g_____ = the force of attraction that causes things to fall to the ground

1 In paragraph 1, why does the author mention "Galileo Galilei"?

   Ⓐ To claim that he made the world's first telescope

   Ⓑ To state that he discovered Saturn in 1601

   Ⓒ To discuss his relationship with Christiaan Huygens

   Ⓓ To note he saw the rings of Saturn for the first time

Factual Information Question

2 According to paragraph 2, which of the following is true about the rings of Saturn?

   Ⓐ Different objects of various sizes comprise them.

   Ⓑ They are slowly moving toward the planet.

   Ⓒ There are only seven individual rings around the planet.

   Ⓓ They are the only rings in the solar system.

Reference Question

3 The word "some" in the passage refers to

   Ⓐ astronomers

   Ⓑ the rings

   Ⓒ two primary theories

   Ⓓ the remains of a moon

Prose Summary Question

4 An introductory sentence for a brief summary of the passage is provided below. Complete the summary by selecting the THREE answer choices that express the most important ideas of the passage. Some sentences do not belong because they express ideas that are not presented in the passage or are minor ideas in the passage.

Saturn has a system of rings that orbits it.

ANSWER CHOICES

   ☐ The most notable feature of the planet is all of the rings that surround it.

   ☐ Astronomers have known about the rings of Saturn since the 1600s.

   ☐ The Cassini Division is the largest gap between the planet's rings.

   ☐ Experts have come up with two major theories about how the rings formed.

   ☐ There are seven major rings and many other smaller ones around Saturn.

Atoll Formation

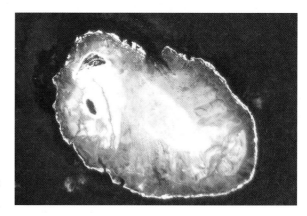

A low-lying group of islands made of coral is an atoll. It typically forms in the shape of a ring that surrounds an inner body of water called a lagoon. Atolls are commonplace in tropical regions, particularly in the Pacific Ocean. British naturalist Charles Darwin developed the main theory of atoll formation while voyaging in the Pacific Ocean from 1831 to 1836. He believed an atoll was once a part of a larger volcanic island. Over time, however, the volcano collapsed and left behind the atoll.

Volcanoes often form beneath the world's oceans. <u>Magma</u> erupts from cracks in the seafloor deep underwater. Over time, the magma cools and develops into an undersea mountain. Eventually, it emerges from the water to form a volcanic island. As more time passes, the island forms a ring of coral around it. Coral is a living organism which grows in warm waters in large colonies. As the coral grows, it releases secretions of calcium carbonate. They form a hard, rocklike structure that the coral anchors onto. This structure is a coral reef.

Sometimes the seafloor beneath a volcano begins sinking. Slowly, as the volcano descends beneath the water, the coral reef grows higher. The reef emerges from the water to form the islands of an atoll. After some time, the volcano sinks entirely under the water, leaving behind only the ring of the coral reef. The inner lagoon is the place where the volcano once stood. The coral reef above the water's surface gets eroded by the action of wind and water over time, resulting in the creation of flat, sandy islands. In some instances, wind, water, and birds bring seeds to the islands, so plants grow. The result is an atoll with sparse amounts of vegetation around the lagoon.

*magma: hot, melted rock beneath the Earth's surface

Vocabulary

- n_____ = a person who studies nature
- s_____ = something that is released from an organism
- a_____ = to connect one thing to another to keep the first thing from moving
- s_____ = rare; uncommon

1 Select the TWO answer choices from paragraph 2 that identify characteristics of atolls. *To receive credit, you must select TWO answers.*

   Ⓐ Most of them have volcanoes that are still active.

   Ⓑ They can be found in regions with warm water.

   Ⓒ The islands that comprise atolls are made of coral.

   Ⓓ They were first discovered by Charles Darwin.

2 The word "emerges" in the passage is closest in meaning to

   Ⓐ rises

   Ⓑ forms

   Ⓒ develops

   Ⓓ exists

3 Which of the sentences below best expresses the essential information in the highlighted sentence in the passage? Incorrect answer choices change the meaning in important ways or leave out essential information.

   The coral reef above the water's surface gets eroded by the action of wind and water over time, resulting in the creation of flat, sandy islands.

   Ⓐ Because the islands are already flat, there is very little erosion of the coral reef over time.

   Ⓑ It takes a long time for the coral reef to become smooth like other islands in the ocean.

   Ⓒ Wind and water erosion smoothes the surface of the coral reef to make it flat and sandy.

   Ⓓ Natural elements cause erosion to occur on the coral reefs that are above the surface.

4 An introductory sentence for a brief summary of the passage is provided below. Complete the summary by selecting the THREE answer choices that express the most important ideas of the passage. Some sentences do not belong because they express ideas that are not presented in the passage or are minor ideas in the passage.

   Atolls form as a result of volcanoes coming above the water's surface and then later sinking beneath it.

   ANSWER CHOICES

   ① As a volcano sinks under the water, the coral reefs come out of the water.

   ② Most experts accept the theory of atoll formation Charles Darwin made.

   ③ The coral reefs form the islands of the atoll while the lagoon is where the volcano was.

   ④ After a volcanic island forms, coral reefs begin forming in the water around it.

   ⑤ Atolls can form anywhere, but they are mostly found in tropical waters.

The Ancient Sea Peoples

One of the great mysteries of early human civilizations in the eastern Mediterranean region concerns the Sea Peoples. They suddenly appeared in the second millennium B.C., and their attacks lasted for roughly a century. They sailed in ships and raided large numbers of coastal cities and towns. The Sea Peoples assaulted places in the modern-day countries of Egypt, Israel, Lebanon, Syria, and Turkey. Most of what is known about them comes from writings from ancient Egypt.

The attacks on Egypt mostly came during the reigns of the three pharaohs: Ramses II, Merneptah, and Ramses III. These men ruled Egypt from 1279 B.C. to 1155 B.C. According to writings found in the nineteenth century, the attackers arrived from the sea with no warning, and nobody was able to stop them. One detailed text claims that the Sea Peoples were the allies of the Hittites, who were enemies of Egypt during the reign of Ramses II. In 1274 B.C., Ramses II managed to defeat the Hittites. He stopped a naval attack on Egypt by the Sea Peoples as well.

Ramses II's son, Merneptah, also had to deal with the Sea Peoples. They allied themselves with another Egyptian enemy, the Libyans. Merneptah defeated both in a great sea battle in which the Egyptians killed more than 6,000 of their enemies. The Egyptians believed they had seen the last of the Sea Peoples. However, they returned yet again during the rule of Ramses III. They attacked and destroyed the great Egyptian trading center of Kadesh. The Sea Peoples then raided several places along the Egyptian coast. Finally, they attacked the Nile River delta region. During the Battle of the Delta in 1175 B.C., the Egyptians ambushed the Sea Peoples. Using archers on land and on ships at sea, the Egyptians killed many of the Sea Peoples with arrows and also destroyed their ships.

In other parts of the eastern Mediterranean, the natives were unable to defeat the Sea Peoples. There is archaeological evidence of the widespread destruction of cities and towns in coastal areas during the same period. However, after the Egyptians defeated them at the Nile delta, the Sea Peoples were barely heard from again. The reason for their disappearance is uncertain. ◼1 What is also uncertain is where the Sea Peoples came from. ◼2 Some scholars claim they came from islands in the Mediterranean such as Sicily or Crete. ◼3 Others believe they were natives of southern Europe and hailed from Italy, Greece, or parts of Turkey. ◼4

There are also a number of theories concerning why they attacked so many lands. A few scholars propose that they were merely pirates looking for plunder. Others theorize that they were migrating people searching for a new homeland. These individuals claim the Sea Peoples had to move after a disaster—perhaps an earthquake, a tsunami, or a drought—destroyed their homes and food supplies. A third theory is that the Sea Peoples' homelands were attacked. So they were simply fleeing from those attackers.

*Glossary

ambush: to hide and then to attack someone

plunder: something that is taken by stealing

1   According to paragraph 1, which of the following is true about the Sea Peoples?

Ⓐ They made written records of their attacks in the Mediterranean.

Ⓑ They raided places in coastal regions for around a hundred years.

Ⓒ They are believed to have come from in the western Mediterranean.

Ⓓ They had powerful navies on the sea and strong armies on land.

2   In paragraph 2, the author's description of the Sea Peoples mentions which of the following?

Ⓐ The name of the people they joined together against Egypt

Ⓑ Some of the pharaohs whom they defeated in battle

Ⓒ The reason that they suddenly made war on the Egyptians

Ⓓ The years in which their biggest battles took place

3   The phrase "deal with" in the passage is closest in meaning to

Ⓐ talk to

Ⓑ handle

Ⓒ conquer

Ⓓ attack

4   In paragraph 3, the author uses "Kadesh" as an example of

  Ⓐ a place in Egypt that the Sea Peoples successfully assaulted

  Ⓑ the site of a battle between the Egyptians and the Sea Peoples

  Ⓒ one of the home cities of the Sea Peoples

  Ⓓ the place Egyptian ships sailed from during Merneptah's reign

5   In paragraph 4, the author implies that the Sea Peoples

  Ⓐ began to live in some of the towns and cities they had captured

  Ⓑ did not recover after losing a battle to the Egyptians

  Ⓒ have been proven to have originated from Sicily or Crete

  Ⓓ left Egypt and attacked other places in the Mediterranean

6   In paragraph 5, the author's description of the theories on why the Sea Peoples attacked so many lands mentions all of the following EXCEPT:

  Ⓐ some possible natural disasters that affected them

  Ⓑ the name of the attackers they were escaping from

  Ⓒ the reason they might have been acting like pirates

  Ⓓ the possibility they were migrants from another land

7   Look at the four squares [■] that indicate where the following sentence could be added to the passage.

  But most historians say it is likely that they suffered too many losses at the hands of Ramses III.

  Where would the sentence best fit?

  Click on a square [■] to add the sentence to the passage.

8   **Directions:** Select the appropriate statements from the answer choices and match them to the Egyptian pharaoh to whom they relate. TWO of the answer choices will NOT be used. **This question is worth 4 points.**

Drag your answer choices to the spaces where they belong. To remove an answer choice, click on it. To review the passage, click on VIEW TEXT.

STATEMENTS

1. Did not win any battles against the Sea Peoples

2. Won a battle at sea in 1274 B.C.

3. Ruled Egypt during the Battle of the Delta

4. Fought both the Sea Peoples and the Hittites

5. Killed over 6,000 enemy soldiers in one battle

6. Had Kadesh destroyed while he was pharaoh

7. Was the first pharaoh to be attacked by the Sea Peoples

8. Battled the Libyans and their allies, the Sea Peoples

9. Ruled when the Sea Peoples were harmed by a tsunami

EGYPTIAN PHARAOH

Ramses II (Select 3)

-
-
-

Merneptah (Select 2)

-
-

Ramses III (Select 2)

-
-

Cotton Spinning Machines

The Industrial Revolution started in England in the 1700s. The textile industry, which involves the making of cloth, was one of the primary early industries in it. The development of water- and steam-powered machines to spin cotton greatly improved the making of textiles.

The first step toward England's textile revolution began in the early 1700s. A series of laws, called the Calico Acts, banned the importing of cotton textiles. These laws were directed at cheap imports from India. The major purpose of the Calico Acts was to protect England's domestic cotton spinning and weaving industries. At that time, they were cottage industries. Entire families—and sometimes villages—were devoted to making cloth from cotton from their homes.

In the early 1700s, the process of making cloth from cotton was laborious and time consuming. Cotton is a plant with fibers that make good cloth, but it also has parts such as the seeds, which are useless for making textiles. The seeds had to be removed first. Then, the cotton fibers could be spun into cotton yarn, which was made into cloth. Cotton fiber spinning machines had been around for centuries. The first was the spinning wheel, which had been invented in the Islamic world in the 1000s. It spread from there to Asia and Europe.

The spinning wheel made the process of twisting cotton fibers into yarn easier and faster. Yet it was still a slow process, so there was a bottleneck in the making of textiles. In 1733, John Kay invented the flying shuttle, which improved the speed of looms that could weave yarn into cloth. But cotton spinners could not produce enough yarn to feed the faster looms. This led several inventers to attempt to improve the process of spinning yarn. In 1738, Lewis Paul and John Wyatt invented the rolling spinning wheel. It spun cotton yarn faster and made it a more even thickness. Their invention became the basis for later spinning machines.

The first of these was James Hargreaves's spinning jenny, which he invented in 1764. It allowed cotton spinners to spin eight threads of cotton yarn at one time. Larger spinning jennies let them spin an even greater number of threads. But all of the work was still done by hand. At the same time, Richard Arkwright invented the water frame, which was the first cotton spinning mechanically powered machine. It could spin up to ninety-six threads at once. A waterwheel provided the mechanical power for the water frame. Arkwright used his machine when, in 1771, he opened the first major textile factory in Cromford, England.

In 1779, Samuel Crompton created the spinning mule, which combined the methods of the spinning jenny and the water frame. **1** This new spinning machine even further improved the speed of yarn production. **2** Another machine, Eli Whitney's cotton gin, invented in 1793, allowed the easy separation of cotton fibers and seeds. **3** This final invention led to the explosion of textile manufacturing and was a major step forward in the Industrial Revolution. **4**

*Glossary

cottage industry: the small-scale production of goods at a person's home

bottleneck: a stage in a process when progress slows down for some reason

9   According to paragraph 2, England passed the Calico Acts to

    Ⓐ reduce the wages of workers in England since they were rising

    Ⓑ protect English workers from imported goods from India

    Ⓒ increase the number of cottage industries in the country

    Ⓓ help English farmers who wanted to grow more cotton

10   The word "laborious" in the passage is closest in meaning to

    Ⓐ difficult

    Ⓑ expensive

    Ⓒ handmade

    Ⓓ precise

11   In paragraph 3, why does the author mention "the spinning wheel"?

    Ⓐ To point out that it relied upon water power to work

    Ⓑ To explain how it could be used by people

    Ⓒ To claim it was invented either in Asia or Europe

    Ⓓ To name the first cotton fiber spinning machine

12 According to paragraph 4, what did the rolling spinning wheel do?

 (A) It provided power for machines that spun cotton yarn.

 (B) It spun cotton yarn that was equally thick in all places.

 (C) It helped looms weave yarn into cloth.

 (D) It separated cotton seeds from cotton fibers.

13 Which of the following can be inferred about James Hargreaves's spinning jenny from paragraphs 4 and 5?

 (A) It made Hargreaves one of the wealthiest men in England.

 (B) It was inspired by the invention of Paul and Wyatt.

 (C) It was the invention that started the Industrial Revolution.

 (D) It was installed in factories all throughout England.

14 In paragraph 5, the author's description of the water frame mentions all of the following EXCEPT:

 (A) one place where it was installed and used

 (B) the name of the man who created it

 (C) the source of power that it used

 (D) the number of people required to run it

15 Look at the four squares [■] that indicate where the following sentence could be added to the passage.

It also led to cotton becoming a huge cash crop in the southern part of the United States.

Where would the sentence best fit?

Click on a square [■] to add the sentence to the passage.

16 **Directions:** An introductory sentence for a brief summary of the passage is provided below. Complete the summary by selecting the THREE answer choices that express the most important ideas of the passage. Some sentences do not belong because they express ideas that are not presented in the passage or are minor ideas in the passage. **This question is worth 2 points.**

There were several inventions that helped the textile industry during the Industrial Revolution.

-
-
-

ANSWER CHOICES

1. People used spinning wheels in Asia and Europe as far back as the eleventh century.

2. The Calico Acts were designed to help the English domestic textile industry.

3. The inventions of Samuel Crompton and Eli Whitney both helped the textile industry.

4. The spinning wheel, the flying shuttle, and the rolling spinning wheel all spun cotton yarn quickly.

5. It was difficult to remove cotton fibers from seeds when people had to do that by hand.

6. The spinning jenny and the water frame could spin large numbers of cotton yarn at one time.

◢ Vocabulary Review

A   Complete each sentence with the appropriate word from the box.

sparse	efficient	reign	ally	flee

1   A place with _____ amounts of vegetation has few plants.

2   The time when a king rules over a land is his _____ .

3   When people run away from something, they _____ from it.

4   You are _____ when you do a job quickly and well.

5   Countries _____ themselves with others by joining together.

B   Complete each sentence with the correct answer.

1   A person who is interested in _____ is a **naturalist**.

    a. the outdoors   b. the indoors

2   When people **stress** certain tasks, they _____ .

    a. ignore those tasks   b. focus on those tasks

3   When one army **defeats** a second one, it _____ a battle against that army.

    a. loses   b. wins

4   **Prominent** features on a planet are _____ .

    a. easy to see   b. hard to find

5   If a disease is **widespread**, then _____ have it.

    a. many people   b. few people

6   Something that is a **mystery** is difficult to _____ .

    a. purchase   b. understand

7   The soldiers plan to **assault** the village by _____ .

    a. attacking it   b. leaving it alone

8   Saturn has the most **extensive** ring system because it _____ .

    a. has few rings   b. has many rings

9   Two pieces that are **glued** together are _____ to each other.

    a. connected   b. apart

Chapter **04**

Negative Factual Information

◢ About the Question

Negative Factual Information questions focus on information that is not included in the passage. You are asked to answer a question asking about facts or information that is NOT covered in the passage. Three of the four answer choices contain accurate information appearing in the passage while the correct answer choice has either incorrect information or information that does not appear in the passage. The information asked about in these questions is always included in a small section of the passage. There are 0-2 Negative Factual Information questions for each passage.

Recognizing Negative Factual Information questions:

- According to paragraph 1, which of the following is NOT true about X?

- The author's description of X mentions all of the following EXCEPT:

- In paragraph 2, all of the following questions are answered EXCEPT:

Helpful hints for answering the questions correctly:

- The question identifies one or two paragraphs where the correct answer can be found. Focus only on that part of the passage when looking for the correct answer.

- The correct answer may contain information that is factually correct but does not appear in the passage.

- The answer choices often restate the information mentioned in the passage but use different words and phrases. Be careful of slight deviations that can make these restatements become the correct answer.

Basic Practice

Check T if the statement is true and F if the statement is false according to each paragraph.

CH04_1A

A

One of the most important documents in the history of England was the Magna Carta. It was signed by King John after his nobles forced him to. They had rebelled against the king due to his harsh rule. The Magna Carta stated that the king was not above the law and also protected the rights of the people. It prohibited the king from making new taxes without consent, too. While King John promptly violated the Magna Carta after signing it, it proved to be influential over time.

1 The Magna Carta was signed by the king of England. T ☐ F ☐

2 According to the Magna Carta, the king had to obey the law. T ☐ F ☐

3 The Magna Carta allowed the king to raise taxes any time. T ☐ F ☐

CH04_1B

B

There are both saturated and unsaturated fats. Both of them are nutrients that provide energy for the body. Yet they also have a few differences. Saturated fats are solid at room temperature whereas unsaturated fats are liquid. Saturated fats are mostly found in meat and other animal products. These include milk and cheese. They tend to increase the body's cholesterol levels. On the other hand, unsaturated fats mainly come from plants. Eating them can lower the cholesterol level of the body.

1 Eating fat can give a person more energy. T ☐ F ☐

2 Saturated fats are liquid in room temperature conditions. T ☐ F ☐

3 Unsaturated fats can cause the body to get higher cholesterol levels. T ☐ F ☐

CH04_1C

C

Carnivorous plants are ones that get some of their nutrients by consuming animals such as insects. These plants usually grow in poor soil, so they are unable to obtain all the nutrients they need to grow well. The Venus flytrap is the best-known of all these types of plants. It has leaves that snap closed to trap insects that touch them. Two other kinds of carnivorous plants are sundews and pitcher plants, which utilize other methods to capture and kill animals.

1 Carnivorous plants get all of their nutrients from eating animals. T ☐ F ☐

2 The leaves of the Venus flytrap close to capture animals. T ☐ F ☐

3 One type of pitcher plant is the Venus flytrap. T ☐ F ☐

A | **Patagonia**

🎧 CH04_2A

The land at the southernmost part of South America belongs to Chile and Argentina. Known as Patagonia, this region starts around the Colorado River and extends south all the way to Tierra del Fuego. There are two main parts of Patagonia: the Patagonian Andes and the Pampa. The Andes Mountains extend down the western part of South America. These rugged mountains can

be thousands of meters high. In Patagonia, the mountains contain valleys, fjords, lakes, and glaciers. The Pampa is a vast grassland.

While large in size, both parts of Patagonia have few human inhabitants. Yet nearly 500 species of animals, most of which are birds, live there. There are also around sixty mammals that reside in this region, which is one of the largest <u>untamed</u> areas of land in the world. In addition, at least 2,500 species of plants ranging from mosses to trees can be found in both the mountainous area and the plains of Patagonia.

*untamed: wild; uncivilized

According to paragraphs 1 and 2, which of the following is NOT true about Patagonia?

Ⓐ There are large ice sheets found in it.

Ⓑ Not many people live in the area.

Ⓒ There are three distinct regions in it.

Ⓓ It includes both mountains and grasslands.

| Vocabulary |

• r_____ = rocky; hilly

• v_____ = extensive; very large

• i_____ = a person who lives in a certain area

B Walking Fish

All fish live in the water, but some can survive on land. Around the world, there are numerous air-breathing fish. Some can live out of the water for weeks or months at a time. Unfortunately, many walking fish are causing problems in their environments.

The main issue is that some walking fish have become **invasive species**. The climbing perch is one such example. It is slowly making its way from Papua New Guinea to Australia. This aggressive fish can survive out of the water for six days. Many fear that the climbing perch will lack natural predators in Australia. It will likely alter local ecosystems by feeding on large numbers of animals in its new environments.

The snakehead is another walking fish that is an invasive species. Native to parts of Asia, it has been found in parts of the United States. The snakehead can grow up to 1.2 meters long and can survive out of water. Highly aggressive, the fish attacks humans and feeds on numerous types of animals, thereby disrupting local ecosystems.

*invasive species: a plant or animal that moves from its native area to a new region

In paragraph 2, all of the following questions are answered EXCEPT:

Ⓐ What will the climbing perch do if it reaches Australia?

Ⓑ What is the behavior of the climbing perch like?

Ⓒ How long can the climbing perch live on land?

Ⓓ When is the climbing perch expected to arrive in Australia?

Vocabulary

- a _____ = tending to attack others without being attacked first
- e _____ = all the living and nonliving things in a certain area
- d _____ = to cause problems; to interrupt

A Art Deco in New York City

🎧 CH04_3A

In the 1920s and 1930s, one popular style of architecture was Art Deco. It was a combination of several modern artistic movements, including Cubism and Fauvism. It also was influenced by the styles of Japan, China, India, and Egypt. Art Deco architecture was characterized by the use of stainless steel, chrome, and concrete. Architects designed towering skyscrapers to show off the new style. This was especially true in New York City, where several Art Deco buildings remain standing today.

Skyscrapers built in New York City had to follow certain laws. For instance, one 1916 law prohibited the shadow of a building from entirely blocking the sunlight on other buildings and the streets. This led to the layer-cake design common for many Art Deco buildings there. These structures have wide bottom sections and then, as they rise, they get narrower, so they are built like layers. Art Deco buildings often have either boxlike shapes or straight sections with rounded corners. Some have spires or **battlements** like those on castles. Another feature is that their exteriors have detailed designs done in stainless steel and concrete.

The two most noted examples of Art Deco architecture in New York City are the Chrysler Building and the Empire State Building. The former was completed in 1930. Its main features are the massive stainless steel terraced crown and spire on its top. The crown's arched exteriors and triangle-shaped windows are considered classics of Art Deco design. The Chrysler Building was the world's tallest structure until the Empire State Building was completed the next year in 1931. It too was noted for its layered design and tall Art Deco spire. Today, the Empire State Building is considered one of the architectural wonders of the world.

*battlement: a raised structure on a castle or similar structure that was originally used for defensive purposes

Vocabulary

- c _____ = to describe something; to mark or distinguish something
- p _____ = not to allow; to ban
- s _____ = a tall, thin, pointed top of a building
- m _____ = very large; enormous

1   The word "towering" in the passage is closest in meaning to

   (A) erect   (B) straight

   (C) high   (D) wide

2   Which of the sentences below best expresses the essential information in the highlighted sentence in the passage? Incorrect answer choices change the meaning in important ways or leave out essential information.

   These structures have wide bottom sections and then, as they rise, they get narrower, so they are built like layers.

   (A) Some of these buildings are very wide at their bottoms, which lets them have multiple layers.

   (B) At their bottoms, the buildings are wide, but their layers become narrower as they get taller.

   (C) These buildings are so narrow that they must be built in layers as they become higher.

   (D) Most of these structures are built in layers that make them look wide at the ground level.

3   In paragraph 3, the author's description of the Chrysler Building mentions all of the following EXCEPT:

   (A) which parts of it are inspired by Art Deco

   (B) how long it was the world's tallest building

   (C) what some of its major characteristics are

   (D) how much shorter than the Empire State Building it is

4   An introductory sentence for a brief summary of the passage is provided below. Complete the summary by selecting the THREE answer choices that express the most important ideas of the passage. Some sentences do not belong because they express ideas that are not presented in the passage or are minor ideas in the passage.

   Many skyscrapers in New York City were influenced by the Art Deco Movement.

   ANSWER CHOICES

   1 New York City skyscrapers in the 1920s often used Art Deco materials and designs.

   2 Both the Chrysler Building and the Empire State Building have Art Deco characteristics.

   3 Many laws that dictated how skyscrapers could be built were passed in New York City.

   4 Lots of skyscrapers in New York City use the layer-cake design as they rise higher.

   5 Art Deco was influenced by several art movements as well as the art of many countries.

B | Economic Bubbles

When the price of an asset is much greater than its true value, an economic bubble occurs. The bubble typically bursts as soon as people realize the asset's actual worth. The price of the asset then dramatically declines. Unfortunately, by that time, most investors have already purchased the asset at inflated prices. When the price goes down, these individuals lose large amounts of money. Two prominent historical examples of economic bubbles are the Dutch Tulip Mania in the 1600s and the South Sea Bubble in the early 1700s. In more recent times, there were the Internet dotcom bubble of the late 1990s and the housing market bubble in 2007 and 2008.

Economists are uncertain how and why economic bubbles occur. They are often identified only after the price of the asset drops. The reason is that people disagree about the asset's true value. It is only afterward that the actual worth is realized. For instance, in the 1990s, many investors believed that the new Internet companies would earn huge profits. **1** They invested heavily in them, so their stock prices rose, creating a bubble. **2** However, most of these companies had poor business plans and failed to attract enough customers. **3** Only a few, such as Amazon.com, survived when the bubble burst. **4**

Once a bubble begins, speculation makes the price of the asset rise. Some investors hold on to the asset while others do not. They try to profit by selling it for an even higher price than what they paid. These new buyers, in turn, also hope to sell for an even higher price. Ultimately, when the price collapses, the people left holding the asset cannot find new buyers and lose their money, causing many of them to go bankrupt.

*speculation: the engagement in business transactions that are risky but which have the potential to provide large profits

Vocabulary

- a _____ = anything that has value
- b _____ = to explode; to blow up
- i _____ = a person who puts money into a business in the hope of earning more money
- p _____ = money a person or company makes from doing business

1   The word "prominent" in the passage is closest in meaning to

    Ⓐ notable

    Ⓑ typical

    Ⓒ past

    Ⓓ individual

2   In paragraph 1, all of the following questions are answered EXCEPT:

    Ⓐ What happens to investors when an economic bubble bursts?

    Ⓑ How long does an economic bubble last before it bursts?

    Ⓒ What is the definition of an economic bubble?

    Ⓓ When did some economic bubbles from the past take place?

3   Look at the four squares [▉] that indicate where the following sentence could be added to the passage.

Practically overnight, people who were once millionaires saw their personal net worth decline rapidly as the market dropped.

Where would the sentence best fit?

4   An introductory sentence for a brief summary of the passage is provided below. Complete the summary by selecting the THREE answer choices that express the most important ideas of the passage. Some sentences do not belong because they express ideas that are not presented in the passage or are minor ideas in the passage.

An economic bubble happens when the price of an asset rises but then suddenly bursts.

ANSWER CHOICES

    1̄ Different types of assets can cause economic bubbles to occur.

    2̄ Large numbers of people usually lose money when an economic bubble takes place.

    3̄ There was an Internet bubble in the 1990s where many people lost money.

    4̄ The Dutch Tulip Mania in the 1600s was the first economic bubble to happen.

    5̄ When the asset's true value becomes known, its price declines.

Thales of Miletus

Thales of Miletus was an ancient Greek philosopher. Born in the city of Miletus in Asia Minor, he lived from around 624 B.C. to 546 B.C. Thales was considered by some to be the first major philosopher of the Greek age. Much of his work was based on scientific philosophy. He produced work in the fields of mathematics, astronomy, and engineering. Thales always sought rational explanations for everything he saw. So he challenged the accepted belief that mythology was sufficient enough to explain the world and the universe. During his lifetime, he was known as one of the Seven Sages of Greece. His work heavily influenced those who came after him, including Socrates, Plato, and Aristotle.

During the time he lived, there were Greek communities in many parts of the eastern Mediterranean Sea. Thales himself spent his life residing in Greece, Egypt, and Babylon. His principal area of expertise was engineering. But he later became adept in both mathematics and astronomy. He was known for predicting solar eclipses and determining the timing of the equinoxes and solstices. He also discovered the seasons and accurately calculated the length of a year. Thales studied geometry and electricity and even discovered static electricity. Finally, he established a school of philosophy, took part in politics, and was a businessman.

There are no known surviving writings of Thales as they were lost over time. The work of Aristotle therefore serves as the primary source of information about him. Aristotle claimed that Thales's philosophical ideas centered on what was known as the First Cause. This was the substance from which all else came. Thales believed that the First Cause was water. Water flowed around everything, could change its shape, and could exist in different states, but it never changed its basic substance. One part of his theory was that the Earth was floating on a vast ocean of water. He further believed that earthquakes were caused by the motion of this ocean's waves. Some experts disagree regarding whether Thales believed the Earth was flat or spherical in shape. But given his expertise in astronomy, it is hard to believe he thought the Earth was flat.

Thales was noted for two famous sayings. The first was "Know thyself." Some believe he meant that a person must know the nature of mankind before he or she could explore other areas. ■ Others claim he meant that a person must know his or her inner self before everything else. ■ His second famous saying has also been interpreted in various ways. ■ Thales supposedly said, "All things are full of gods." ■ This is a somewhat odd statement considering that Thales overtly rejected the influence of the gods on nature. However, Plato later popularized the saying and attributed it to Thales. Still, the precise meaning of this sentence is unclear to modern scholars.

*Glossary

equinox: the time when the sun crosses the celestial equator, making the day and the night last the same amount of time

solstice: the time when the sun is farthest away from the celestial equator, making either the day or the night the shortest one of the year

1   In paragraph 1, the author's description of Thales mentions all of the following EXCEPT:

    Ⓐ which of his works have survived

    Ⓑ what some people used to call him

    Ⓒ the time during which he lived

    Ⓓ which areas he did work in

2   Which of the following can be inferred from paragraph 1 about Socrates, Plato, and Aristotle?

    Ⓐ They rejected the ideas that Thales promoted.

    Ⓑ They knew less about philosophy than Thales did.

    Ⓒ They all read some of the writings of Thales.

    Ⓓ They became famous thanks to the influence of Thales.

3   According to paragraph 2, which of the following is NOT true about Thales?

    Ⓐ He knew how to use electricity as a source of energy.

    Ⓑ He was both a scientist and engineer.

    Ⓒ He made several scientific discoveries.

    Ⓓ He spent time living in several different places.

4 The author discusses "the First Cause" in paragraph 3 in order to

Ⓐ point out some of the problems with this theory

Ⓑ explain that water is the most important substance

Ⓒ show how it relates to the philosophy of Thales

Ⓓ mention that Thales wrote an entire book on it

5 According to paragraph 3, Thales believed earthquakes happened because

Ⓐ the flat shape of the Earth sometimes rose and fell

Ⓑ waves of water below the land were moving

Ⓒ plates in the Earth's crust collided with one another

Ⓓ the First Cause became heated and thus expanded

6 The word "overtly" in the passage is closest in meaning to

Ⓐ steadily

Ⓑ openly

Ⓒ repeatedly

Ⓓ carefully

7 Look at the four squares [■] that indicate where the following sentence could be added to the passage.

There are many supporters of both interpretations.

Where would the sentence best fit?

Click on a square [■] to add the sentence to the passage.

8 **Directions:** An introductory sentence for a brief summary of the passage is provided below. Complete the summary by selecting the THREE answer choices that express the most important ideas of the passage. Some sentences do not belong because they express ideas that are not presented in the passage or are minor ideas in the passage. **This question is worth 2 points.**

Thales of Miletus was talented in a wide range of fields.

-
-
-

ANSWER CHOICES

1. Thales believed everything could be explained rationally, so he looked for scientific explanations.

2. The First Cause was a belief of Thales's that had a great influence on his philosophy.

3. Thales did work in science and made discoveries such as the seasons and static electricity.

4. The Greek community in which Thales lived was spread out over the eastern part of the Mediterranean Sea.

5. "Know thyself" was a sentence by Thales that has a large number of different interpretations.

6. None of the works that were written by Thales has survived to the present day.

American Colonial Farmers in New England

The majority of early settlers in England's American colonies in the seventeenth and eighteenth centuries were farmers. They arrived with their families, settled the land, and began growing crops. Many lived in New England, where plenty of land was available.

However, farming in New England was difficult. Much of the area was not arable as the poor soil was unsuitable for farming. The region also had short summers and long winters, resulting in shorter growing seasons. In many places, there were thick forests and numerous rocks in the soil. Farmers and their families worked hard to get rid of trees and rocks before planting crops. There was also the problem of forest regrowth, so farmers usually had to clear new trees from their land every few years.

Initially, farmers in New England grew only enough to feed themselves. ◼1 Their main crops were grains, pumpkins, corn, squash, and beans. ◼2 They practiced crop rotation if they had enough cleared land to make it practical. ◼3 Some New England farmers grew tobacco, but the soil was not suitable for this cash crop everywhere. ◼4 Most of the work was with simple tools. Iron-tipped hoes and plows prepared the land for planting, which was usually done by hand. In fall, farmers harvested their crops with sickles and scythes. More fortunate farmers had animals to do hard labor. A horse or ox could help them prepare the rocky soil for planting. Sometimes a single horse or ox was shared by many families. Cows provided milk, butter, and cheese while chickens provided eggs and meat.

Despite their hard work, many families could not grow enough food to survive each season. They therefore acquired extra food from nearby sources. Colonists hunted the plentiful game, such as deer and rabbits, living in forests, and they picked fruits and berries that ripened in summer. As a result of the poor land and low crop yields, many New England colonists turned to the Atlantic Ocean for extra food. The nearby water had enormous schools of cod and haddock as well as lobsters, crabs, and other shellfish. Some colonists began hunting whales for oil, so a lively whaling industry soon developed in New England.

As for residences, the typical colonial farmer's home in New England in the seventeenth century was a log cabin with a dirt floor. It was often a single room in which the entire family cooked, ate, and slept. Stone fireplaces burned wood for heating and cooking. The smoke departed the house through stone chimneys. Over time, these cabins were expanded into large multiroom homes. There were many rivers and waterfalls in the area to run machines, so sawmills eventually began turning out cut wood for building houses. This led to the growth of wood-frame housing. Farmers also constructed wooden barns to store grain and to protect animals in. Most farms had a small toolshed as well. By the mid-eighteenth century, the wood-frame house had become the normal home for most New England farmers.

*Glossary

scythe: a tool with a long, curved blade that is used to cut plants

game: wild animals that people hunt for food

9 The word "clear" in the passage is closest in meaning to

    (A) plant

    (B) trim

    (C) remove

    (D) prune

10 According to paragraph 2, much of the land in New England was bad for farming because

    (A) there were not enough sunny days during the year

    (B) there was not enough water for farmers to use on their crops

    (C) there are large areas of land covered with mountains and hills

    (D) there were large numbers of rocks found in the soil

11 In paragraph 3, the author's description of colonial farming mentions all of the following EXCEPT:

    (A) the ways that farmers used animals for food

    (B) the types of tools that farmers used while working

    (C) the various crops that farmers grew in their fields

    (D) the sizes of the harvests that farmers reaped

12 In paragraph 4, why does the author mention "the Atlantic Ocean"?

Ⓐ To point out that people crossed it to get to America

Ⓑ To name some of the animals caught for food in it

Ⓒ To show how some colonists used its water for farming

Ⓓ To prove that Americans developed the first whaling industry

13 According to paragraph 5, which of the following is true about American colonial homes in the seventeenth century?

Ⓐ The single room that most of them had served many purposes.

Ⓑ Smoke was a major problem in the majority of houses.

Ⓒ Coal was used to heat many homes by burning it in fireplaces.

Ⓓ Most of them were wooden-frame houses with several rooms.

14 In paragraph 5, the author implies that sawmills

Ⓐ were owned and operated by wealthy colonial farmers

Ⓑ created wood that was used to build sailing ships

Ⓒ were able to run thanks to the use of water power

Ⓓ led to the destruction of many forests in New England

15 Look at the four squares [■] that indicate where the following sentence could be added to the passage.

This allowed them to grow different crops in their fields each year to keep the soil fertile.

Where would the sentence best fit?

Click on a square [■] to add the sentence to the passage.

16 Directions: An introductory sentence for a brief summary of the passage is provided below. Complete the summary by selecting the THREE answer choices that express the most important ideas of the passage. Some sentences do not belong because they express ideas that are not presented in the passage or are minor ideas in the passage. **This question is worth 2 points.**

Colonists who farmed the land in New England during colonial times lived difficult lives.

-
-
-

ANSWER CHOICES

1. The land in New England was poor for farming, and growing seasons were short as well.

2. The whaling industry became a major source of money for some New England colonists.

3. Because farmers could not grow enough crops, they relied upon other sources of food, too.

4. Wood-frame houses became more popular thanks to the building of sawmills.

5. Cash crops such as tobacco provided large amounts of money for some farmers.

6. Farmers had to use simple tools to work the land, but some luckier ones had animals.

■ Vocabulary Review

A Complete each sentence with the appropriate word from the box.

aggressive	disrupted	investors	predict	substance

1. The storm knocked down power lines and _____ electric service.

2. That animal is very _____ and often attacks other animals.

3. What _____ is this item made of?

4. Nobody knows what will happen since we cannot _____ the future.

5. The _____ put a lot of their own money into the project.

B Complete each sentence with the correct answer.

1. **Rugged** mountains are always very _____.

   a. rough   b. smooth

2. They _____ since they earned a **profit** from their store.

   a. made money   b. lost money

3. The balloon **burst**, so it _____ in his face.

   a. got bigger   b. exploded

4. A **rational** thinker is one who uses _____ thoughts.

   a. logical   b. imaginary

5. A **vast** amount of land covers a _____.

   a. small area   b. large area

6. She _____ about that topic since it is her area of **expertise**.

   a. knows a lot   b. knows a bit

7. Gold is a valuable **asset** since it is _____.

   a. easy to buy   b. worth a lot of money

8. Because the world is shaped like a _____, it is **spherical**.

   a. square   b. circle

9. Because that event happened _____, it took place during **ancient** times.

   a. a long time ago   b. a few weeks ago

Chapter **05**

Sentence Simplification

Question Type | Sentence Simplification

◢ About the Question

Sentence Simplification questions focus on a single sentence. You are asked to choose a sentence that best restates the information in the sentence that is highlighted in the passage. You need to note the primary information that is found in the sentence and make sure that it is included in the answer choice that you select. The words, phrases, and grammar in the answer choices vary from those in the highlighted sentence. There are 0-1 Sentence Simplification questions for each passage.

Recognizing Sentence Simplification questions:

- Which of the sentences below best expresses the essential information in the highlighted sentence in the passage? Incorrect answer choices change the meaning in important ways or leave out essential information.

  [You will see a sentence in bold.]

Helpful hints for answering the questions correctly:

- The highlighted sentence typically contains at least two separate clauses. Make sure that you know what the main point or idea of each clause is.

- The answer choice you select must contain all of the important information that is in the highlighted sentence.

- Do not select answer choices that contain incorrect information or that omit important information.

- The answer choices for these questions are approximately half the length of the sentences being asked about. Therefore, you should consider how to summarize information in long sentences.

Basic Practice

Read each sentence below and choose the answer choice that has basically the same meaning.

A

> Insects frequently use camouflage, so they may be the same color as tree bark or leaves or resemble sticks, making them harder to be seen by predators.

(A) Many insects have a variety of methods they can use to employ camouflage.

(B) Some predators use camouflage to be able to hunt insects better.

(C) Insects may blend in with their surroundings to hide from other animals.

B

> Even though there are many glaciers around the world that are retreating, many others are expanding and growing bigger by the day.

(A) Most of the world's glaciers are steadily decreasing in size these days.

(B) While some glaciers are getting smaller, others are becoming larger.

(C) There are some glaciers becoming bigger than they ever were before.

C

> In the roughly twenty-seven days it takes the moon to orbit the Earth, the moon goes through several phases.

(A) The moon goes around the Earth, and a single phase lasts nearly a month.

(B) The moon completes one orbit of the Earth in about twenty-seven days.

(C) The moon has a number of different phases as it goes around the Earth.

D

> One leading theory about Stonehenge is that it was an ancient observatory, but other anthropologists dispute this belief.

(A) Some theorize that Stonehenge was used to look at the stars, but not everyone agrees.

(B) The theory about Stonehenge which most anthropologists believe is that it was an observatory.

(C) Not all anthropologists agree about what ancient people used Stonehenge for.

A | The Renaissance of the Twelfth Century

⌒ CH05_2A

The Italian Renaissance is well known, but there was another one that took place three centuries earlier. It is called the Renaissance of the Twelfth Century. It would go on to have a great amount of influence throughout Europe in several different fields.

One reason this revival of knowledge happened was the **Crusades**. The First Crusade occurred at the end of the eleventh century. During the twelfth century, the Second and Third Crusades took place. One result of these wars was increased contact between the East and the West. European scholars in the West thereby gained access to scientific, philosophic, and other knowledge that was known to people in the East. This helped increase the amount of knowledge in the West.

In addition, learning became more formal during this time. The first universities were founded in the eleventh century, and they continued to grow in the following hundred years. Eager students flocked to these new schools. There, they mostly studied theology. But some students also learned law, medicine, and other subjects.

*Crusades: a series of wars in which armies from Europe went to the Middle East to free the Holy Land from Muslim invaders

Which of the sentences below best expresses the essential information in the highlighted sentence in the passage? Incorrect answer choices change the meaning in important ways or leave out essential information.

European scholars in the West thereby gained access to scientific, philosophic, and other knowledge that was known to people in the East.

Ⓐ There was a lot of scientific and philosophic knowledge in the East.

Ⓑ Scholars from Europe traveled to the East to obtain more knowledge.

Ⓒ Knowledge from the East was obtained by people living in the West.

Ⓓ The people in the East knew more than those living in the West did.

Vocabulary

- e _____ = willing to do something
- f _____ = to go somewhere in great numbers
- t _____ = the study of religion

B | Robert Goddard

American Robert Goddard was one of the most influential people in the history of rocketry. His effect was so great that he is called the father of modern rocket propulsion. Thanks to his work, the American space program was eventually able to send astronauts to the moon.

Goddard was born in 1882 and became interested in rockets during his youth. In 1914, he was awarded two patents. One was for a rocket using liquid fuel while the other was for a two- or three-stage rocket. Both would become standard in the American space program of the 1950s and 1960s.

In 1926, Goddard successfully tested the first rocket to use liquid fuel. Some people mocked his suggestion that a rocket powered by liquid fuel could fly to the moon, but Goddard did not abandon his belief. He continued working on rockets until his death in 1945. He never saw his rockets travel into space, but it was his research that allowed it to happen.

*propulsion: the act of driving or moving something forward through force

---

Which of the sentences below best expresses the essential information in the highlighted sentence in the passage? Incorrect answer choices change the meaning in important ways or leave out essential information.

Some people mocked his suggestion that a rocket powered by liquid fuel could fly to the moon, but Goddard did not abandon his belief.

Ⓐ Goddard strongly believed that rockets would be able to fly to the moon one day.

Ⓑ Goddard felt a liquid fuel-powered rocked could fly to the moon despite the doubts of others.

Ⓒ Most people supported Goddard's belief that his rocket was able to reach the moon.

Ⓓ Many people made fun of Goddard for believing that humans would be able to fly to the moon.

Vocabulary

- p_____ = the legal right to an invention
- m_____ = to make fun of
- a_____ = to give up

A | Sediment in Rivers

🎧 CH05_3A

Sediment is a combination of soil particles and <u>organic matter</u>. It typically consists of clay, silt, sand, gravel, and decaying plant and animal matter. It is often carried from land into water. Rainfall, wind, and ice all help move sediment to rivers. Human activities, such as farming and cutting down trees, also move sediment toward water. Finally, gravity plays a role by moving some sediment from high elevations to lower ones.

Sediment is small in size, so rather than sink to the bottom, it is often suspended in water. In rivers, as the water moves, sediment is carried downstream. When the water begins to slow, the heavier particles get dropped to the riverbed. As for fine particles, they are carried all the way to where the river ends. This is usually a lake or an ocean. When sediment is deposited, it can influence the shape of the river. When a river bends, the water tends to flow more slowly, so sediment may build up and thereby create a wider riverbank. At river mouths, sediment that gets deposited can create estuaries, deltas, or large marshlands. The deltas at the Mississippi River and the Nile River are both places with large sediment deposits.

Deposits of sediment are important to river ecosystems. They create nutrition-rich environments that support a wide range of aquatic and land-based plant and animal life. But the sediment needs to be balanced. Too little sediment can lead to the erosion of deltas, estuaries, and marshes and destroy habitats. Too much sediment clouds the river. Not enough sunlight penetrates. Marine vegetation therefore dies. The sediment kills fish by clogging their gills. Finally, sediment that is too fine chokes fish eggs laid in riverbeds. Most fish require loose gravel beds for their eggs to provide them with enough oxygen.

*organic matter: anything that contains or once contained something living

| Vocabulary |

- d_____ = to rot
- s_____ = to be held up in the air or in another substance; to be above the ground
- e_____ = the part of a river where it meets the ocean
- c_____ = to block

1 According to paragraph 1, which of the following is true about sediment?

    Ⓐ Most of it gets into rivers due to human actions.

    Ⓑ It can move from low elevations to higher ones.

    Ⓒ People sometimes try to remove it from rivers.

    Ⓓ Some of it is made of matter from plants and animals.

Sentence Simplification Question

2 Which of the sentences below best expresses the essential information in the highlighted sentence in the passage? Incorrect answer choices change the meaning in important ways or leave out essential information.

    When a river bends, the water tends to flow more slowly, so sediment may build up and thereby create a wider riverbank.

    Ⓐ When there is very much sediment in rivers, it often creates wide riverbanks.

    Ⓑ Wide riverbanks result in rivers having many bends, which makes the water move slowly.

    Ⓒ If a river has a lot of sediment, the water in it moves slower than the water in other rivers.

    Ⓓ Sediment can make wide riverbanks when a river bends, so the water moves slowly.

Negative Factual Information Question

3 In paragraph 3, the author's description of the problems caused by sediment mentions all of the following EXCEPT:

    Ⓐ how it causes problems for fish eggs

    Ⓑ how it can cause water plants to die

    Ⓒ how it makes deltas and marshes too big

    Ⓓ how it kills many fish

Prose Summary Question

4 An introductory sentence for a brief summary of the passage is provided below. Complete the summary by selecting the THREE answer choices that express the most important ideas of the passage. Some sentences do not belong because they express ideas that are not presented in the passage or are minor ideas in the passage.

    Sediment gets into rivers in many ways and has a number of effects on them.

    ANSWER CHOICES

    ☐ Sediment often accumulates at the mouths of rivers and forms deltas and marshes.

    ☐ Many plants and animals depend on the environments created by large amounts of sediment.

    ☐ Sometimes fish can die when there is too much sediment in a small area.

    ☐ Rain, wind, and the action of gravity can move sediment from the ground to rivers.

    ☐ Because sediment can be very heavy, it often moves very slowly through water.

Venomous Insects

Large numbers of the insects that live on the Earth have venom. This is a liquid which an insect delivers either by stinging or biting another animal. The venom then causes some sort of harm to the animal in which it is injected. In many cases, it merely results in pain or <u>tissue</u> damage, such as a rash. In other cases, more powerful venom may paralyze or even kill the animals that are stung or bitten. Some insects use venom for offensive purposes, but others use it only to defend themselves.

Flies, beetles, and wasps are some insects that use their venom for offensive purposes. The horsefly is one such insect. This predator captures prey and then injects it with a powerful venom that paralyzes its victim. The horsefly can then feed upon its victim at its leisure. Many species of wasps also use venom to attack their prey. Wasps have stingers which can be used multiple times, thereby making them dangerous predators. Some of them can even be deadly to humans if they sting an individual several times.

Many more insects utilize their venom for defensive purposes. For the most part, they only attack others with venom when they are protecting their homes, eggs, or larvae. Ants, bees, beetles, and numerous other species use this kind of venom. Honeybees, for instance, protect their hives by stinging attackers. This prevents them from getting the bees' supplies of honey, which they need to survive. Likewise, ants may use venom to protect their nests. The harvester ant is widely considered the most venomous insect in the world. Only a few stings by this ant are capable of killing small mammals, and they can cause intense pain in any humans that they inject with their venom.

*tissue: cells that combine to form a part of an animal's body

Vocabulary

- i＿＿＿＿＿ = to put some sort of liquid into a person or animal
- p＿＿＿＿＿ = to prevent someone or something from moving
- d＿＿＿＿＿ = able to kill
- l＿＿＿＿＿ = insects that have just hatched

1   The author discusses "The horsefly" in paragraph 2 in order to

  Ⓐ show how it uses venom to attack animals

  Ⓑ compare its venom with that of the wasp

  Ⓒ claim it uses venom for defensive purposes

  Ⓓ state it has the most powerful venom of all insects

Reference Question

2   The word "them" in the passage refers to

  Ⓐ numerous other species

  Ⓑ honeybees

  Ⓒ their hives

  Ⓓ attackers

Sentence Simplification Question

3   Which of the sentences below best expresses the essential information in the highlighted
    sentence in the passage? Incorrect answer choices change the meaning in important ways or
    leave out essential information.

    **Only a few stings by this ant are capable of killing small mammals, and they can cause
    intense pain in any humans that they inject with their venom.**

  Ⓐ Some ants are capable of killing mammals like humans with their venom.

  Ⓑ The ant's venom can hurt humans badly and kill small mammals.

  Ⓒ The venom of some ants is powerful enough to kill some small animals.

  Ⓓ Some small mammals have enough venom to cause pain in humans.

Fill in a Table Question

4   Select the appropriate statements from the answer choices and match them to the type of
    venom to which they relate. TWO of the answer choices will NOT be used.

Offensive Purposes	Defensive Purposes
•	•
•	•

STATEMENTS

1 Is the more common usage of venom   4 Can be used by some types of wasps

2 May be powerful enough to paralyze victims   5 Is used against attackers trying to steal food

3 May result in the instant death of animals   6 Can often kill humans with one or two stings

The Norwich School of Art

In the early nineteenth century, there was an art movement based in Norwich, England. Noted for the landscape works made by its members, it was eventually called the Norwich School of Art. Norwich lies northeast of London in East Anglia. It is known for its beautiful and diverse landscape. John Crome, a landscape artist, established the school in 1803 and called it the Norwich Society at that time.

Crome was interested in examining the state of painting, architecture, and sculpture. He wanted to do that to discover the best methods to achieve perfection in those arts. Despite his lofty thoughts, the society primarily became a school of landscape painters. It was small at first but grew in size and reputation. Meetings involving the members were held every few weeks to discuss their ongoing works and other matters. In 1805, the Norwich School held an exhibition in Norwich. Eighteen artists contributed more than 220 works, most of which were oil and watercolor paintings. The exhibition, the first of its kind in England outside of London, was a success, and it raised the profile of the school.

Crome was the president of the society until he died in 1821. He was aided by John Sell Cotman, who served first as vice president and later as president from Crome's death until 1834. The society was dominated by these two men, and other artists followed the style of one or the other. While Crome favored strict realism for landscape works, Cotman differed. At times, he added fanciful, unrealistic touches. He also did not believe it was necessary to visit a site to paint it. He preferred to send other artists to sketch places and then used their drawings to make paintings of his own.

Most of the works produced by the members of the Norwich School were landscapes. Typical subjects included the coastal areas, forests, countryside, and towns of Norwich and the nearby Norfolk region. A prime example is Crome's *Yarmouth Harbour – Evening* (1817). The painting shows the harbor and its sailing vessels under an evening sky with everything reflected in the water. Another famous example is Cotman's *Norwich Market* (1807). It depicts a crowded market full of people, horses, and stalls between rows of buildings. The colors in both paintings are muted as they have faded over time. A more vibrant example is James Stark's *Woody Landscape*, whose date of completion is unknown. It shows some people on a road emerging from a forest. The trees are massive and dominate the entire scene.

The style of the Norwich School retained its popularity through the 1820s. However, the school began to lose favor in the 1830s. Cotman moved to London in 1834, so the school was deprived of its leader. An exhibition in 1839 was unsuccessful and showed the school's time had passed. Nevertheless, many artists of the school continued painting well into the late nineteenth century. Today, many of their works are displayed at the Norwich Castle Museum and in the Tate Museum in London.

*Glossary

landscape work: art that shows the natural scenery of an area

muted: drab; dark

1 The word "It" in the passage refers to

 (A) The Norwich School of Art

 (B) Norwich

 (C) London

 (D) Its beautiful and diverse landscape

2 Which of the sentences below best expresses the essential information in the highlighted sentence in the passage? Incorrect answer choices change the meaning in important ways or leave out essential information.

The exhibition, the first of its kind in England outside of London, was a success, and it raised the profile of the school.

 (A) No exhibitions in England had ever been held outside London until this one took place.

 (B) There was an exhibition of the works of some artists that made people aware of the school.

 (C) Until the exhibition took place outside London, few people had ever heard of the school.

 (D) The exhibition that made the school better known was the first in England not to be in London.

3 In paragraph 2, which of the following can be inferred about John Crome?

(A) He was more interested in architecture than in art.

(B) Most of the paintings at the 1805 exhibition were his.

(C) He held regular lectures to instruct the school members.

(D) His original goals for the school were not met.

4 According to paragraph 3, how did John Sell Cotman like to paint landscapes?

(A) By basing his works on drawings others had made

(B) By looking at photographs of places

(C) By imagining how he thought places looked

(D) By visiting the sites first

5 In paragraph 4, the author uses "*Woody Landscape*" as an example of

(A) a typical painting made by the Norwich School

(B) the best work of art made by John Crome

(C) a drab landscape showing the local region

(D) one of the early Norwich School paintings

6 In paragraph 4, the author's description of the works produced by the Norwich School mentions all of the following EXCEPT:

(A) the names of some more famous examples

(B) the reason so many landscapes were painted

(C) what types of scenes most of them showed

(D) the places that were often shown in their works

7 In stating that the school began to "lose favor," the author means that the school was

(A) unknown

(B) ignored by critics

(C) less popular

(D) closed down

8 **Directions:** An introductory sentence for a brief summary of the passage is provided below. Complete the summary by selecting the THREE answer choices that express the most important ideas of the passage. Some sentences do not belong because they express ideas that are not presented in the passage or are minor ideas in the passage. **This question is worth 2 points.**

The Norwich School of Art was founded by John Crome, and its members mostly created landscapes.

-
-
-

ANSWER CHOICES

1. John Crome remained the head of the school for nearly twenty years until he died.

2. The paintings of the Norwich School influenced a large number of artists in later years.

3. John Crome and John Sell Cotman were the two biggest influences on the school.

4. Many of the landscapes that the members created featured scenes from the surrounding area.

5. Large numbers of paintings made by the Norwich School are on display in museums today.

6. The Norwich School started to gain popularity thanks to an exhibition of its works in 1805.

The Roles of Bees in Nature

Bees play vital roles in their ecosystems. Without them, the world would be different by having fewer plants and much less food. The reason is that bees are responsible for pollinating many crops people eat. They also pollinate numerous species of wild plants. In addition, bees provide food for both people and animals. Finally, they play a key role in building their ecosystems, and they ensure biodiversity in nature, which helps ecosystems survive.

Pollination is the act of moving pollen between the female and male parts of a plant. Many plants cannot pollinate themselves. Without doing so, they cannot produce fruits, seeds, or berries. They need outside help. Bees often provide this. They suck nectar from plant flowers and tree blossoms to make honey. As they do so, their bodies brush up against the pollen in flowers and trees. While they move from flower to flower, the pollen gathered on their bodies is spread around. This starts the reproductive cycles of plants. It is estimated that around thirty percent of human crops need help pollinating. Bees pollinate many crops, including apples, cherries, melons, avocados, cranberries, and broccoli. They also pollinate wild nuts, fruits, and berries, which are food sources for numerous animals. In addition, common forest trees such as willows and poplars rely on bees to pollinate their blossoms.

Bees provide food for people and animals in two other ways. First, they produce honey, which both people and animals enjoy eating. Nowadays, farmers raise bees in large colonies not only for their pollination abilities but also for the honey they produce. Bears and other wild animals are known to ravage entire hives just to obtain the honey inside them. Second, bees are eaten by many wild animals. Large numbers of bird species consume them. So do spiders and insects such as moths, dragonflies, and praying mantises.

In many ecosystems, bees are considered keystone species because they are so essential. The primary reason for this is that bees help ecosystems develop by pollinating so many plants. By taking pollen from a wide variety of plants, bees contribute to making ecosystems diverse. This allows a wide variety of plants, many of which would not survive without bees, to grow in a single area. The more diverse an ecosystem is with regards to plant life, the greater its chances of surviving and prospering as it provides a home for a wide range of animal life.

Unfortunately, bees are not thriving everywhere. In some places, entire colonies are dying in what biologists call colony collapse disorder. Experts are struggling to understand why this is happening. The main theory is that chemical pesticides and insecticides are killing bees. If these chemicals get into plants, bees can absorb them when they suck nectar from flowers. Many scientists are alarmed by this. The reason is that if too many bees die, ecosystems will undergo changes. This could result in the collapse of future human and animal food supplies in some places.

*Glossary

biodiversity: the act of there being a wide range of plant and animal species in an area

nectar: a sweet liquid that is produced by plants and attracts birds and insects

9   According to paragraph 1, which of the following is NOT true about bees?

    Ⓐ They pollinate all of the wild plants growing in forests.

    Ⓑ They help make food that humans and animals eat.

    Ⓒ They are considered important in the places they live.

    Ⓓ They contribute to the wide number of plant species on the Earth.

10   According to paragraph 2, bees pollinate plants by

    Ⓐ moving nectar from male trees to female ones

    Ⓑ creating pollen that can be used by various plants

    Ⓒ transferring pollen to different plants

    Ⓓ using pollen created from honey in their hives

11   The author's description of the types of plants bees pollinate in paragraph 2 mentions all of the following EXCEPT:

    Ⓐ nuts planted by people

    Ⓑ trees that grow in forests

    Ⓒ berries that grow in the wild

    Ⓓ crops planted by humans

12 The word "ravage" in the passage is closest in meaning to

  (A) find

  (B) destroy

  (C) protect

  (D) look for

13 In paragraph 3, the author uses "moths, dragonflies, and praying mantises" as examples of

  (A) animals that are known to hunt bees

  (B) insects that cause harm to plants that bees pollinate

  (C) insects that bees often consume for food

  (D) animals that help bees pollinate plants

14 Which of the sentences below best expresses the essential information in the highlighted sentence in the passage? Incorrect answer choices change the meaning in important ways or leave out essential information.

This allows a wide variety of plants, many of which would not survive without bees, to grow in a single area.

  (A) Bees that live in a single area typically pollinate most of the plants in it.

  (B) When there are no bees in a certain area, most of the plants there do not survive.

  (C) Without bees, most of the Earth's plants would not have survived.

  (D) Many plant species that would otherwise die without bees manage to grow.

15 In paragraph 5, the author implies that colony collapse disorder

  (A) has made it difficult for bees to reproduce

  (B) is not fully understood by scientists yet

  (C) has killed most bees around the world

  (D) is definitely caused by human actions

16 **Directions:** An introductory sentence for a brief summary of the passage is provided below. Complete the summary by selecting the THREE answer choices that express the most important ideas of the passage. Some sentences do not belong because they express ideas that are not presented in the passage or are minor ideas in the passage. **This question is worth 2 points.**

Bees are important animals in their ecosystems for several reasons.

-
-
-

ANSWER CHOICES

1. Colony collapse disorder is killing bees on account of pesticides and insecticides.

2. There are many different species of bees, and most of them help pollinate plants.

3. Bees are eaten by many wild animals and also make honey that people and animals consume.

4. The pollination of both planted crops and wild plants is done by bees in many places.

5. Thanks to bees, there are a wide variety of plants growing all around the world.

6. Bees are known to live in beehives that have a queen bee and thousands of worker bees.

■ Vocabulary Review

A   Complete each sentence with the appropriate word from the box.

| theology | patent | mocked | decaying | exhibition |

1   A _____ gives a person ownership of an invention.

2   _____ matter rots and falls apart over time.

3   The children _____ the young boy by making fun of him.

4   The study of religion is known as _____.

5   At an _____, works of art are put on display.

B   Complete each sentence with the correct answer.

1   When you **abandon** work on a project, you _____ on it.
    a. stop working   b. complete your work

2   People who are **depicted** in a work of art are _____ in it.
    a. small   b. featured

3   Students who are **eager** to study are very _____.
    a. bored by school   b. willing to learn

4   A **prime** example is one that is more _____ than others.
    a. ideal   b. expensive

5   When fish have **clogged** gills, there is _____ their gills.
    a. nothing in   b. something blocking

6   A person _____ if he is **paralyzed**.
    a. is very athletic   b. cannot move

7   A person who **favors** something _____ more than others.
    a. likes it   b. ignores it

8   When people **flock** to a new place, they go there _____.
    a. by flying   b. in great numbers

9   Something that is **deadly** is capable of _____ others.
    a. killing   b. healing

Chapter **06**

Inference

Question Type | Inference

�__ About the Question

Inference questions focus on the implications that are made in the passage. You are asked to analyze the information presented in the passage and then to come to logical conclusions about it. The answers to these questions are never explicitly written in the passage. Instead, you need to infer what the author of the passage means. These questions often require you to understand cause and effect and also to compare and contrast various events, people, or ideas. There are 0-2 Inference questions for each passage. Most passages have at least 1 Inference question though.

Recognizing Inference questions:

- Which of the following can be inferred about X?

- The author of the passage implies that X . . .

- Which of the following can be inferred from paragraph 1 about X?

Helpful hints for answering the questions correctly:

- Inference questions often focus on various cause and effect relationships. Think about the possible unstated effects of various events, ideas, or phenomena that are presented in the passage.

- You need to be able to read between the lines to answer these questions properly. Focus not only on what the author is overtly writing but also on what the author is hinting at in the text.

- Avoid selecting answer choices because they contain words that are found in the passage. These are frequently misleading.

- The correct answer will never contradict the main point of the passage. Avoid answer choices that go against the main point or theme of the passage.

- Some questions use words such as *suggest* rather than *imply* or *infer*.

- The difficulty level of these questions has increased. In some cases, test takers must be able to understand an entire paragraph rather than only a part of it.

Read the following paragraphs and answer the questions.

🎧 CH06_1A

A

Light moves in a straight line faster than anything in the universe. But upon encountering a dense object, it slows down and refracts, or bends. This refraction lets people who wear eyeglasses see better. Eyeglasses are made of curved glass or plastic since both cause light to refract. Depending upon how much light bends, it may look like it is coming from closer or farther away. Thus, refraction alters how images are viewed, so people's vision can be improved.

What can be inferred about refraction?

Ⓐ It happens when light passes through an object.

Ⓑ It causes the speed of light to increase.

Ⓒ It only takes place when light encounters glass.

🎧 CH06_1B

B

Every continent except for Antarctica has at least one continental divide. This is an elevated area of land that divides two drainage basins. The most famous continental divide is the one that runs in a north-south direction in North America. Starting in Alaska, it goes south through Canada. It runs through the United States and then enters Mexico. Water on the western side of the line drains in the Pacific Ocean. Water on the eastern side empties into the Arctic Ocean, the Atlantic Ocean, or the Gulf of Mexico.

What can be inferred about the continental divide in North America?

Ⓐ It is longer than any other continental divide.

Ⓑ It is nearer the Atlantic Ocean than the Pacific Ocean.

Ⓒ It is on land higher than the surrounding area.

🎧 CH06_1C

C

Thomas Malthus was a British economist known for his writings on population. In the 1700s and 1800s, the global population was rising. Many philosophers thought the increase in population was sustainable. Malthus took a more pessimistic view. He believed the human population would continue to grow while the food supply would not. Thus, Malthus set limits on the population. He said the population would decline at some point.

What can be inferred about Thomas Malthus?

Ⓐ He disagreed with most philosophers on population.

Ⓑ He lived during a time when the population declined.

Ⓒ He worked on ways to improve the food supply.

A | The Kangaroo

🎧 CH06_2A

In the eastern part of Australia, the world's largest marsupial lives. The kangaroo can stand more than two meters tall. It has powerful hind legs and a strong tail and is known for its leaping ability. Some are capable of leaping more than nine meters in a single jump.

As a marsupial, the female kangaroo gives birth to a joey, as its baby is called, before it is fully developed. The joey then lives in a pouch at the front of the mother. There, the mother <u>nurtures</u> the joey by providing it with milk. The joey can leave the pouch for short periods of time after four months, and it leaves the pouch for good when it is around ten months old.

As a large animal, the kangaroo does not have many natural predators. Nevertheless, its habitats are shrinking as they become developed by humans. It is also vulnerable to periods of extreme heat and drought. Still, there are millions of kangaroos living in Australia, so it is not in any immediate danger.

*nurture: to provide food and protection

In paragraph 3, the author implies that kangaroos

- (A) can be killed by extreme weather conditions
- (B) should be placed on the endangered species list
- (C) have expanding areas in which they can live
- (D) are predators that hunt smaller animals

Vocabulary

- h_____ = back
- p_____ = a pocket
- v_____ = able to be hurt or killed by

James Fenimore Cooper

James Fenimore Cooper was born in 1789. A year later, his family moved to Cooperstown in upstate New York. Growing up there, he was tremendously influenced by the land and the people. They would feature in the novels that made him famous.

In 1820, Cooper wrote his first novel, *Precaution*, in imitation of the style of Jane Austen. Three years later, he authored *The Pioneers*, the first of the five books in *The Leatherstocking Tales*. It featured the woodsman Natty Bumppo. This book told a tale about life on the American frontier. It is widely considered the first real American novel, and Bumppo is the first fictional American hero.

The Pioneers was an instant success, so the reading public wanted more. Cooper subsequently published *The Last of the Mohicans* in 1826, which also featured Bumppo. This would become his most famous work. Cooper was a prolific author and wrote several more works until his death in 1851. While his works have often been criticized, they have influenced numerous authors.

*prolific: highly productive

Which of the following can be inferred from paragraphs 1 and 2 about *The Pioneers*?

Ⓐ It was inspired by Cooper's life as a child.

Ⓑ It was based on a true story Cooper's parents told him.

Ⓒ It was considered the best of Cooper's works.

Ⓓ It was written in a style no author had tried before.

Vocabulary

- w_____ = a person who spends a lot of time in the forest and is skilled at hunting
- f_____ = the land at the edge of a country that has few people living in it
- s_____ = later; next

A | Language Acquisition by Children

🎧 CH06_3A

Children are not born with the ability to speak but must instead acquire their language skills. They accomplish this primarily by being together with people who are talking. Children who are surrounded by older individuals that speak will learn the language skills of the family's <u>native tongue</u>. However, some steps must be taken to ensure that the children learn to speak well.

First, the type of speech must be both conversational and dynamic. It cannot be static talking, such as that coming from a radio or television set. There must be some interactive aspect, such as two people having a conversation during which they speak back and forth. When children observe these conversations, they desire to do the same thing. In addition, talking to children in simple terms—often called baby talk—can improve their ability to learn. Baby talk utilizes short, simple sentences. It also uses basic structures, includes repetitions, and employs exaggerated pronunciation. Children can learn languages more easily if they are presented in these manners.

All children learn to speak at different times in their lives. Most babies make simple sounds such as *ooh*, *aah*, and *ee* when they are around six weeks old. *Mama* or *papa* is often the first understandable word children say. Later, they begin to utter single words, such as *dog*, *cat*, *cookie*, or *run*. This normally happens when they are around a year and a half old. As children grow older, they need to play with others their age. Doing so can improve their language skills. Play activities are dynamic situations, so children must use language to do activities with others. By doing this, they can learn to make sentences. At first, they are short and simple. However, they grow in complexity as children improve their language skills.

*native tongue: the language that is spoken by the people of a certain place

Vocabulary

- d_____ = active
- s_____ = inactive
- e_____ = overstated
- c_____ = how complicated something is

1 The word "interactive" in the passage is closest in meaning to

    Ⓐ intermediate

    Ⓑ appropriate

    Ⓒ cooperative

    Ⓓ approved

Factual Information Question

2 In paragraph 2, the author's description of baby talk mentions which of the following?

    Ⓐ The number of words that it contains

    Ⓑ The methods of communication that it consists of

    Ⓒ The time when babies begin to utilize it

    Ⓓ The best way for parents to learn to speak it

Inference Question

3 In paragraph 3, which of the following can be inferred about children?

    Ⓐ It would be better for them to study than to play with others.

    Ⓑ Those with more friends can develop better language skills.

    Ⓒ Most of them cannot speak until they are older than two.

    Ⓓ They can speak correct sentences only after they attend school.

Prose Summary Question

4 An introductory sentence for a brief summary of the passage is provided below. Complete the summary by selecting the THREE answer choices that express the most important ideas of the passage. Some sentences do not belong because they express ideas that are not presented in the passage or are minor ideas in the passage.

Children acquire their language skills in several ways over an extended period of time.

ANSWER CHOICES

    1️⃣ Babies can make a wide variety of sounds when they are a couple of months old.

    2️⃣ Observing people talking to one another can help children learn how to speak.

    3️⃣ Dynamic situations such as playing with other individuals can be useful to children.

    4️⃣ Speech that is static is useful for improving the vocabulary of many children.

    5️⃣ Baby talk is effective for language learning thanks to the simple structures it uses.

B The Effects of Public Transportation on Urban Life

In modern times, public transportation is available in most cities. This normally consists of a combination of bus, rail, streetcar, train, and subway systems. Public transportation is relatively new as it was not introduced to most cities until the 1800s. It has had a tremendous effect on both the appearances of cities and the people living in them.

Prior to the advent of public transportation, cities were extremely crowded. The main reason concerned mobility. Without a quick and easy method of transportation, most people had to live near their workplaces. People who worked in cities therefore had to live in them. The closer they lived to their places of employment, the less time they had to spend traveling to their jobs in factories and other places. Since cities were so crowded, people lived in homes that were small and cramped. City streets also tended to be narrow and were not maintained well.

In the mid-1800s, large urban centers began developing public transportation systems. At first, streetcars were introduced. In 1863, the world's first subway system was introduced in London, England. In the twentieth century, bus systems were established. These forms of public transportation could carry people long distances for low prices. They resulted in several changes in urban life. First, people started moving from their homes to places located farther away from the city center. They still worked there, but they no longer had to live close to their jobs. Roads expanded in size since streetcars had to share lanes with horses and, later, cars. The tourism industries in some places also grew. For instance, Coney Island in New York and Brighton Beach in England were connected to big cities by railways. Thus, people living in nearby cities were easily able to visit them.

*cramped: overcrowded; small and having little open space

Vocabulary

- r_____ = fairly; quite
- w_____ = the location where a person's job is
- e_____ = to start, found, or create
- l_____ = a part of a road wide enough for vehicles to drive on

1   In paragraph 2, the author implies that streets in cities before public transportation

   Ⓐ were often in very poor condition

   Ⓑ were made from cheap materials

   Ⓒ were built in straight lines

   Ⓓ were located close to houses and buildings

2   In paragraph 3, the author uses "Coney Island in New York" as an example of

   Ⓐ a place that became very popular due to tourism

   Ⓑ a destination near New York that had streetcars running to it

   Ⓒ a tourist site that benefitted from public transportation

   Ⓓ a beachside area that got many visitors from trains

3   According to paragraph 3, which of the following is true about public transportation systems?

   Ⓐ They were inexpensive for people to use.

   Ⓑ They were found in every major city in the world.

   Ⓒ They consisted mostly of buses and subways.

   Ⓓ They required large monetary investments by cities.

4   An introductory sentence for a brief summary of the passage is provided below. Complete the summary by selecting the THREE answer choices that express the most important ideas of the passage. Some sentences do not belong because they express ideas that are not presented in the passage or are minor ideas in the passage.

   Developments in public transportation changed urban centers in many ways.

   ANSWER CHOICES

   ① Coney Island and Brighton Beach became popular resorts.

   ② Roads became wider and were better maintained for public transportation.

   ③ Public transportation allowed people to travel to places for low prices.

   ④ People moved from downtown areas to places farther away from cities.

   ⑤ Fewer people lived in houses that were small in the centers of cities.

CH06_4A

The Venetian Water System

The city of Venice, Italy, sits atop islands surrounded by water. This water, however, is salty and thus unfit for drinking. Throughout the city's history, it has dealt with the problem of providing fresh water for its people. The people of Venice have therefore had to be creative in their endeavors.

One simple solution was to collect water in barrels from the many rivers and streams on the mainland. Then, the barrels were transported to the city. This was extremely labor intensive though, so it was the least desired option. The Venetians also built a system of wells to collect rainwater. It was collected in clay-lined cisterns kept underground. Every major square in Venice had manholes where rainwater could drain underground. Beneath the squares were cisterns, which contained layers of sand. The rainwater filtered through the sand, thereby removing any impurities. In the center of each square was a well about five meters deep. The cistern bottoms were slanted so that the water flowed toward the wells after it was filtered. People could then draw water from the wells in buckets.

Each well had a raised stone or brick circular top, many of which still exist today. The stone ones normally had detailed carvings on them. Each well had a cover called a wellhead. This was tightly fitted to cover the entire well opening. It was also locked because control of the wells was strict. Local officials or priests from nearby churches controlled the keys to the wells. They were opened twice a day for people to draw fresh water.

The wells tended to become social gathering places. As people stood in line waiting for their turn at the well, they talked with one another. However, there were rules governing behavior around the wells. For instance, animals were forbidden from drinking from the wells. The people taking water were required to have clean hands as well. These were both intended to keep the well water clean. In addition, during the periodic times of flooding, the manholes and wellheads were protected from the floodwaters. This prevented salt water from seeping into the cisterns.

Because Venice got an adequate amount of rainfall, the system was effective for many centuries. Historians estimate its population to have been between 100,000 and 150,000 for most of its history. But in the late 1800s, the city's population grew to more than 160,000. City officials decided to obtain a better source of fresh water. Like their Roman ancestors had done many centuries before them, the people of Venice decided to construct an aqueduct to import water from the mainland. It was built alongside a railway bridge connecting the mainland to the city. The aqueduct was completed in 1886 and became the main source of fresh water for Venice. Soon afterward, many cisterns were closed down and their manholes covered over. Today, the well tops remain in many squares and serve as reminders to tourists interested in the city's history.

*Glossary

cistern: a tank used to hold water or other liquids

periodic: happening from time to time

1   The word "endeavors" in the passage is closest in meaning to

    Ⓐ proposals

    Ⓑ decisions

    Ⓒ investments

    Ⓓ efforts

2   The word "slanted" in the passage is closest in meaning to

    Ⓐ installed

    Ⓑ angled

    Ⓒ constructed

    Ⓓ focused

3   According to paragraph 2, which of the following is NOT true about the cisterns in Venice?

    Ⓐ Sand was used in them to clean the water they collected.

    Ⓑ The water that was collected in them was moved to wells.

    Ⓒ Numerous barrels were kept in them to store fresh water.

    Ⓓ They were used to collect water that fell when it rained.

4   Which of the following can be inferred from paragraph 3 about priests in Venice?

    Ⓐ They were considered people who could be trusted.

    Ⓑ Some of them were employed as city officials.

    Ⓒ They helped design the city's water collection system.

    Ⓓ Some of them received money from people taking water.

5   In paragraph 4, the author implies that floods

    Ⓐ caused seawater to cover the city's streets

    Ⓑ happened in Venice on an annual basis

    Ⓒ were rare so were not worried about much

    Ⓓ made the water in some wells undrinkable

6   Which of the sentences below best expresses the essential information in the highlighted sentence in the passage? Incorrect answer choices change the meaning in important ways or leave out essential information.

Like their Roman ancestors had done many centuries before them, the people of Venice decided to construct an aqueduct to import water from the mainland.

    Ⓐ The aqueduct that the Venetians decided to build was constructed by using Roman technology.

    Ⓑ Even though there was a Roman aqueduct nearby, the Venetians never used it to bring in water from the mainland.

    Ⓒ An aqueduct constructed centuries ago by the Romans was used to supply the Venetians with water.

    Ⓓ The Venetians satisfied their water needs by imitating the Romans and building an aqueduct.

7   According to paragraph 5, the city stopped using many cisterns because

    Ⓐ they became too old and unusable

    Ⓑ saltwater created cracks in them

    Ⓒ water was obtained from another source

    Ⓓ trains started bringing fresh water to Venice

8 **Directions**: An introductory sentence for a brief summary of the passage is provided below. Complete the summary by selecting the THREE answer choices that express the most important ideas of the passage. Some sentences do not belong because they express ideas that are not presented in the passage or are minor ideas in the passage. **This question is worth 2 points.**

The city of Venice had an effective system of getting fresh water for its residents.

-

-

-

ANSWER CHOICES

1 Rainwater was collected in large cisterns and then filtered in to wells.

2 People waited in line to draw fresh water from wells on a daily basis.

3 An aqueduct was built to import fresh water from an inland source.

4 Despite being surrounded by water, Venice had trouble getting fresh water.

5 The wells were controlled to keep them clean and to restrict how much water people got.

6 Most of the city's water was collected from rivers and brought to it in barrels.

Portraiture

One major type of painting is portraiture. This is a painting of a person, called a portrait, with the person's face being featured prominently. Sometimes a portrait is of a group of people or of the artist, which is a self-portrait. Portraiture is one of the oldest forms of art and dates back to ancient Egypt.

Great artists in history, such as Leonardo da Vinci, Michelangelo, Raphael, Cézanne, and Goya, all created portraits. Leonardo's *Mona Lisa* is considered one of the most famous ever done. The aim of the portrait artist is to show the inner essence of the subject. Some artists, especially the Dutch, strove for realism. But in the past, most portraits were done in a flattering light with a serious tone. The subject was usually not portrayed smiling. The artist also had to protect the subject from ridicule. Any ugly features, such as scars, moles, a large nose, and a weak chin, were overlooked. As a result, many portraits are not true likenesses of their subjects.

To capture an image of an individual requires the person or people to sit for the artist. This means posing for a long time, often in a certain position, wearing certain clothing, or holding an object. This is tiring and may require several sessions before the artist is satisfied. The subject may be painted standing, sitting, or reclining. The subject poses in a straight-on position or at an angle to give a profile. In the past, many subjects for portraits were military men and members of royal families. They were often painted in full uniform and sometimes with a horse.

Historically, most subjects of portraiture were the rich and famous of the time. This was due to the high costs of portraits. Many wealthy individuals became great patrons of the arts. In the past, patrons were major sources of artists' incomes. Some worked for great families, such as the Medici of Florence, while others were appointed court artists of royal families. Having a portrait of one's self and one's family was deemed important for royalty. As artists became well known, they were frequently commissioned to do portraits for other notable people.

Once a portrait is done, the subject views it. If the person is satisfied, the portrait may be put on display in the subject's home for others to view and enjoy. However, if the subject is unsatisfied, the artist may be required to touch it up or redo it entirely. Sometimes the subject is so displeased that the portrait is destroyed. One famous example of this is Graham Sutherland's 1954 portrait of Winston Churchill. Churchill had his portrait burned after a public viewing left him unhappy. While this happens on occasion, many of history's most famous portraits still hang in museums and galleries around the world for the public to enjoy.

*Glossary

profile: the outline of a human face as viewed from the side

patron of the arts: a person who sponsors the works of artists

9   According to paragraph 1, which of the following is true about portraiture?

 Ⓐ It takes longer to create than other types of paintings.

 Ⓑ It focuses on the entire body of the person being painted.

 Ⓒ It has been practiced by people since ancient times.

 Ⓓ It may only be a picture of a single person.

10 The word "aim" in the passage is closest in meaning to

 Ⓐ result

 Ⓑ intention

 Ⓒ mark

 Ⓓ orientation

11 In paragraph 2, the author uses "scars, moles, a large nose, and a weak chin" as examples of

 Ⓐ body parts that were emphasized in portraits

 Ⓑ features that Dutch artists always painted

 Ⓒ aspects of people that artists spent time painting

 Ⓓ features not painted by portrait artists

12 According to paragraph 3, which of the following is NOT true about posing for a portrait?

(A) Artists make their subjects take identical positions.

(B) People may do it while holding various objects.

(C) Subjects of paintings often do it several times.

(D) It can make the subjects tired when they do it.

13 The word "deemed" in the passage is closest in meaning to

(A) considered

(B) made

(C) appointed

(D) purchased

14 Which of the sentences below best expresses the essential information in the highlighted sentence in the passage? Incorrect answer choices change the meaning in important ways or leave out essential information.

If the person is satisfied, the portrait may be put on display in the subject's home for others to view and enjoy.

(A) People enjoy looking at the portraits of others in their homes.

(B) A person who likes a portrait will hang it up for others to see.

(C) People usually like their portraits and hang them in their homes.

(D) Most portraits can be found in people's homes, where others can view them.

15 In paragraph 5, the author implies that Graham Sutherland's portrait of Winston Churchill

(A) is worth a lot of money

(B) has been sold several times

(C) no longer exists

(D) is hanging in a museum

16 **Directions**: An introductory sentence for a brief summary of the passage is provided below. Complete the summary by selecting the THREE answer choices that express the most important ideas of the passage. Some sentences do not belong because they express ideas that are not presented in the passage or are minor ideas in the passage. **This question is worth 2 points.**

Many artists paint portraits, which are pictures focusing on people's heads, of people notable during their times.

-

-

-

ANSWER CHOICES

1 Artists like Raphael, Cezanne, and Michelangelo painted portraits of famous people.

2 Members of royal families and military men often had their portraits painted in the past.

3 Portraiture has been used as a form of art from ancient Egypt to the modern day.

4 Winston Churchill disliked a portrait of himself, so he destroyed it.

5 Some portrait artists use realism, but others paint flattering pictures of their subjects.

6 The subjects of portraits sit in various positions and must keep those poses for long periods of time.

◼ Vocabulary Review

A Complete each sentence with the appropriate word from the box.

pouch	frontier	complexity	flow	aqueduct

1 The _____ is an area that has few people living in it.

2 Water in a river or stream must _____ downhill, not uphill.

3 The _____ of the machine makes using it difficult.

4 The city gets most of its water from a large _____.

5 A kangaroo has a _____ that its joey stays in.

B Complete each sentence with the correct answer.

1 She is taking an **intensive** class, so she has to study _____.

   a. a little   b. all the time

2 An animal's **hind** legs are its _____ legs.

   a. front   b. rear

3 You need to _____ to give her a **reminder** about the meeting.

   a. call her   b. ignore her

4 A place that is _____ safe is considered **relatively** free of danger.

   a. fairly   b. very

5 The group's **dynamic** events are always very _____.

   a. boring   b. active

6 Water is _____ the floor because it is **seeping** from the pipes.

   a. not on   b. all over

7 Some **exaggerated** movements are _____.

   a. overdone   b. underdone

8 The man is **forbidden** from that place, so he _____ there.

   a. cannot go   b. sometimes goes

9 An animal that is **vulnerable** is _____ other animals.

   a. in danger from   b. safe from

Chapter **07**

Rhetorical Purpose

■ About the Question

Rhetorical Purpose questions focus on the reasons that certain information is included in the passage. You are asked to answer a question about why the author decided to write about something in the passage. The function of the material rather than its meaning is important for these kinds of questions. The information asked about in these questions is always included in a small section of the passage. There are 1-2 Rhetorical Purpose questions for each passage.

Recognizing Rhetorical Purpose questions:

- The author discusses "X" in paragraph 2 in order to . . .

- Why does the author mention "X"?

- The author uses "X" as an example of . . .

Other Rhetorical Purpose questions ask about the function or purpose of an entire paragraph. The questions are phrased like this:

- Paragraph 4 supports which of the following ideas about . . . ?

- Paragraphs 2 and 3 support which of the following ideas about . . . ?

- What is the author's purpose in paragraph 4 of the passage?

Helpful hints for answering the questions correctly:

- Read only the paragraph that is mentioned in the question itself. Then, think about how the topic mentioned in the question relates to that paragraph or the entire passage.

- The words that are used in the answer choices, particularly the verbs, are very important when you try to find the answer. Look for words such as *define, illustrate, explain, argue, compare, contrast, criticize, refute, note, example,* and *function.*

- There is a special emphasis on these questions. Some questions ask about entire sentences, not just words or phrases.

Read the following paragraphs and answer the questions.

🎧 CH07_1A

A

　　While most artists prefer oil paints, there are some who like watercolor paints better. Painting with watercolors can present challenges though. One is that mistakes are virtually impossible to correct, which is not true for oil paints. Nevertheless, watercolors have some advantages. They are cheaper and easier to clean up than oil paints. They do not contain any harmful chemicals. They are also unique when it comes to colors. If properly applied, they appear clear and transparent, which makes them look unlike any other type of paint.

Why does the author mention "watercolor paints"?

Ⓐ To explain how to use them

Ⓑ To make a comparison

Ⓒ To name some art made with them

🎧 CH07_1B

B

　　Two of the main causes of air pollution are factories releasing various chemicals and vehicles burning fossil fuels. Air pollution has numerous negative effects. First, polluted air can cause health problems for the people and animals that breathe it. It can also result in "acid rain". It contains harmful chemicals. When it falls, it kills plants, hurts animals, and makes lakes and ponds unfit for life. Acid rain can even harm buildings over time.

Why does the author mention "acid rain"?

Ⓐ To point out the damage it can do

Ⓑ To explain what chemicals are in it

Ⓒ To state where it usually falls

🎧 CH07_1C

C

　　Before the American space program sent anyone to the moon, it needed to gain more experience in space. So in 1965 and 1966, the American space agency NASA flew ten *Gemini* missions. The astronauts that went into space accomplished a number of feats. For instance, the first spacewalk by an American was conducted on the *Gemini 4* mission. The *Gemini 6* and *Gemini 7* space capsules met each other while in orbit at the same time. And the astronauts on *Gemini 7* stayed in orbit for two weeks.

Why does the author mention the "*Gemini* missions"?

Ⓐ To argue that they were unnecessary to get to the moon

Ⓑ To show how the astronauts trained for their missions

Ⓒ To name their contributions to the American space effort

A | **Whirlpools**

 CH07_2A

In places where two currents of water meet, the water may begin to swirl around. This often results in what is termed a whirlpool. While sailors have warned about whirlpools for centuries, they are not nearly as dangerous as they have been portrayed.

There are both permanent and temporary whirlpools. How large and powerful they are depends upon the strengths of the currents that comprise them. One of the largest natural whirlpools in the world is the Old Sow Whirlpool. It is located in the Atlantic Ocean near Canada and the United States. It has been measured with a **diameter** of seventy-six meters at times, and its waters move so powerfully that it sometimes makes sounds like a pig.

Despite the large sizes of many whirlpools, it is rare for them to harm large ships. There are only a few stories throughout history of ships being sunk by whirlpools. While they have sunk small boats and killed sailors, most whirlpools are fairly harmless, yet interesting, parts of their environment.

*diameter: the length of a straight line passing through the center of a circle and going from one side to the other

---

In paragraph 2, the author uses "the Old Sow Whirlpool" as an example of

Ⓐ a whirlpool that has a great size

Ⓑ a whirlpool that formed in a river

Ⓒ a whirlpool that is temporary

Ⓓ a whirlpool that has killed people

Vocabulary

- s _____ = to move around in a circle
- t _____ = lasting a short amount of time; not permanent
- h _____ = to cause damage or injury to

The Composition of Comets

There are countless objects orbiting the sun. Among them are the planets, their moons, asteroids, meteors, and comets. Of all the objects moving around the sun, comets have the most unique composition.

All comets have three parts: the nucleus, the coma, and the tail. The nucleus is the solid part and is the reason why many people refer to it as a dirty snowball. Comets are believed to have rocky centers. Around them, the rest of the nucleus is comprised mostly of frozen water. Along with ice, there are other frozen substances, including carbon dioxide, methane, ammonia, and carbon monoxide.

When comets pass near the sun, they develop both a coma and a tail. The sun's heat melts part of the nucleus, so a coma forms. It contains water, various gases, and dust. Finally, comets have a dust tail and an ion tail. The dust tail is formed of tiny dust particles and may be ten million kilometers long. The ion tail is made of **plasma** and may extend hundreds of millions of kilometers.

*plasma: an ionized gas that has almost the same number of positive electrons and ions

In paragraph 2, why does the author mention "frozen water"?

Ⓐ To show how cold space is

Ⓑ To prove that comets lack rocky matter

Ⓒ To state what is in the nucleus

Ⓓ To explain how comets' tails form

Vocabulary

- s _____ = a material
- m _____ = to change from a solid to a liquid
- e _____ = to stretch; to reach from one place to another

A | The Golden Age of Piracy

🎧 CH07_3A

Piracy has existed ever since ancient times and still exists today. When most people think of pirates, they imagine ships flying flags with the skull and crossbones and filled with pirates attacking and plundering other ships. This popular conception of pirates comes from the period known as the Golden Age of Piracy. It lasted from the 1650s to the 1730s. At this time, piracy was at its height, and most of it took place in the Atlantic Ocean and Caribbean Sea.

The Golden Age of Piracy was a time of increased international trade. There was little naval protection on the seas, and there were many weak colonies. This was especially true of places in the Caribbean Sea and along the coast of North America. These conditions made trade routes vulnerable to pirate attacks. A large number of wars were also fought during this time. European countries built large navies to fight them. When the wars ended, many trained sailors suddenly had no jobs. Piracy was one way for them to use their skills to become rich.

One of the primary targets of pirates during this era was the rich Spanish treasure ships. They sailed from Spain's New World colonies to the Spanish homeland while carrying gold, silver, and other treasures. Other merchant ships were also preyed upon by pirates. Blackbeard, Captain Kidd, Black Bart, and Henry Morgan were some of the most famous pirates of that time. For many decades, pirates struck fear in the hearts of sailors. However, in the end, most pirate captains were captured and executed. The British Royal Navy played a major role in doing that. The British wanted to keep the seas safe for their growing empire and international trade. By the 1730s, piracy in the Atlantic and Caribbean was almost entirely ended.

*New World: North and South America

Vocabulary

- p_____ = to steal something after attacking a person or place
- c_____ = an idea, belief, or thought about something
- h_____ = the place where a person is from
- e_____ = to kill, often for committing a crime

1   The phrase "vulnerable to" in the passage is closest in meaning to

   Ⓐ aware of

   Ⓑ available to

   Ⓒ exposed to

   Ⓓ result in

2   In paragraph 2, all of the following questions are answered EXCEPT:

   Ⓐ Which places had colonies that were not powerful?

   Ⓑ What did pirates do when they attacked ships on the sea?

   Ⓒ Where did many pirates learn how to sail on ships?

   Ⓓ Why were some trade routes attacked by pirates?

3   In paragraph 3, why does the author mention "The British Royal Navy"?

   Ⓐ To state that many pirates were once in it

   Ⓑ To point out who captured Black Bart

   Ⓒ To claim that it sometimes sank pirate ships

   Ⓓ To discuss its role in ending piracy

4   An introductory sentence for a brief summary of the passage is provided below. Complete the summary by selecting the THREE answer choices that express the most important ideas of the passage. Some sentences do not belong because they express ideas that are not presented in the passage or are minor ideas in the passage.

   There were many pirate attacks on ships during the Golden Age of Piracy.

   ANSWER CHOICES

   ☐1 There were frequent attacks on Spanish treasure ships and other merchant ships.

   ☐2 Blackbeard and Henry Morgan were two of the most famous pirates.

   ☐3 Many sailors became pirates after they stopped serving in their country's navy.

   ☐4 There were a large number of pirate attacks on ships in the 1600s and 1700s.

   ☐5 Colonies in North America and the Caribbean were poorly protected and easy to attack.

Trout Streams

Trout are a type of **game fish** common in rivers and streams in North America. There are several species, including brown trout, rainbow trout, brook trout, and bull trout. While each type of trout has its own unique characteristics, all have some similarities. One of these is the type of water in which they live.

Virtually all species of trout can be found in streams. In the United States and Canada, there are trout living in streams across both countries. However, trout only live in water which is cold or cool. Most trout thrive when the water temperature ranges between ten and sixteen degrees Celsius. When the temperature increases, they have trouble surviving. Most die when the water temperature exceeds twenty-three degrees Celsius.

Trout prefer living in areas of streams which are shaded from the sun by vegetation, rocks, or overhangs. This helps keep them cool and provides them with cover when they hunt. Trout are predators and eat smaller fish, but the majority of their diet comes from insects. They feed on insects in the water in addition to those flying above it. Many trout hide at the bottom of the water or between rocks and then strike their prey when it cannot see them.

Another feature of trout streams is that trout prefer pools where the current does not move too swiftly. This allows trout to rest without having to swim against the current. Additionally, it provides them with places to lay their eggs where they will not be swept away by rapidly moving water.

*game fish: a fish that gives fishermen a challenge when they try to catch it

Vocabulary

- t＿＿＿＿＿ = to do well
- e＿＿＿＿＿ = to go past or beyond
- s＿＿＿＿＿ = to cast a shadow over something to block it from the sun
- s＿＿＿＿＿ = to hit; to attack

1   According to paragraph 2, which of the following is true about the water in which trout live?

   Ⓐ It should be fast moving as well as fairly shallow.

   Ⓑ The water temperature should be more than twenty-three degrees Celsius.

   Ⓒ The water can either be fresh or have a small amount of salt in it.

   Ⓓ It needs to be cool and is best between ten and sixteen degrees Celsius.

Reference Question

2   The word "**those**" in the passage refers to

   Ⓐ trout

   Ⓑ predators

   Ⓒ smaller fish

   Ⓓ insects

Rhetorical Purpose Question

3   The author discusses "**pools**" in paragraph 4 in order to

   Ⓐ note how big they should be for most trout

   Ⓑ point out how they are formed in some streams

   Ⓒ explain why many trout like living in them

   Ⓓ recommend them as places to find trout eggs

Prose Summary Question

4   An introductory sentence for a brief summary of the passage is provided below. Complete the summary by selecting the THREE answer choices that express the most important ideas of the passage. Some sentences do not belong because they express ideas that are not presented in the passage or are minor ideas in the passage.

   The streams that trout live in have many common features.

   ANSWER CHOICES

   1️⃣ There are many species of trout that can be found living all around the world.

   2️⃣ Trout prefer to rest and lay their eggs in pools that have weak currents.

   3️⃣ There is a specific temperature range for the water in which trout live.

   4️⃣ The places in streams where trout live often have some sort of shade.

   5️⃣ Fishermen enjoy trying to catch trout in streams across Canada and the United States.

Maslow's Hierarchy of Needs

Maslow's Hierarchy of Needs is a theory of motivation in psychology. It centers on human needs and the things people both require and desire in life. American <u>psychologist</u> Abraham Maslow first presented the theory named after him in 1943 in a paper entitled "A Theory of Human Motivation." Maslow's Hierarchy of Needs theory is often presented as a pyramid containing five levels. From bottom to top, the levels are called physiological, safety, belongingness, esteem, and self-actualization.

Physiological needs are basic ones that every person must have to survive. They include food, water, warmth, shelter, clothing, and rest. If people lack these basic needs, they will die. Therefore, motivations to acquire basic needs are very strong, and they are the first ones that people try to obtain each day.

Safety needs deal with obtaining freedom from fear. This means that people are protected from danger and have a desire for law and order. People begin to concern themselves with their physical safety once their basic needs have been met. Among them are protection from natural disasters, criminals, and enemies. In modern society, firefighters, police, and military forces provide a great amount of this protection. Individuals can also take steps to ensure their economic safety by getting job security, by purchasing health insurance, and by accumulating savings in banks. These will all help protect people during times of trouble. People who do not have a <mark>sense</mark> of security often feel uneasy and fearful.

As for belongingness, it is related to the need for love, intimacy, and friendship. Most people get this through their families. In addition, as they grow older, they make friends and expand their circles of belongingness. Many people also join clubs and other similar organizations. The ultimate fulfillment of this need is to find love with another person and to start a family. This sense of belongingness can be negatively affected when people are ignored by others.

<mark>Esteem</mark> is the need to be respected by others. Most people want others to regard them in a positive manner. To be esteemed, people do their best to be recognized for their achievements. Being successful in their work, education, and community activities can bring respect from others. Some people aspire to reach higher levels of esteem. They develop both self-confidence and inner strength. Being esteemed by others helps people be more self-confident. On the other hand, those who are not well regarded will lack it.

The final level of Maslow's pyramid is self-actualization. In simple terms, it means that people try to be the best they can be. The first step to success is recognizing one's <u>potential</u>. ◼1 People can become self-aware of what they are capable of doing. ◼2 They can then try to fulfill their potential. ◼3 Most of the time, they strive to become high achievers regarding their relationships, work, education, the arts, and sports. ◼4

*Glossary

psychologist: a specialist in the study of the human mind

potential: something that could happen in the future

1　In paragraph 1, the author implies that Abraham Maslow

　　Ⓐ worked as a professor at a university

　　Ⓑ announced his theory by printing it in a journal

　　Ⓒ conducted most of his research with a partner

　　Ⓓ took more than a decade to develop his ideas

2　According to paragraph 2, which of the following is NOT true about physiological needs?

　　Ⓐ They are the primary motivations for people.

　　Ⓑ Some of them are food, shelter, and clothing.

　　Ⓒ People need to fulfill them in order to live.

　　Ⓓ A few of them are difficult to obtain for people.

3　Paragraph 3 supports which of the following ideas about safety?

　　Ⓐ The only way to ensure it is through law and order.

　　Ⓑ Few people care enough about it to act.

　　Ⓒ People can guarantee it in several different ways.

　　Ⓓ It is considered one of the basic needs of people.

4 The word "sense" in the passage is closest in meaning to

(A) feeling

(B) logic

(C) display

(D) wealth

5 According to paragraph 4, people may not feel belongingness if

(A) they rarely meet their family members

(B) they fail to associate with others

(C) they do not succeed at their jobs

(D) they never join any organizations

6 The author discusses "Esteem" in paragraph 5 in order to

(A) compare its importance with physiological needs

(B) give examples of some people who have it

(C) explain how people can have it in their lives

(D) show why many people are unable to obtain it

7 Look at the four squares [■] that indicate where the following sentence could be added to the passage.

They can accomplish this in a variety of ways.

Where would the sentence best fit?

Click on a square [■] to add the sentence to the passage.

8 **Directions:** Select the appropriate statements from the answer choices and match them to the human need to which they relate. TWO of the answer choices will NOT be used. **This question is worth 4 points.**

Drag your answer choices to the spaces where they belong. To remove an answer choice, click on it. To review the passage, click on VIEW TEXT

STATEMENTS

1 It may be obtained when people develop friendships.

2 A lack of it can cause people to experience fear.

3 It can be provided by police and firefighters.

4 It allows people to fulfill their potential during their lives.

5 Doing well at work can help people develop it.

6 People who have families may experience this.

7 It is the most basic need that all people must have.

8 Public recognition can result in it being fulfilled.

9 It may be required when there are disasters.

HUMAN NEED

Safety (Select 3)

-
-
-

Belongingness (Select 2)

-
-

Esteem (Select 2)

-
-

Volcanic Eruptions

A volcanic eruption occurs when lava, gas, ash, or rocks shoot out from a mountain called a volcano. The nature of the eruption depends on many factors. Some are lava viscosity, gas content, and the presence of water. There are two basic types of eruptions: effusive and explosive. Within these two categories are six major subtypes of eruptions.

Effusive eruptions are mild and often involve lava oozing out of the ground. The lava ejected has a low viscosity and low gas content. There are two major effusive eruption types: Icelandic and Hawaiian. Icelandic eruptions happen when there are long cracks in the surface where lava comes out and spreads on the surface. They create plateaus of basalt but do not form cones. Hawaiian eruptions also see lava slowly coming out of the ground. They tend to make low, wide cones, called shield cones. As they progress, lava flows from both the summit and from cracks in the mountains' sides. This type is named for volcanoes found in Hawaii such as Mauna Loa.

Lava from explosive eruptions has a higher gas content and higher viscosity. These volcanoes tend to erupt with massive ejections of lava, gas, ash, and sometimes steam. The mildest is the Strombolian type. It is named after a volcano in Italy. Strombolian eruptions happen when gas buildup underground forms bubbles. They then burst and shoot lava into the air. Some volcanoes of this type almost continually erupt. **1** However, these eruptions are not too violent. **2** A more violent eruption is the Vulcanian one. **3** In this eruption, large gas bubbles burst violently and hurl lava, ash, and rocks high into the air while forming dense ash columns up to twenty kilometers high. **4**

The most violent explosive eruptions are the Peléan and Plinian types. Peléan eruptions are named for Mount Pelée on the island of Martinique. They are characterized by massive ejections of ash and gas in pyroclastic flows. These are thick clouds of hot ash, rocks, and gas that flow down the slopes of volcanoes and that destroy everything in their path. Plinian eruptions are the most violent of all. They are named for Pliny the Younger, a Roman who recorded the eruption of Mount Vesuvius in Italy in 79 A.D. The eruptions involve huge explosions that shoot masses of ash, lava, gas, and rocks into the air. The ash columns can reach great heights in the atmosphere and spread ash over a huge geographical area.

A rarer type of volcanic eruption is the Surtseyan, which is named for an island near Iceland. This happens in shallow water when a volcano forms near the surface. As gas bubbles up, it bursts and shoots lava into the water. The interaction of hot lava and cool water causes the water to flash into steam. This produces a violent eruption on the surface of the water. This kind of eruption sometimes happens on land when magma underground interacts with a large water source that is also underground.

*Glossary

viscosity: the thickness of a liquid that causes it to flow quickly or slowly

ooze: to flow slowly, as in the way a liquid moves

9   In paragraph 2, the author uses "shield cones" as an example of

    (A) the major result of Icelandic eruptions

    (B) geographical areas that tend to have many volcanoes

    (C) a land formation created by Hawaiian eruptions

    (D) types of land that are found at the top of Mauna Loa

10 According to paragraph 2, which of the following is true about effusive eruptions?

    (A) They eject lava that has little gas in it.

    (B) They can be violent at times.

    (C) They produce volcanic islands over time.

    (D) They are found mostly on plateaus.

11 The word "hurl" in the passage is closest in meaning to

    (A) produce

    (B) throw

    (C) rain

    (D) drop

12 In paragraph 4, why does the author mention "Pliny the Younger"?

    Ⓐ To note that he conducted research on volcanoes in Italy

    Ⓑ To point out he was the first person to write about volcanoes

    Ⓒ To claim that he discovered the volcano Vesuvius

    Ⓓ To explain how a certain type of eruption got its name

13 In paragraphs 3 and 4, which of the following can be inferred about Peléan eruptions?

    Ⓐ Their eruptions produce more lava than Vulcanian ones.

    Ⓑ They are more destructive in nature than Strombolian eruptions.

    Ⓒ Their eruptions can affect the atmosphere on a global scale.

    Ⓓ They have killed more people than other volcanic eruptions.

14 According to paragraph 5, Surtseyan eruptions produce steam because

    Ⓐ the lava that they eject has a high viscosity

    Ⓑ they shoot gas and ash high into the atmosphere

    Ⓒ lava erupts from them in places where there is water

    Ⓓ they eject lava into rivers and streams

15 Look at the four squares [■] that indicate where the following sentence could be added to the passage.

It is also named after a volcano in Italy.

Where would the sentence best fit?

Click on a square [■] to add the sentence to the passage.

16 Directions: Select the appropriate statements from the answer choices and match them to the type of volcanic eruption to which they relate. TWO of the answer choices will NOT be used. This question is worth 3 points.

Drag your answer choices to the spaces where they belong. To remove an answer choice, click on it. To review the passage, click on VIEW TEXT

STATEMENTS	TYPE OF VOLCANIC ERUPTION
1 Are able to produce large amounts of steam	**Effusive** (Select 2)
2 Include Strombolian and Plinian eruptions	•
3 Have lava that is low in viscosity	•
4 Include eruptions that happen in Hawaii	**Explosive** (Select 3)
5 Happen mostly underneath the ocean	•
6 May produce dangerous pyroclastic flows	•
7 Are known to shoot ash high into the air	•

■ Vocabulary Review

A **Complete each sentence with the appropriate word from the box.**

swirl	melt	conception	homeland	exceeds

1 A person's _____ of something is what that individual thinks of it.

2 Water may _____ around a bathtub when it moves in a circle.

3 When the temperature _____ the freezing point, it is above zero degrees Celsius.

4 He plans to see his family by returning to his _____, where he was born.

5 Ice will _____ and become a liquid when the temperature rises.

B **Complete each sentence with the correct answer.**

1 The criminals were _____ for their crimes, so they were **executed**.
   a. killed   b. imprisoned

2 People who are **respected** by others are _____ by them.
   a. looked down on   b. looked up to

3 **Temporary** measures are ones that last for a _____.
   a. short time   b. long time

4 All people should **obtain** nutrition by _____ the vitamins and minerals they need.
   a. looking for   b. getting

5 When a whirlpool **harms** a ship, it _____.
   a. does nothing to it   b. causes damage to it

6 When people **ensure** someone's safety, they _____ that the person will be fine.
   a. guarantee   b. hope

7 A **basic** need is _____ that all people need to have.
   a. an expensive one   b. an elementary one

8 **Shaded** areas in streams are those places that _____.
   a. are blocked from the sun   b. have fast-moving water

9 People **thrive** in a new location when they _____ there.
   a. do well   b. have problems

Chapter **08**

Insert Text

▪ About the Question

Insert Text questions focus on an additional sentence that could be included in the passage. You are asked to read a new sentence and then to determine where in the passage it could be added. These questions require you to consider several factors, including grammar, logic, flow, and connecting words, when you are trying to determine the correct answer. There are 0-1 Insert Text questions for each passage. There is a special emphasis on these questions. Almost every passage now has 1 Insert Text question.

Recognizing Insert Text questions:

- Look at the four squares [■] that indicate where the following sentence could be added to the passage.

  [You will see a sentence in bold.]

  Where would the sentence best fit?

Helpful hints for answering the questions correctly:

- The squares are always placed after four consecutive sentences.

- Try reading the passage to yourself by adding the sentence after each square. That can help you determine where it should be added.

- Many times, the sentence to be added contains a connecting word or phrase. Pay attention to words or phrases such as *in addition, for instance, for example, therefore, consequently, on the other hand, finally*, and *as a result*. These connecting words and phrases can affect the flow of the passage.

Basic Practice

Read the sentences below and put them in the correct order.

CH08_1A

A

Ⓐ They are among the most important of all ocean ecosystems.

Ⓑ They dwell in coral reefs thanks to the food found in abundance in them.

Ⓒ The reason is that numerous species of fish and other animals live in them.

Ⓓ Coral reefs are normally found in shallow water in tropical and subtropical areas.

Ⓔ In addition, coral reefs protect coastlines during storms.

Correct Order: (   ) – (   ) – (   ) – (   ) – (   )

CH08_1B

B

Ⓐ The making of pottery helped improve standards of living in ancient times.

Ⓑ Doing that enabled people to improve their diets by eating cooked food.

Ⓒ They were also able to make large ceramic pots for cooking food in.

Ⓓ For one, people could make containers to store their food in.

Ⓔ This allowed them to keep food for longer periods of time.

Correct Order: (   ) – (   ) – (   ) – (   ) – (   )

CH08_1C

C

Ⓐ When the battle came to an end, the William and his men were victorious.

Ⓑ The Battle of Hastings took place on October 14, 1066.

Ⓒ During it, King Harold of England led his army against Duke William of Normandy.

Ⓓ Only two months later, William became the new king of England.

Ⓔ Harold was killed by Norman soldiers near the conclusion of the battle.

Correct Order: (   ) – (   ) – (   ) – (   ) – (   )

A | Terrestrial Planets

CH08_2A

Of the eight planets in the solar system, four are terrestrial planets while the others are considered gas giants. The four terrestrial planets are Mercury, Venus, Earth, and Mars. Each planet shares a number of characteristics with the others.

The most apparent similarities are their sizes and orbits. All the terrestrial planets are fairly small in size and are much smaller than the gas giants. Earth, the largest terrestrial planet, has a diameter around 12,500 kilometers, but Jupiter, the largest gas giant, has a diameter of more than 138,000 kilometers. ■ The terrestrial planets orbit close to the sun whereas the gas giants are much farther away. ■ The terrestrial planets therefore have short orbits. ■ Mercury's is almost eighty-eight days while that of Mars is 687 days. ■

The terrestrial planets additionally have few or no moons. Earth has a single moon while Mars has two. Every gas giant has a large number of moons. A final characteristic concerns their composition. The terrestrial planets are all made of rocky material and have a core, mantle, and crust. The gas giants are made of various gases.

*terrestrial: relating to the Earth

Look at the four squares [■] that indicate where the following sentence could be added to the passage.

Neptune, meanwhile, takes more than 164 years to complete a single revolution around the sun.

Where would the sentence best fit?

• g_____ = someone or something that is much larger than normal

• a_____ = clear; obvious

• r_____ = made of rocks and stones

Stalactites and Stalagmites

In many caves, particularly those formed in **limestone**, there are long, thin formations. Some are suspended from the ceilings while others rise from the floors. These are called stalactites and stalagmites.

Stalactites form from the ceilings of caves while stalagmites emerge from the floors of caves. Water typically flows from the surface down to the ceilings of limestone caves. **1** In the process, it dissolves calcite. **2** As water drips to the floor, some of the calcite in the water gets left behind. **3** Slowly, the calcite on the ceiling hardens so that, over time, it extends toward the ground and forms a stalactite. **4**

At the same time, dripping water lands on the floor. More calcite gets left there, so a formation grows from the cave floor, too. This is a stalagmite. In some instances, stalactites and stalagmites grow for so many years that they combine to create a column. However, this requires tens of thousands of years because each formation only grows around one or two centimeters a century.

*limestone: a type of sedimentary rock made mostly from the remains of various organisms

Look at the four squares [■] that indicate where the following sentence could be added to the passage.

It is a mineral that is a major component of limestone.

Where would the sentence best fit?

- e＿＿＿＿＿＿＿＿　＝ to come out from
- d＿＿＿＿＿＿＿＿　＝ to break down when exposed to a liquid
- d＿＿＿＿＿＿＿＿　＝ to fall in drops, as in water

A **The Human Eye**

CH08_3A

Vision is one of the five senses. The eye is what gives people vision and enables them to see. The eye itself has a complicated structure with many parts. Working together, they enable signals to be sent from the eye to the brain, where they can be interpreted as images. The major parts of the eye are the eyeball, pupil, cornea, iris, lens, retina, and optic nerve. There are also tear glands, which provide fluid to prevent the eyeball from drying, the eyelid to wash the fluid over the eyeball, and eyelashes to protect the eye from dust and other objects.

The eyeball houses the other major parts of the eye. Round in shape, it is filled with fluid. In the center of the eye is the pupil, a hole allowing light into the eye. The pupil is surrounded by the colorful iris. The iris acts like a muscle as it opens and closes to allow more or less light into the eye. In front of the pupil is the cornea, which is clear and functions mostly to focus light into the pupil toward the lens. The lens, in turn, further focuses light back into the eye toward the retina.

It is the retina that absorbs light by using photoreceptor cells called rods and cones to **distinguish** between different types of light. Rods are on the edges of the retina and are mainly used for night vision. **1** Thus, they cannot easily distinguish colors. **2** Cones are in the center of the retina. **3** The light that hits the retina is then converted to electronic signals. **4** These pass from the retina to the optic nerve. It carries the signals to the brain, where they are changed into images. The visual cortex is the part of the brain that does this.

*distinguish: to tell the difference between two or more things

Vocabulary

- i_____ = to understand
- f_____ = a liquid
- a_____ = to soak up; to take in
- c_____ = to change from one form to another

1　The word "they" in the passage refers to

(A) people

(B) many parts

(C) signals

(D) images

2　According to paragraph 2, the role of the iris is to

(A) control the amount of light that gets into the eye

(B) help light get focused onto the lens

(C) prevent fluid from leaving the eyeball

(D) protect the eye from any foreign substances

3　Look at the four squares [▓] that indicate where the following sentence could be added to the passage.

Unlike rods, they are able to identify a wide variety of colors.

Where would the sentence best fit?

4　An introductory sentence for a brief summary of the passage is provided below. Complete the summary by selecting the THREE answer choices that express the most important ideas of the passage. Some sentences do not belong because they express ideas that are not presented in the passage or are minor ideas in the passage.

There are many parts of the eye that work together to give people sight.

ANSWER CHOICES

1　All of the signals sent to the brain are interpreted as images in people's minds.

2　It is the rods and cones that allow the retina to absorb light.

3　There are many ways the eye can suffer damage and thus cause a person to go blind.

4　The pupil and the iris combine to let varying amounts of light enter the eye.

5　Light is transformed into images for the brain to interpret in the retina.

The Ladybug

The ladybug is a tiny, colorful insect. There are approximately 5,000 species of ladybugs around the world. Most of them have dome-shaped bodies with two wings and six legs. Many have colorful patterns on their backs. The most familiar one is a North American species called the seven-spotted ladybug. It has a colorful reddish-orange back and seven black spots. There are three spots on each side of this ladybug and another one in the middle near its head while it also has two white spots on its head.

1 The colored markings of the ladybug serve a purpose. 2 The colors indicate that it is unsafe for other animals to eat the ladybug. 3 When attacked, the ladybug secretes an oily, foul-tasting fluid from its legs. 4 While this helps the ladybug avoid attacks from some animals, other predators have become accustomed to the taste. Birds, frogs, spiders, and dragonflies are among these animals. The ladybug itself eats other insects, with its favorite being the aphid. This pest feeds on farmers' crops, so the ladybug is a welcome sight on farms. It is the most active from spring to fall during the farming season, and it hibernates in large colonies during winter.

The ladybug lays its eggs on the undersides of leaves. It usually does so near aphid colonies, which provide its young with a food supply when they hatch. The eggs hatch a few days after being laid, and a larva comes out from each egg and begins eating. The larva sheds its skin several times until it is big enough to transform. It then attaches itself to a leaf by its tail and forms a pupa. Roughly a week later, a full-grown adult ladybug emerges.

*secrete: to release; to give off

Vocabulary

- a_____ = around; about
- be a_____ to = to be used to
- h_____ = to sleep for a long period of time during winter
- s_____ = to lose one's skin, hair, or fur

1   Which of the sentences below best expresses the essential information in the highlighted sentence in the passage? Incorrect answer choices change the meaning in important ways or leave out essential information.

There are three spots on each side of this ladybug and another one in the middle near its head while it also has two white spots on its head

Ⓐ If a ladybug has spots on its head, then it also has some spots on its back.

Ⓑ The ladybug has seven spots on its back and two other spots on its head.

Ⓒ Some of these ladybugs have spots on their backs while others have them on their heads.

Ⓓ Along with the three spots on its back, the ladybug has two more on its head.

Inference Question

2   In paragraph 2, the author implies that birds, frogs, spiders, and dragonflies

Ⓐ are animals that hunt ladybugs and eat them

Ⓑ do not like to consume any oily fluids

Ⓒ are effective at hunting all kinds of insects

Ⓓ prefer to eat the ladybug instead of the aphid

Insert Text Question

3   Look at the four squares [■] that indicate where the following sentence could be added to the passage.

They are a warning to predators.

Where would the sentence best fit?

Prose Summary Question

4   An introductory sentence for a brief summary of the passage is provided below. Complete the summary by selecting the THREE answer choices that express the most important ideas of the passage. Some sentences do not belong because they express ideas that are not presented in the passage or are minor ideas in the passage.

There are many species of ladybugs, but most have colorful markings and are hunters.

ANSWER CHOICES

① All species of ladybugs have black and white spots on their bodies.

② Ladybug larvae often hatch near aphids so that they can feed on them.

③ The ladybug's markings tell predators that it secretes a bad-tasting fluid.

④ There are several thousand species of ladybugs living all over the Earth.

⑤ Since the ladybug eats other insects, farmers like having it on their land.

CH08_4A

Ancient Amazonian Agriculture

The Amazon Rainforest in South America is known for its heavy vegetation. For centuries, people believed the presence of so much of it prevented any large-scale farming from being done. Anthropologists also thought that only small groups of primitive people dwelled in the rainforest. New research suggests that the Amazon was once a land of farms though. They supported millions of people and existed for thousands of years. It was only when the Europeans began arriving after 1492 that their way of life was destroyed.

The new research centers on the nature of the soil and plants in the Amazon. Researchers discovered that ancient Amazonians had domesticated more than eighty different plants. Among them were the sweet potato, cacao, pineapple, cassava, pepper, and numerous fruit and nut trees. They further came to realize that thousands of other plants had been used in a variety of ways by pre-Columbian societies even though they had not been domesticated. The people in the Amazon region lived close to nature. As a result, over the course of centuries, they learned which plants could be beneficial.

More evidence of farming comes from the soil. In many parts of the Amazon, there is dark nutrient-rich soil just beneath the surface topsoil. This was called *terra preta*, or black soil, by Portuguese colonists. The dark soil exists for two reasons. First, people in the Amazon region practiced slash-and-burn agriculture. They burned trees and then planted crops in the cleared areas. Burning trees deposited charcoal that was rich in nutrients in the soil. The charcoal gave the black soil its characteristic color. Second, large numbers of people—perhaps millions—left behind deposits of human waste. This too was beneficial to the soil. Together, they produced the rich black soil of the Amazon.

In the writings of early European explorers, the Amazon is described as being highly populated. These explorers found large numbers of people living close to the rivers, which they used for transportation. Most of the people they saw looked healthy and well fed. Their villages tended to be large, and their crops were plentiful. ■ Unfortunately, these people had no defenses against European diseases such as smallpox. ■ Visiting sailors often carried it and other sicknesses. ■ When they made contact with the natives, their lack of immunity led to widespread epidemics. ■ Millions died in the decades following the arrival of the Europeans.

One reason it has taken so long to learn about pre-Columbian agricultural societies concerns the lack of remains. Unlike the Aztecs and Mayans in Central America, the Amazonian people did not build with stone. Their main building material was wood. As people died out, their villages became unpopulated. Over time, the jungle reclaimed the villages and the croplands. The huts and other buildings quickly decayed in the rainy, humid environment. Today, all that remains of this once-large community are a few scattered tribes living like their ancestors once did.

*Glossary

topsoil: fertile soil found at ground level

slash-and-burn agriculture: the act of burning the plants on land to clear it and then farming on that land

1   According to paragraph 1, what was the Amazon Rainforest like before the Europeans arrived?

   Ⓐ It was a highly populated land with many farms.

   Ⓑ It was grasslands that had few trees or people.

   Ⓒ It was an area with small primitive populations of people.

   Ⓓ It was a region that was not heavily farmed.

2   The phrase "centers on" in the passage is closest in meaning to

   Ⓐ argues about

   Ⓑ appears with

   Ⓒ moves by

   Ⓓ focuses on

3   Which of the sentences below best expresses the essential information in the highlighted sentence in the passage? Incorrect answer choices change the meaning in important ways or leave out essential information.

   They further came to realize that thousands of other plants had been used in a variety of ways by pre-Columbian societies even though they had not been domesticated.

   Ⓐ Some pre-Columbian societies managed to domesticate thousands of different types of plants.

   Ⓑ It became possible for some pre-Columbian societies to use large numbers of plants in ways that benefited them.

   Ⓒ It was discovered that pre-Columbian societies learned how to use large numbers of plants without domesticating them.

   Ⓓ Unless they discovered to domesticate plants, pre-Columbian societies were unable to use thousands of different plants.

4 According to paragraph 3, which of the following is NOT true about *terra preta*?

(A) It was created through the actions of people.

(B) It gained its color because of charcoal in it.

(C) It has a large number of nutrients in it.

(D) It can be found in a layer above the topsoil.

5 The word "they" in the passage refers to

(A) these explorers

(B) large numbers of people

(C) the rivers

(D) most of the people

6 In paragraph 5, why does the author mention "the Aztecs and Mayans"?

(A) To describe their building methods

(B) To explain their connection with the Europeans

(C) To compare them with the Amazonians

(D) To note that they made buildings from wood

7 Look at the four squares [■] that indicate where the following sentence could be added to the passage.

They therefore appeared to have no problems obtaining enough food for themselves.

Where would the sentence best fit?

Click on a square [■] to add the sentence to the passage.

8 **Directions**: An introductory sentence for a brief summary of the passage is provided below. Complete the summary by selecting the THREE answer choices that express the most important ideas of the passage. Some sentences do not belong because they express ideas that are not presented in the passage or are minor ideas in the passage. **This question is worth 2 points.**

According to recent research, the pre-Columbian Amazonians farmed the land in great numbers.

-
-
-

ANSWER CHOICES

1 A large number of Amazonians died after many Europeans came in contact with them.

2 Farmers in the Amazon created *terra preta,* which made the soil very nutrient rich.

3 The Europeans wrote about seeing large villages in the Amazon with extensive farms.

4 Ancient Amazonians domesticated many plants and learned how to benefit from many others.

5 The Amazonians used wood and stone for construction, but their wood buildings disappeared.

6 Much of the soil in the Amazon Rainforest is very dark and rich in nutrients.

Science and Technology in the Apple Industry

Apples are among the most popular fruits that people eat around the world. There are more than 7,000 varieties of apples, and large numbers of them are grown in apple orchards. Modern-day apple farmers rely heavily on science and technology. They use it to improve crop yields, to protect apples from insects and disease, and to harvest their crops. In fact, science and technology are involved in practically the entire growing process.

Unlike regular people, apple farmers do not plant seeds directly into the ground. If they did that, the resulting trees would contain unwanted characteristics, such as sour fruit. To make sure their apples are all the same variety and have the same characteristics, farmers graft parts of growing trees onto rootstocks to make new seedlings. Grafting is the process through which a part of one plant is joined to a part of another to make a new plant. Seedlings created in this way thrive in greenhouses and are planted in orchards when they mature. Organic compost or chemical fertilizers are typically spread around the trees to induce growth.

To produce fruit, apple tree blossoms must be pollinated. Many varieties of apple trees have male and female parts on the same flower. Nevertheless, apple tree blossoms are unable to self-pollinate. Bees assist in this process, so apple farmers often care for beehives. A large orchard might require tens of thousands of bees to carry out the act of pollination. Once the blossoms are pollinated, they transform as the petals fall off and fruit starts growing.

Apple trees are susceptible to damage from a variety of insects and diseases. ■ Aphids are the primary insects that attack them. ■ Other harmful pests are moths and maggots. ■ Diseases that hurt apple trees include fire blight, apple scab, apple rust, and several molds and mildews. ■ Insects and diseases are controlled with chemical pesticides and insecticide sprays, but they cannot be used when trees are being pollinated since they may harm bees.

Some farmers avoid using chemicals to control insects and instead utilize a variety of ingenious traps, which usually look like ripe apples. These devices are coated with a sticky substance that traps insects. Animals such as mice, rabbits, and deer are also problems since they enjoy eating apples. Strong fences are built around orchards to keep large animals out. Wire mesh wrapped around tree trunks stops smaller animals from climbing the trees.

At harvest time, some farmers gather apples by hand to avoid damaging the fruit. But most large orchards utilize machinery for this work. Some machines shake trees to loosen apples. Other machines then scoop up apples from the ground. More modern machines that can pick apples directly from trees have been invented in recent years. By using machines, the number of people needed to work on apple orchards has been reduced tremendously.

*Glossary

rootstock: the root of a plant and the buds that grow from it

maggot: the larva of a fly

9   Which of the sentences below best expresses the essential information in the highlighted sentence in the passage? Incorrect answer choices change the meaning in important ways or leave out essential information.

To make sure their apples are all the same variety and have the same characteristics, farmers graft parts of growing trees onto rootstocks to make new seedlings.

   Ⓐ Farmers graft apple trees onto rootstocks to ensure that all their plants are identical.

   Ⓑ It is possible to graft parts of trees onto rootstocks and then to get fruit from those trees.

   Ⓒ Most farmers prefer apple trees that are the same variety so that their trees are identical.

   Ⓓ To make sure all the trees have the same characteristics, the same variety should be grafted.

10   According to paragraph 3, many apple farmers raise bees because

   Ⓐ the honey that bees produce makes apples sweeter

   Ⓑ bees assist in pollinating the apple trees

   Ⓒ bees kill harmful insects such as aphids and maggots

   Ⓓ apple trees make good locations for beehives

11   In paragraph 4, the author implies that apple trees

   Ⓐ only live a few years before they are killed by diseases

   Ⓑ frequently lose their leaves because of insects eating them

   Ⓒ are more vulnerable to diseases at certain times of the year

   Ⓓ require more pesticides than most other fruit trees do

12 The word "ingenious" in the passage is closest in meaning to

  (A) serious

  (B) traditional

  (C) clever

  (D) high-tech

13 Select the TWO answer choices from paragraph 5 that identify how farmers prevent animals from eating their crops. *To receive credit, you must select TWO answers.*

  (A) By wrapping wire mesh around tree trunks

  (B) By setting traps to capture large animals

  (C) By putting up fences around their orchards

  (D) By using dogs as guard animals in their orchards

14 According to paragraph 6, which of the following is NOT true about machines that farmers use in their apple orchards?

  (A) They require more workers in orchards.

  (B) They gather apples lying on the ground.

  (C) They pick apples while they are on trees.

  (D) They are able to knock apples out of trees.

15 Look at the four squares [■] that indicate where the following sentence could be added to the passage.

These diseases can harm trees in many ways, including by even killing them.

Where would the sentence best fit?

Click on a square [■] to add the sentence to the passage.

16 Directions: An introductory sentence for a brief summary of the passage is provided below. Complete the summary by selecting the THREE answer choices that express the most important ideas of the passage. Some sentences do not belong because they express ideas that are not presented in the passage or are minor ideas in the passage. **This question is worth 2 points.**

Many apple farmers rely upon science and technology to ensure that they can grow apples successfully.

-

-

-

ANSWER CHOICES

1 Farmers raise bees to pollinate their trees and use chemicals to kill diseases and insects.

2 Automation has resulted in fewer people working in apple orchards that utilize many machines.

3 Machinery can be used to remove apples from trees and to pick them up off the ground.

4 Most apple trees start growing fruit in spring, and then the fruit ripens in either summer or fall.

5 Farmers use grafting to ensure that their trees are of the same variety and have the same characteristics.

6 There are many kinds of insects that are known to cause harm to certain varieties of apple trees.

◪ Vocabulary Review

A Complete each sentence with the appropriate word from the box.

apparent	convert	vegetation	deposits	immunity

1 South Africa is known for its huge _____ of diamonds.

2 There are some _____ similarities if you look at both of them.

3 A battery is able to _____ energy into power.

4 She has _____ to that disease so cannot get sick from it.

5 Rainforests are places that have large amounts of _____.

B Complete each sentence with the correct answer.

1 When a computer **interprets** images, it is able to _____.

   a. print them   b. understand them

2 A place that is _____ often has a **humid** environment.

   a. very wet   b. very cold

3 When a stalagmite **emerges** from the floor, it _____.

   a. comes out   b. disappears

4 A severe **epidemic** affected the people, so many of them _____.

   a. got sick   b. lost their jobs

5 People _____ animals after they learned to **domesticate** them.

   a. hunted   b. tamed

6 When the object **dissolves** in water, it _____.

   a. comes together   b. breaks down

7 The retina **absorbs** light by _____.

   a. taking it in   b. keeping it out

8 This **populated** area has _____ people living in it.

   a. lots of   b. no

9 Vitamins are **beneficial** to people because they can _____.

   a. get them sick   b. make them healthy

Chapter **09**

Prose Summary

Question Type | Prose Summary

◢ About the Question

Prose Summary questions focus on the main theme or idea of the passage. First, you must read a thesis sentence that covers the main points in the passage. Then, you must read six sentences that cover parts of the passage and choose the three sentences that describe the main theme or idea of the passage the closest. These questions always appear last, but they do not always appear. When there is a Fill in a Table question, there is not a Prose Summary question. However, Prose Summary questions are much more common than Fill in a Table questions. Almost every passage now has 1 Prose Summary question.

Recognizing Prose Summary questions:

- **Directions:** An introductory sentence for a brief summary of the passage is provided below. Complete the summary by selecting the THREE answer choices that express the most important ideas of the passage. Some sentences do not belong because they express ideas that are not presented in the passage or are minor ideas in the passage. This question is worth 2 points.

  [You will see an introductory sentence and six answer choices.]

Helpful hints for answering the questions correctly:

- Try to understand the main theme or idea of the passage as you are reading it.
- Only select answer choices that focus on the main theme. Ignore answer choices that focus on minor themes.
- Do not select answer choices that contain incorrect information. In addition, ignore answer choices that contain information which is correct but which is not mentioned in the passage.

Basic Practice

Read the following paragraphs and choose the correct summary for each paragraph.

CH09_1A

A   Lying between the crust and the core, the mantle is the largest of the Earth's three layers. While the mantle has never been visited, geologists have managed to study it. It begins approximately thirty kilometers beneath the surface and descends roughly 2,900 kilometers. The upper mantle contains both the lithosphere and the asthenosphere. The lithosphere, which includes the crust, is comprised of solid rock, but the asthenosphere is not. It is exposed to great amounts of heat and pressure, so the rock there is viscous and flows like a liquid. This movement in the asthenosphere is what causes the tectonic plates resting above it to move. This results in both earthquakes and continental drift. As for the lower mantle, the rock in it is believed to be solid.

(A) Scientists have not visited the mantle but still know very much about it.

(B) The mantle is the most important of the Earth's three layers because of its size.

(C) The mantle has both solid and viscous rock, which causes the crust to move.

CH09_1B

B   One of the greatest artists in history was Diego Velázquez. A Spaniard, he lived from 1599 to 1660. Velázquez produced a large number of works during his lifetime but is known mostly for the portraits he painted. He became the court painter for King Philip IV of Spain, which let him make paintings of many members of the Spanish royal family and other nobles. Velázquez was influenced by Italian painters such as Caravaggio, Titian, and Tintoretto. He particularly adopted their use of color, which tended to be dark. His paintings are noted for their realism and simplicity. His works, including his masterpiece, *Las Meninas*, would later influence large numbers of artists. These included Francis Bacon, Edouard Manet, and Pablo Picasso.

(A) Velázquez was a great Spanish painter who influenced other artists after him.

(B) *Las Meninas* is the most famous and influential work that Velázquez ever made.

(C) The influence of Caravaggio and other Italians on Velázquez is obvious.

A | Star Carr

🎧 CH09_2A

Stonehenge is the most famous prehistoric site in England. However, there are many others that can be found throughout the land. One of them is Star Carr. It is a settlement that existed during the **Mesolithic Period**.

Star Carr is a site in Yorkshire that was occupied sometime around 9000 B.C. Archaeologists believe people lived there for around 200 to 300 years. It appears to have been a permanent residence for a group of people in the area. That is noteworthy since humans at the time were hunter-gatherers, so they primarily lived nomadic lives.

One reason Star Carr is so important is that a large number of artifacts have been excavated there. These include spearheads, various tools, and even masks. Many of these items have been well presevered so are in excellent condition. As for the site itself, it covers an area almost five hectares in size. There are some remains of wooden buildings that served as homes for people. The buildings were extremely advanced for the time and have caused archaeologists to reconsider many of their theories on humans from this period.

*Mesolithic Period: the Middle Stone Age period that lasted from around 10,000 B.C. to 5000 B.C.

An introductory sentence for a brief summary of the passage is provided below. Complete the summary by selecting the THREE answer choices that express the most important ideas of the passage. Some sentences do not belong because they express ideas that are not presented in the passage or are minor ideas in the passage.

Star Carr is an important archaeological site in England.

ANSWER CHOICES

1. Stonehenge and Star Carr are two of the most famous ancient sites in England.
2. The people who lived at Star Carr made several wooden buildings.
3. People who lived in the Mesolithic Period were mostly hunter-gatherers.
4. The site at Star Carr was occupied for around two or three centuries.
5. Many well-preserved artifacts have been excavated at Star Carr.

Skyscraper Design

The first skyscrapers were constructed in the mid-1800s. Prior to then, there were limits regarding how tall buildings could be made. Thanks to improvements in building materials and developments in technology though, it became possible to make buildings more than a few stories high.

For centuries, brick and stone were common building materials. However, both had various limitations, especially regarding how high buildings using them could be constructed. For instance, brick and stone weighed so much that buildings made from them could only be a few stories high. Upon reaching a certain height, they became too heavy and collapsed. In the 1800s, advances were made in iron and steel technology. Thanks to their strength, people could use them to make buildings higher than ten stories.

Once this problem was solved, another appeared. Few people wanted to walk up and down stairs in skyscrapers. The invention of the elevator solved that problem by making going up and down tall buildings simple. It enabled architects to design buildings ten or more stories high. With that problem solved, skyscrapers in the 1800s and 1900s began to rise higher and higher.

*collapse: to fall down

An introductory sentence for a brief summary of the passage is provided below. Complete the summary by selecting the THREE answer choices that express the most important ideas of the passage. Some sentences do not belong because they express ideas that are not presented in the passage or are minor ideas in the passage.

Two developments allowed people to make skyscrapers in the 1800s.

ANSWER CHOICES

1. Steel and iron were strong enough to support buildings many stories high.
2. The first elevators were installed in buildings in the middle of the 1800s.
3. A lot of buildings collapsed because their materials were too heavy to support their weight.
4. It was difficult to make tall buildings with stone and brick because of their weight.
5. The invention of the elevator allowed people to go up and down skyscrapers easily.

A   The Amazon Reef

🎧 CH09_3A

A new coral reef was recently discovered in the South Atlantic Ocean. Located off the coasts of Brazil, Suriname, and French Guiana, it is named the Amazon Reef since it is located near the mouth of the Amazon River. It is one of the world's largest coral reefs. It exists between fifty and 100 meters underwater. And it covers an area of 9,500 square kilometers. The reef also stretches nearly 1,000 kilometers.

Since the 1970s, scientists had hypothesized that a reef existed in the area. The outflow of muddy sediment from the Amazon River makes the nearby water very <u>murky</u>. The region also has very choppy water. Both conditions make exploring underwater difficult. In 2012, a team of researchers found evidence of the reef. Another team then conducted a broader search of the area and found it. News of their discovery as well as photographs were later released.

The Amazon Reef is different from most of the other coral reefs in the world. The fresh water coming from the Amazon River gives the ocean water a low salt content and a high acid content. **1** Coral does not grow well in these conditions. **2** However, the Amazon Reef is deep enough that it is below the level of much of the Amazon's outflow. **3** So the coral is not affected by the lack of salt in the water near the surface. **4** During their studies, scientists found dozens of species of fish, shellfish, and marine plants living in and around the reef. Still, this reef appears to be less suitable for life than other coral reefs, particularly those in shallow tropical waters. As a result, it has less marine life than other reefs do.

*murky: dark; muddy; unclear

Vocabulary

- h_____ = to believe; to theorize
- c_____ = rough
- s_____ = appropriate; acceptable
- s_____ = not deep

1 In paragraph 2, the author implies that the coral reef

(A) is the biggest in the entire world

(B) is found in water that is difficult to see in

(C) was not expected to exist by scientists

(D) is in the process of slowly dying

2 The word "it" in the passage refers to

(A) the reef

(B) another team

(C) a broader search

(D) the area

3 Look at the four squares [■] that indicate where the following sentence could be added to the passage.

In fact, a lack of salt in the water will cause coral to die.

Where would the sentence best fit?

4 An introductory sentence for a brief summary of the passage is provided below. Complete the summary by selecting the THREE answer choices that express the most important ideas of the passage. Some sentences do not belong because they express ideas that are not presented in the passage or are minor ideas in the passage.

There is a recently discovered coral reef in the Atlantic Ocean near the Amazon River.

ANSWER CHOICES

1 Several dozen new species of fish have been discovered in the waters of the reef.

2 The coral reef is located in salt water beneath fresh water coming from the Amazon River.

3 The coral reef is found in very deep water, so the water is much cooler there.

4 The reef is one of the biggest in the world and extends around 1,000 kilometers.

5 Scientists had long believed the reef existed and finally found it after many years of looking.

B | Michael Faraday

Michael Faraday was a British scientist. He was born in the 1700s but did work in the 1800s. Today, most people remember him for his work with gases and electromagnetism. During his youth, Faraday's family had little money. As a result, he did not receive a proper education. He dropped out of school at the age of thirteen to work at a bookshop. There, he read science books in his free time. He also went to lectures by scientists when he had a chance.

When he became older, Faraday began his career as a chemist by becoming the apprentice of Sir Humphry Davy. He later became a professor at the noted Royal Institution. He stayed there for fifty-four years. Much of Faraday's early chemistry work was on the liquefaction of gases. He learned how to turn chlorine and ammonia into liquids. He also learned that when mechanical pumps liquefied ammonia and then let it evaporate, it had a cooling effect. This became the principle upon which modern refrigeration is based. Later, in 1825, Faraday discovered the gas benzene.

Faraday did work in the field of electromagnetism as well. He started by doing basic experiments. They led him to find out that moving a magnet over a wire could produce electricity in the wire. This is called electromagnetic induction. It is a form of kinetic energy. Modern electric motors rely on this method to make electricity. Faraday also discovered some of the laws of electrochemistry that describe the relationship between chemicals and electricity. Another of his discoveries is called the Faraday Effect. He learned that a magnetic field caused the plane of a light source to rotate. This is used to study remote sensing in magnetic fields. It also has applications for fiber optic systems used today.

*evaporate: to change from a liquid or a solid into a gas

Vocabulary

- e_____ = the science of electric and magnetic fields
- l_____ = the act of making something a liquid
- p_____ = an accepted rule or belief
- r_____ = to turn around in a circle

1 According to paragraph 1, how did Michael Faraday start learning science?

   (A) By studying with a tutor

   (B) By attending school

   (C) By working with his father

   (D) By reading on his own

Vocabulary Question

2 The word "apprentice" in the passage is closest in meaning to

   (A) student

   (B) colleague

   (C) trainee

   (D) advisor

Inference Question

3 Which of the following can be inferred from paragraphs 2 and 3 about Michael Faraday?

   (A) Many of his discoveries have uses in modern times.

   (B) He became very wealthy from his discoveries.

   (C) He preferred teaching students to doing research.

   (D) The electric motor he invented is still used today.

Prose Summary Question

4 An introductory sentence for a brief summary of the passage is provided below. Complete the summary by selecting the THREE answer choices that express the most important ideas of the passage. Some sentences do not belong because they express ideas that are not presented in the passage or are minor ideas in the passage.

Michael Faraday made several discoveries that contributed to the advancement of scientific knowledge.

ANSWER CHOICES

1 One of the discoveries that Faraday made was the gas benzene.

2 Faraday was employed as a teacher at the same place for more than five decades.

3 Faraday's work in electromagnetism resulted in a method that electric motors use today.

4 Faraday did some experiments on how to turn certain gases into liquids.

5 The principles of modern refrigeration were discovered by Faraday.

🎧 CH09_4A

The Woolly Mammoth

The woolly mammoth was an enormous elephant-like animal that once lived across the northern parts of Eurasia and North America. Today, it is extinct, but there is evidence that it lived together alongside prehistoric men. Around 10,000 years ago, the mammoth began to die out. However, it did not disappear everywhere at the same time. Its extinction was a long process, and the last one is believed to have died around 4,000 years ago.

The main causes of the mammoth's decline were the changing climate and human hunting. The mammoth flourished during the last ice age. ■1 It was much better adapted to cold climates than most other animals and humans were. ■2 When the last ice age ended, the glaciers retreated, and vegetation began growing again in many places. ■3 This could have been an advantage to the mammoth, an herbivore. ■4 But it also led to various animals encroaching on its territory, which resulted in increasing competition for food sources. The more southerly mammoth herds died out first. Over time, the surviving mammoths migrated north to find better feeding grounds.

The mammoth could not, however, escape from human hunters. Over thousands of years, hunters pushed them further north. Many remains of mammoth bones have spear marks and other tool marks to show they were hunted, killed, and then butchered. By 6,000 years ago, most mainland mammoths had been hunted to extinction. The only remaining ones lived on two remote islands in the far north. They had moved to them when ice covered the oceans and got stuck when the ice retreated.

Some mammoths lived on St. Paul Island. It is located in the Bering Sea between Alaska and Russia. It is a small island and supported a small group of mammoths. It is also a dry island, having a single lake with fresh water. Scientists believe some St. Paul mammoths died of thirst during a dry spell 5,600 years ago. Others also likely ate all the limited amount of vegetation on the island, making them starve to death. Their actions could have also destroyed the lake by allowing it to fill with sediment from erosion.

The last remaining mammoths lived on Wrangel Island, which is located in the Arctic Ocean near Russia. It is much larger than St. Paul Island, so it could support a bigger mammoth population. Still, this herd was smaller than the ones that roamed the mainland. Experts believe that around 300 mammoths lived on the island. This led to a small gene pool for them to reproduce from. Over time, this caused several mutations in generations of mammoths.

One such mutation could have caused their hair to be less able to protect them from the cold. Another one could have disrupted their sense of smell. This might have caused reproduction problems since smell is often important for animals when choosing mates. Eventually, these problems led to the death of the final woolly mammoth around 4,000 years ago.

*Glossary

Eurasia: the continents of Europe and Asia

butcher: to cut up an animal for its meat

1   According to paragraph 1, which of the following is true about the woolly mammoth?

  Ⓐ It died out before it encountered men.

  Ⓑ It went extinct around 10,000 years ago.

  Ⓒ It was smaller than the modern elephant.

  Ⓓ It lived in the northern parts of many places.

2   In paragraph 2, why does the author mention "the last ice age"?

  Ⓐ To explain how its end affected the woolly mammoth

  Ⓑ To point out when it both began and ended

  Ⓒ To state that the woolly mammoth declined during it

  Ⓓ To note how much food animals found during it

3   The word "remote" in the passage is closest in meaning to

  Ⓐ distant

  Ⓑ empty

  Ⓒ large

  Ⓓ cold

4   According to paragraph 4, the woolly mammoths on St. Paul Island likely died because

(A) humans hunted them

(B) they had no food or water

(C) a disease killed them

(D) there was a natural disaster

5   The word "it" in the passage refers to

(A) Wrangel Island

(B) the Arctic Ocean

(C) Russia

(D) St. Paul Island

6   In paragraph 5, the author's description of Wrangel Island mentions all of the following EXCEPT:

(A) how many woolly mammoths lived there

(B) why the woolly mammoths there died

(C) where in the world it can be found

(D) how the woolly mammoths got there

7   Look at the four squares [■] that indicate where the following sentence could be added to the passage.

For instance, its long hair protected it from cold temperatures, snow, and wind.

Where would the sentence best fit?

Click on a square [■] to add the sentence to the passage.

8 **Directions**: An introductory sentence for a brief summary of the passage is provided below. Complete the summary by selecting the THREE answer choices that express the most important ideas of the passage. Some sentences do not belong because they express ideas that are not presented in the passage or are minor ideas in the passage. **This question is worth 2 points.**

The woolly mammoth population went extinct for a variety of reasons.

-
-
-

ANSWER CHOICES

1. It is possible that a deadly disease killed large numbers of them around the world.

2. The ending of the ice age forced many woolly mammoths to move to more northern lands.

3. Woolly mammoths lived alongside humans for a long period of time.

4. Humans killed large numbers of woolly mammoths in some places.

5. The meat of the woolly mammoth could feed many humans for several days.

6. Woolly mammoths trapped on island starved to death and suffered from genetic mutations.

PASSAGE 2

European and Native American Cultures

When European explorers began arriving in the New World in the 1500s, they came into contact with the natives of the land who already lived there. They discovered that each of them had very different cultures. This was particularly true regarding their views of property, the roles of women in society, and attitudes toward trade. Some of these differences help explain why the two sides often clashed with each other.

Europeans viewed land as private property. They needed land to grow food in order to survive. Getting more land increased a person's wealth. They also passed land on within their families to help provide for their children's futures. Native Americans regarded land as being something that everyone in the community could use though. To them, all of nature was for everyone. Agreements between tribes often set boundaries. But within a tribal area, no person owned any land. The members could hunt and fish anywhere. They also planted crops in temporary plots. They normally changed the locations of their fields each year to ensure the soil stayed fertile.

Another major difference was men's and women's roles. In Europe, men led their families and controlled all aspects of their wives' and children's lives. Women had few rights and were expected to obey their father or husband. European women ran the home and looked after the children. They did not often engage in labor, do a trade, or get involved in business. But women had greater roles in Native American society. They helped run their families and made decisions with their husbands. They even partook in tribal discussions. In many tribes, women had a say in whom they married. They also did heavy labor. Women also often did the farming while men hunted and fished.

Once they made contact, Europeans and Native Americans engaged in trade. The Europeans provided many kinds of goods while the Natives mostly offered furs. The two sides viewed trade differently. To Europeans, the purpose of trade was to acquire more wealth. So they wanted to get the best deal for the least amount. ■ Natives considered trade more of a ceremonial activity. ■ It was a way to build relationships with others. ■ It often involved exchanging gifts. ■ The giving and receiving of gifts was considered an integral part of tribal life. Acquiring gifts led to greater status while giving them showed generosity. The Europeans did not understand this importance. Thus they often unintentionally insulted Natives during trade talks.

In the 1500s and 1600s, Europeans moved to the New World in great numbers. Then, they built large communities. They erected fences to control the land and its resources. This shut out Natives from places they had lived for generations. The inevitable result of these cultural differences was war. The Europeans had superior weapons of war. So they won and pushed the Natives westward. Over time, they were able to conquer almost the entire New World.

*Glossary

New World: the name for North and South America at the time when it was first discovered by Europeans

fur: the fine, soft fur of animals such as beavers and minks

9   The phrase "clashed with" in the passage is closest in meaning to

  Ⓐ mismatched with

  Ⓑ distrusted

  Ⓒ fought against

  Ⓓ talked about

10 According to paragraph 2, which of the following is true about how Native Americans regarded land?

  Ⓐ They thought that having more of it increased their wealth.

  Ⓑ They believed it was important enough to place restrictions on its use.

  Ⓒ They did not think that individual people could own any of it.

  Ⓓ They considered it property they could pass on to their children.

11 In paragraph 3, the author's description of European and Native American views on the roles of women mentions all of the following EXCEPT:

  Ⓐ how women had to behave toward men

  Ⓑ how each culture had different thoughts

  Ⓒ what type of work women often did

  Ⓓ why each culture was so different in its attitudes

12 In paragraph 4, why does the author mention "a ceremonial activity"?

Ⓐ To describe how Native Americans thought of trade

Ⓑ To compare Europeans' attitude with those of other people

Ⓒ To argue that trade was too important to Europeans

Ⓓ To discuss why Native Americans fought with Europeans

13 According to paragraph 4, what happened during trade talks between Europeans and Native Americans?

Ⓐ They occasionally ended in fighting.

Ⓑ The Native Americans were sometimes offended.

Ⓒ The Europeans usually felt they got bad bargains.

Ⓓ The two sides often traded with gold and silver.

14 The word "inevitable" in the passage is closest in meaning to

Ⓐ desired

Ⓑ rumored

Ⓒ unfortunate

Ⓓ predictable

15 Look at the four squares [■] that indicate where the following sentence could be added to the passage.

In other words, they were focused on making a profit.

Where would the sentence best fit?

Click on a square [■] to add the sentence to the passage.

16 **Directions**: An introductory sentence for a brief summary of the passage is provided below. Complete the summary by selecting the THREE answer choices that express the most important ideas of the passage. Some sentences do not belong because they express ideas that are not presented in the passage or are minor ideas in the passage. **This question is worth 2 points.**

There were many cultural differences between Europeans and Native Americans in the New World.

-

-

-

ANSWER CHOICES

☐1 Women had much greater roles in Native American society than they did in European society.

☐2 The Europeans and the Native Americans frequently exchanged gifts with each other when they met.

☐3 The Native Americans welcomed the Europeans when they first arrived, but then they later became hostile.

☐4 The Europeans and the Native Americans had varying opinions on the purposes and uses of trade.

☐5 There were many fights between Europeans and Native Americans, and the Europeans wound up winning in the end.

☐6 Native Americans did not believe in private property, but Europeans had strong views about owning land.

◢ Vocabulary Review

A Complete each sentence with the appropriate word from the box.

| artifacts | limitations | invention | shallow | herbivore |

1 This _____ has never been made by anyone before.

2 They can walk in the water because it is very _____.

3 An _____ is an animal that does not eat any meat.

4 Since there are _____, we cannot do everything we want to.

5 The _____ were all relics that were buried in the ground.

B Complete each sentence with the correct answer.

1 The _____ water is very **choppy** today because of the storm.
   a. calm   b. rough

2 The animals are trying to **escape** so that they can _____ the hunters.
   a. attack   b. get away from

3 Since the award is **noteworthy**, many people _____ about it.
   a. care a lot   b. do not care

4 Because there have been many **mutations**, the organisms _____ over time.
   a. have changed   b. have remained the same

5 When the scientist **hypothesized** about the experiment, he _____.
   a. did another experiment   b. came up with an idea

6 When those flowers **flourished**, they grew _____ in that area.
   a. poorly   b. very well

7 If an area can **support** many animals, then they _____.
   a. can live in it   b. have no food there

8 The archaeologists _____ many items when they **excavated** the site.
   a. did not find   b. dug up

9 The glaciers **retreated** by _____ at the end of the last ice age.
   a. getting larger   b. moving back

Chapter 10

Fill in a Table

Question Type | Fill in a Table

About the Question

Fill in a Table questions focus on the entire passage. You are asked to answer a question that breaks down the passage into two or three major theme or topics. There will be a number of sentences about these themes. You have to determine which theme each of the sentences you read refers to. These questions may ask about cause and effect, problem and solution, and compare and contrast, or they may focus on other themes. These questions always appear last, but they do not always appear. When there is a Prose Summary question, there is not a Fill in a Table question. Fill in a Table questions rarely appear anymore. Prose Summary questions are much more common than Fill in a Table questions.

Recognizing Fill in a Table questions:

- **Directions:** Select the appropriate statements from the answer choices and match them to X to which they relate. TWO of the answer choices will NOT be used. This question is worth 3 points.

  [You will see seven statements.]

- **Directions:** Select the appropriate statements from the answer choices and match them to X to which they relate. TWO of the answer choices will NOT be used. This question is worth 4 points.

  [You will see nine statements.]

Helpful hints for answering the questions correctly:

- These questions only ask about the major themes or topics in the passage.

- Passages that have two or three major themes or topics frequently have this type of question.

- Ignore any minor themes or topics in the passage. These are not covered on this type of question.

- There are always two answer choices that are incorrect. They may have irrelevant information, incorrect information, or information that is correct but which does not appear in the passage.

Read the paragraph below about the Cherokee and the Apache tribes. <u>Underline</u> the information about the Cherokee and <u>double underline</u> the information about the Apache.

🎧 CH10_1A

Two well-known tribes of Native Americans are the Cherokee and the Apache. The Cherokee were one of the major tribes in the southeastern part of the United States. They were among the first tribes to make contact with European settlers after they arrived in the New World. As for the Apache, they lived in the central part of North America. They dwelled primarily on the Great Plains. The Apache were nomadic hunter-gatherers. The men hunted bison, deer, and other animals while the women gathered nuts and berries. The Cherokee had permanent settlements. They lived an agrarian lifestyle in which they farmed the land. While both tribes fought wars against the United States government, the Cherokees ended their battles in the 1700s. The Apaches fought during the 1800s and even had some battles with the U.S. government in the 1920s.

Now use the underlined parts of the paragraph to help you complete the table below.

	Cherokee	Apache
Southeastern United States		
Great Plains		
Nomads		
Permanent Dwellings		
Wars in the Eighteenth Century		
Wars in the Nineteenth Century		

A | Telescopes

🎧 CH10_2A

Amateur and professional astronomers around the world use telescopes to observe the sky. For the most part, they use two: refracting and reflecting telescopes.

Each one allows its user to see distant objects more clearly. Yet they operate differently. Refracting telescopes use lenses whereas reflecting telescopes rely upon mirrors. In 1611, Galileo Galilei became the first person to use a telescope to look at the stars. The one he used was a refractor with two lenses. The first bent light rays and sent them to the second lens. This lens, called the eyepiece, magnified the object being viewed. Modern-day refracting telescopes use the same method as ones from 400 years ago.

A few decades later, Sir Isaac Newton invented the reflecting telescope in 1680. His telescope contained two mirrors. The first **gathered** light and sent it to the second mirror. That mirror then reflected the light to the eyepiece. A person would then look through it. Newton's telescope improved upon Galileo's because people were able to make better mirrors in the past. Today, both types of telescopes are popular. But reflecting telescopes tend to be bigger and cost less than refracting telescopes.

*gather: to collect

Select the appropriate statements from the answer choices and match them to the telescope to which they relate. TWO of the answer choices will NOT be used.

Refracting Telescope	Reflecting Telescope
•	•
•	•

STATEMENTS

1 Has no limits on how big it can be

2 Is not used by many astronomers

3 Was used by Galileo Galilei

4 Relies on mirrors to collect light

5 Was invented in 1680

6 Uses lenses to magnify objects

B Economic Downturns

There are periods when economies improve and become bigger. Later, they stagnate and get worse. There are two types of economic downturns. Mild ones are recessions while more serious ones are depressions.

A recession is a period of negative economic growth for at least two **quarters**. Most recessions last a few months, but others may last up to two years. During a recession, the economy declines since production decreases. Unemployment rises as many people lose their jobs. In the United States, recessions frequently occur when wars conclude. For instance, there were recessions in both 1945, when World War II ended, and in 1953, when the fighting in the Korean War ceased.

Depressions are more severe than recessions. Economists do not always agree on the exact definition of a depression. However, most state that it is an extended period of economic decline lasting at least two years. A country's economy may decline more than ten percent during this period. And the unemployment rate may be twenty percent or higher. The Great Depression of the 1930s is the most famous one. But there were several that took place during the 1800s.

*quarter: a period lasting three months

Select the appropriate statements from the answer choices and match them to the economic downtown to which they relate. TWO of the answer choices will NOT be used.

Recession	Depression
•	•
•	•

STATEMENTS

1 May have an unemployment rate of twenty percent

2 Often lasts for less than a year

3 Happens every couple of decades

4 Results in the unemployment rate getting lower

5 Lasts for more than two years

6 Commonly happens after a war ends

A | Sleeping Positions

🎧 CH10_3A

When people sleep, they put their bodies into a number of different positions. There are three main sleeping positions: sleeping on the stomach, on the side, and on the back. Each of these positions affects people's bodies in different ways. Some of them are positive while the others are more negative in nature.

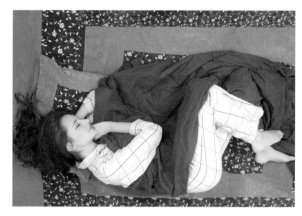

Sleeping on the stomach is considered the worst of the three major sleeping methods. The primary reason for this is that stomach sleepers need to turn their heads in order to breathe. This can cause stress both on their necks and their lower backs. In addition, these individuals often suffer from restlessness as they must constantly toss and turn to become more comfortable.

Those individuals who sleep on their sides do not suffer pain in the neck. But they could develop nerve problems in their arms and legs instead. **1** Scientists have noted that these people sometimes develop **acid reflux** problems as well. **2** The reason is that stomach acid is able to get into the esophagus when people sleep on their sides. **3** In addition, individuals are more likely to suffer from nightmares when sleeping in this position. **4**

Most experts believe that sleeping on the back is the ideal sleeping position. This is especially true for people who suffer from neck or back pain. Sleeping on the back eases these issues, which allows for a more peaceful sleep. On the other hand, people who sleep on their backs are more likely to snore. This position could also result in a person suffering from sleep apnea, a condition in which a person stops breathing for a short period of time.

*acid reflux: a condition in which acid in the stomach flows into the esophagus, which can cause a variety of problems

Vocabulary

- n＿＿＿＿＿＿＿＿ = bad; not positive
- r＿＿＿＿＿＿＿＿ = being unable to relax or rest
- e＿＿＿＿＿＿＿＿ = the passage connecting the mouth to the stomach
- s＿＿＿＿＿＿＿＿ = to make a loud sound while one is sleeping

1 The word "them" in the passage refers to

(A) people

(B) their bodies

(C) these positions

(D) three main sleeping positions

2 In paragraph 3, all of the following questions are answered EXCEPT:

(A) Why might side sleepers develop acid reflux problems?

(B) What can happen to people while they are sleeping on the side?

(C) What body parts could develop problems when a person sleeps on his or her side?

(D) How serious is the neck pain people who sleep on their sides suffer?

3 Look at the four squares [■] that indicate where the following sentence could be added to the passage.

They tend to be vivid and are more easily remembered as well.

Where would the sentence best fit?

4 Select the appropriate statements from the answer choices and match them to the sleeping position to which they relate. TWO of the answer choices will NOT be used.

On the Stomach	On the Side	On the Back
•		•
•	•	•

STATEMENTS

1 Can cause a person to have bad dreams

2 Is the best position for people to sleep

3 Causes sleepers to have no stress on their legs

4 Stops people from waking up in the middle of the night

5 Is the least ideal sleeping position

6 May result in people not breathing well

7 May result in strain on the neck

Types of Precipitation

One part of the <u>water cycle</u> occurs when water on the ground evaporates, ascends into the sky, and then forms clouds. When these clouds become too heavy, they release their water droplets, which fall to the Earth as precipitation. Depending upon the weather conditions, this precipitation typically assumes two different types: liquid or frozen.

The most common type of liquid precipitation is rain. Rain is commonly believed to comprise all liquid precipitation, but that is not correct. Rain falls when the water droplets are 0.5 millimeters or larger in diameter. Droplets smaller than that are considered drizzle. For rain to fall to the ground, the temperature in the air must be higher than zero degrees Celsius. That is the temperature at which water freezes. In some situations, rain may begin to fall from clouds but evaporates before it reaches the ground. This is known as virga. It appears as streaks of gray underneath a cloud.

There are more types of frozen precipitation than liquid precipitation. Snow frequently falls when the temperature is below zero. Snowflakes consist of water droplets that freeze around a core that could be dust or something similar. Hail is another type of frozen precipitation. Hailstones are chunks of ice which usually fall during thunderstorms. Sleet starts as snow but then melts as it is falling to the ground. Then, these raindrops freeze again on their way down and become pellets of ice. Likewise, freezing rain begins as snow but melts when it hits warm air. Then, it enters colder air, so it freezes again. This can coat the ground and streets in ice.

*water cycle: the sequence through which water falls to the ground from clouds, remains there, evaporates, and then rises into the air to form clouds again

Vocabulary

- a＿＿＿＿＿ = to rise; to go up
- d＿＿＿＿＿ = a small bit of a liquid shaped like a drop
- a＿＿＿＿＿ = to believe to be true
- p＿＿＿＿＿ = something small, round, and hard

1   According to paragraph 1, precipitation falls when

   Ⓐ the air temperature becomes very hot or cold

   Ⓑ the wind begins to blow against clouds

   Ⓒ the water in clouds makes them too heavy

   Ⓓ a low pressure system makes it rain or snow

Inference Question

2   In paragraph 2, which of the following can be inferred about drizzle?

   Ⓐ It is smaller than raindrops.

   Ⓑ It can fall in cold weather.

   Ⓒ It happens more often than virga.

   Ⓓ It is the least common liquid precipitation.

Vocabulary Question

3   The word "core" in the passage is closest in meaning to

   Ⓐ edge

   Ⓑ ingredient

   Ⓒ speck

   Ⓓ center

Fill in a Table Question

4   Select the appropriate statements from the answer choices and match them to the type of precipitation to which they relate. TWO of the answer choices will NOT be used.

Liquid	Frozen
●	●
●	●

STATEMENTS

☐1 Falls more often at very high elevations

☐2 Can consist of both hail and sleet

☐3 Can be drops that are smaller than 0.5 millimeters in diameter

☐4 Happens when the air temperature is under zero degrees Celsius

☐5 Can result in flooding when it falls in great amounts

☐6 May fall but evaporate before reaching the ground

CH10_4A

The Neanderthals

Several humanoids populated the Earth in the past. Among them were the Neanderthals. They lived in Europe and parts of Western Asia between 400,000 and 40,000 years ago. They are named for the Neander Valley in Germany. That was where evidence of them was first found. While the Neanderthals thrived for many years, they eventually went extinct. Anthropologists have several theories about their disappearance. None of them is universally accepted though.

Modern humans are thought to have arrived in Europe and Western Asia from Africa around 45,000 years ago. Within the next 5,000 years, the Neanderthals were gone. This suggests that the interaction between the two species was fatal for the Neanderthals. Some experts believe they fought wars against each other. Modern humans then proved superior at making weapons and at coming up with battle tactics. The evidence for this is that modern humans had bows and arrows, which their opponents lacked. While this theory appeals to many, there is no real evidence of wars between the two species. It may be true, however, that humans were better hunters and thus outcompeted the Neanderthals for limited food resources. A comparison of the tools that each used in the past shows that human ones were much better.

The DNA evidence shows that humans and the Neanderthals interacted as the two bred with each other. A small percentage—less than four percent—of human DNA comes from the Neanderthals. So some believe that the Neanderthals were simply assimilated by humans through interbreeding. Others disagree. They argue that the DNA evidence suggests the large number of interactions necessary for this to occur simply did not happen.

It is possible that the close interaction between the two groups led to the rapid spread of diseases and then death. Some speculate that humans carried diseases which the Neanderthals had no defense against. The Neanderthals then got sick and could not recover. This would have been similar to what happened when the Europeans visited the Americas. Sicknesses from the Old World killed millions of people living in the Americas. While this theory is intriguing, there is no evidence so far showing that the Neanderthals were killed by diseases in large numbers.

A final theory is that modern humans had nothing to do with the extinction of the Neanderthals. Instead, some anthropologists believe they were almost all gone by the time humans arrived. When the Neanderthals disappeared, for some reason, forests began to vanish. They were then replaced by plains. This may have happened because ash from a massive volcanic eruption changed the temperatures and growing periods in the region. This would have hurt the Neanderthals' ability to get food. They hunted animals by ambushing them in forests. Their short, squat bodies were suitable for living in cold weather and for running short distances. Their bodies were not suitable for stalking game in warm climates over long distances on plains. So the change in the climate might have caused the Neanderthals to disappear.

*Glossary

battle tactics: methods that are used during fights
Old World: Europe, Africa, and Asia

1   In paragraph 1, the author's description of the Neanderthals mentions all of the following EXCEPT:

- Ⓐ when they used to live on the Earth
- Ⓑ what caused them to become extinct
- Ⓒ where they were discovered for the first time
- Ⓓ which part of the Earth they lived on

2   The word "fatal" in the passage is closest in meaning to

- Ⓐ dangerous
- Ⓑ deadly
- Ⓒ harmful
- Ⓓ worse

3   The word "ones" in the passage refers to

- Ⓐ superior hunters
- Ⓑ the Neanderthals
- Ⓒ limited food resources
- Ⓓ the tools

4 According to paragraph 2, which of the following is true about the Neanderthals?

Ⓐ They died out around 5,000 years after meeting humans.

Ⓑ They had weapons better than those that humans had.

Ⓒ They sometimes fought wars against human tribes.

Ⓓ They were driven out of Europe and into Africa by humans.

5 The author discusses "human DNA" in paragraph 3 in order to

Ⓐ show that humans and the Neanderthals bred with each other

Ⓑ argue that the Neanderthals had a small percentage of it

Ⓒ claim that it is unlikely humans mated with the Neanderthals

Ⓓ discuss the importance of human DNA in the Neanderthals

6 The word "intriguing" in the passage is closest in meaning to

Ⓐ factual

Ⓑ fascinating

Ⓒ worthwhile

Ⓓ transparent

7 Which of the following can be inferred from paragraph 5 about the Neanderthals?

Ⓐ They adapted and learned how to hunt from humans.

Ⓑ They preferred to live in wide, open areas than in forests.

Ⓒ They may have died out due to a natural disaster.

Ⓓ They lived in both warm and cold climates.

8 **Directions**: Select the appropriate statements from the answer choices and match them to the possible reason for the disappearance of the Neanderthals to which they relate. TWO of the answer choices will NOT be used. **This question is worth 3 points.**

Drag your answer choices to the spaces where they belong. To remove an answer choice, click on it. To review the passage, click on VIEW TEXT.

STATEMENTS

1. Had no defenses to protect themselves
2. Did not have effective weapons
3. Died off at a very fast rate
4. Had encounters with tribes that came from Africa
5. Saw millions killed in a single year
6. Were killed when a volcano erupted
7. Were unable to hunt well enough

REASON FOR THE DISAPPEARANCE OF THE NEANDERTHALS

Modern Humans (Select 3)

•
•
•

Disease (Select 2)

•
•

Animal Navigation

Some animals undergo lengthy migrations. They may migrate because they are avoiding bad weather, going to places where there is food, or heading to breeding grounds. In all cases, they need the ability to navigate over long distances. Over time, animals have developed four primary ways of doing this.

Some animals retain memories of places they have visited before. They can recall certain locations and know where they are. By following landmarks which they remember, they can navigate long distances. Basically, they form a mental map of their course by following these landmarks. Migratory birds, for example, visit the same trees and ponds year after year on their journeys north and south. Herd animals in Africa often take the same paths for generations. They do this while following the seasonal rains that produce rich grasslands. And gray whales swim along the Pacific coast of North America when they migrate between Alaskan and Mexican waters.

The positions of the sun and the stars help other animals migrate. The angle of the sun above the horizon changes as one moves north and south. The sun also rises in the east and sets in the west, making it a natural navigation tool. Biologists believe the monarch butterfly navigates by using the sun as it travels from Canada to Mexico. Other species that travel at night use the positions of the stars to assist them. Experiments with the bird called the indigo bunting proved it uses the stars to navigate.

The ability of some species to navigate suggests genetic coding hardwired in their brains. For example, salmon always return to the same stream where they hatched. It is as if the way there was encoded when they hatched from eggs. Sea turtles also return to the same beach where they hatched to breed and to lay eggs. Some species of birds and insects seem to innately know where to go the first time they migrate. Biologists are unsure whether this is a genetic trait or if some other factor is at work. One alternative theory is that these animals utilize their sense of smell to follow a route laid by others of the same species.

Finally, the Earth's magnetic field may be another factor that animals use to navigate. Homing pigeons appear to have the ability to sense the magnetic field and can use it to find their way. In some experiments, magnets were strapped to their backs. The pigeons' navigational skills were then disrupted. That suggested to biologists that the birds rely upon the magnetic field to determine where to go. However, how animals use the Earth's magnetic field to navigate is uncertain. Some biologists believe these animals have special cells or structures in their bodies that respond to magnetism. These send signal to animals' brains to let them navigate. More recent studies seem to disprove this theory though, so more research must be done in the future.

*Glossary

landmark: a prominent object on land that is used as a guide

hardwired: relating to something that is instinctive

9   The word "retain" in the passage is closest in meaning to

(A) update

(B) lose

(C) keep

(D) resolve

10   In paragraph 2, the author's description of animals that use mental maps to navigate while migrating mentions all of the following EXCEPT:

(A) the destination that butterflies go to on their migrations

(B) the reason that some animals in Africa migrate

(C) the places migratory birds stop at on their journeys

(D) the path that whales follow while migrating

11   In paragraph 3, the author uses "the monarch butterfly" as an example of

(A) an insect which has genetic coding hardwired into it

(B) an animal that uses the position of the sun to navigate

(C) an insect which has a mind map it uses to guide it

(D) an animal that relies on the Earth's magnetic field for guidance

12 The word "innately" in the passage is closest in meaning to

    (A) repeatedly

    (B) clearly

    (C) apparently

    (D) naturally

13 Which of the sentences below best expresses the essential information in the highlighted sentence in the passage? Incorrect answer choices change the meaning in important ways or leave out essential information.

    One alternative theory is that these animals utilize their sense of smell to follow a route laid by others of the same species.

    (A) By smelling, some animals are able to locate other animals belonging the same species.

    (B) Some scientists think that animals have a much keener sense of smell than humans do.

    (C) It is possible that some animals can find their way back to their homes by using their sense of smell.

    (D) A different idea is that animals smell the route that other members of their species followed previously.

14 According to paragraph 4, which of the following is true about sea turtles?

    (A) They know where to go when they migrate across the ocean.

    (B) They lay their eggs on the beaches where they hatched.

    (C) They swim upstream to find places to lay their eggs.

    (D) They use the sun for guidance when swimming in the ocean.

15 According to paragraph 5, homing pigeons' ability to navigate may be disrupted by

    (A) changing their diets

    (B) having them fly at night

    (C) making them fly in stormy weather

    (D) placing magnets on them

16 **Directions:** Select the appropriate statements from the answer choices and match them to the type of navigation method to which they relate. TWO of the answer choices will NOT be used. This question is worth 4 points.

> Drag your answer choices to the spaces where they belong. To remove an answer choice, click on it. To review the passage, click on VIEW TEXT

STATEMENTS

1 Is used by the indigo bunting

2 Requires animals to follow landmarks on their treks

3 Needs to be researched more in the future

4 Allows salmon to find the streams where they hatched

5 Is the method used by homing pigeons

6 Can be used as natural navigation tools for animals migrating at night

7 Explains why some animals visit the same places on their migrations

8 May be an inborn trait allowing animals to find their birthplaces

9 Is used by gray whales while they swim in the ocean

TYPE OF NAVIGATION METHOD

Using Memories (Select 3)

-
-
-

Using the Sun and Stars (Select 2)

-
-

Using Genetic Coding (Select 2)

-
-

▰ Vocabulary Review

A Complete each sentence with the appropriate word from the box.

unemployment	magnify	ascend	droplets	lack

1 A telescope can _____ objects to make them seem larger.

2 Some small _____ of water are falling to the ground.

3 The plane will take off and _____ high in the sky soon.

4 A country with low _____ has many jobs.

5 We _____ money, so we cannot purchase anything.

B Complete each sentence with the correct answer.

1 He suffers from **restlessness** every night, so he _____.
   a. cannot sleep well   b. falls asleep quickly

2 When the object **vanished**, we _____.
   a. could not see it   b. saw it clearly

3 When an economy **stagnates**, it _____.
   a. gets much better   b. does not get better

4 People who are **assimilated** are _____ by another culture.
   a. taken in   b. thrown out

5 Because she is an **amateur** athlete, she _____.
   a. makes a lot of money   b. does not get paid

6 This **massive** mountain is _____ than those hills over there.
   a. bigger   b. smaller

7 Because the economy is **thriving**, it is doing _____.
   a. well   b. poorly

8 You _____ at night when you **snore**.
   a. have dreams   b. make lots of noise

9 She will _____ from her illness as she starts to **recover**.
   a. get better   b. suffer a lot

Actual Test

Reading Section Directions

This section measures your ability to understand academic passages in English. You will have **54 minutes** to read and answer questions about **3 passages**. A clock at the top of the screen will show you how much time is remaining.

Most questions are worth 1 point but the last question for each passage is worth more than 1 point. The directions for the last question indicate how many points you may receive.

Some passages include a word or phrase that is underlined. Click on the word or phrase to see a definition or an explanation.

When you want to move to the next question, click on **NEXT**. You may skip questions and go back to them later. If you want to return to previous questions, click on **BACK**. You can click on **REVIEW** at any time, and the review screen will show you which questions you have answered and which you have not answered. From this review screen, you may go directly to any question you have already seen in the Reading section.

Click on **CONTINUE** to go on.

Water on Mars

The *Mars Reconnaissance Orbiter*

Astronomers have long wondered if there is water on Mars. Research has revealed that there is water in ice, gas, and liquid forms on the planet. Most of the ice is found in its polar ice caps. These are comprised of a huge mass of ice lying beneath a thin layer of frozen carbon dioxide. Astronomers estimate that there is enough frozen water on Mars to cover the entire planet if it all melts. As for water in its gaseous form, some water vapor exists in the atmosphere. There is also strong evidence that liquid water flows on the planet's surface at times.

It is believed that billions of years ago, Mars was warmer and had free-flowing water. Some astronomers think that the planet could have supported some small life forms then, but this has yet to be verified. The conditions on Mars were not stable enough for the water to remain on the planet though. Mars is smaller than Earth and also has less gravity and a thinner atmosphere. In addition, it has low temperatures and low atmospheric pressure. These conditions combined to allow evaporated water to escape into space. After some time, there was not enough water vapor in the atmosphere for it to rain. The remaining water on or beneath the surface today was frozen so did not evaporate.

Most of the water on the planet today exists in the ice caps. The northern one is larger than the southern one. It is about two kilometers thick and 1,000 kilometers in diameter. It may contain more than 1.5 million square kilometers of ice. The southern one is only around 350 kilometers in diameter yet is around three kilometers thick. So it contains approximately the same amount of frozen water as the northern ice cap. Both grow and shrink as the seasons change. Like Earth, Mars experiences warm and cool periods each year. In the warm summertime, the frozen carbon dioxide in the upper layer of the ice caps melts. The carbon dioxide undergoes sublimation and transforms from a solid state to a gaseous one. The reverse happens in winter. Then, carbon dioxide in the atmosphere freezes, causing the ice caps to grow again.

Mars also has frozen water underground. The *Mars Reconnaissance Orbiter*, a NASA space probe, took hundreds of ground-penetrating radar images of the Martian surface. It discovered a wide region that contains frozen water. It is between eighty and 170 meters thick and may be as large as Lake Superior. This frozen lake is fifty to eighty percent water. The remainder is dust and rock particles. It is located about halfway between the northern ice cap and the Martian equator. Other smaller patches of underground water have also been found, and more may be discovered in the future.

New research indicates that if the proper conditions are met, liquid water flows freely on the surface. Many geological features on Mars appear to have been made by the carving action of flowing water. At first, astronomers believed this happened in the distant past. Yet continuous observation in recent years has shown some changes in the planet's geology. The *Mars Reconnaissance Orbiter* discovered dark streaks on mountain slopes that appear and disappear. They appear during warm periods and vanish in cool times. It is believed that these slopes contain high levels of hydrated salts. They are used on the Earth to melt snow and ice on roads. If a layer of frozen ice is located just below the surface, the hydrated salts could melt it in warm conditions. Then, the water flows downhill. When it gets colder, the temperature is too low for the salts to melt the ice.

The flowing of water on Mars may mean that there is life on the planet. It is likely that this will not be determined until more missions are carried out on the planet. They would most likely have to be manned missions. But nobody is sure when humans will ever set foot on Mars. Nevertheless, the possibility of there being free-flowing water on Mars increases the likelihood that the planet is not completely sterile but that it instead may have life on it.

*Glossary

sublimation: the process through which a solid or liquid changes into a gas
hydrated salt: a type of salt that has some water in it which it crystallizes

Water on Mars

➡ Astronomers have long wondered if there is water on Mars. Research has revealed that there is water in ice, gas, and liquid forms on the planet. Most of the ice is found in its polar ice caps. These are comprised of a huge mass of ice lying beneath a thin layer of frozen carbon dioxide. Astronomers estimate that there is enough frozen water on Mars to cover the entire planet if it all melts. As for water in its gaseous form, some water vapor exists in the atmosphere. There is also strong evidence that liquid water flows on the planet's surface at times.

⇨ It is believed that billions of years ago, Mars was warmer and had free-flowing water. Some astronomers think that the planet could have supported some small life forms then, but this has yet to be verified. The conditions on Mars were not stable enough for the water to remain on the planet though. Mars is smaller than Earth and also has less gravity and a thinner atmosphere. In addition, it has low temperatures and low atmospheric pressure. These conditions combined to allow evaporated water to escape into space. After some time, there was not enough water vapor in the atmosphere for it to rain. The remaining water on or beneath the surface today was frozen so did not evaporate.

1 In paragraph 1, the author's description of Mars mentions all of the following EXCEPT:

   Ⓐ what covers the ice at its polar caps

   Ⓑ where the oceans on Mars can be found

   Ⓒ which forms the water on it takes

   Ⓓ how much water exists on the planet

   Paragraph 1 is marked with an arrow (➡).

2 Which of the sentences below best expresses the essential information in the highlighted sentence in the passage? Incorrect answer choices change the meaning in important ways or leave out essential information.

   Some astronomers think that the planet could have supported some small life forms then, but this has yet to be verified.

   Ⓐ People are waiting to verify that there are some life forms on the planet.

   Ⓑ Astronomers are considering the possibility that life exists on Mars.

   Ⓒ It is thought that life could have existed there, but nobody is sure yet.

   Ⓓ There is now definite proof that life existed on Mars in the past.

3 According to paragraph 2, one of the reasons water on Mars escaped into space is that

   Ⓐ the planet has such high gravity

   Ⓑ rain was never able to fall there

   Ⓒ the temperature does not rise above freezing

   Ⓓ it has a thin atmosphere

   Paragraph 2 is marked with an arrow (⇨).

4   The word "transforms" in the passage is closest in meaning to

   (A) melts

   (B) changes

   (C) appears

   (D) reveals

5   What is the author's purpose in paragraph 4 of the passage?

   (A) To claim the *Mars Reconnaissance Orbiter* was the first satellite to map Mars

   (B) To describe the role of the *Mars Reconnaissance Orbiter* in finding water on Mars

   (C) To discuss the discoveries in the ice caps made by the *Mars Reconnaissance Orbiter*

   (D) To state that the *Mars Reconnaissance Orbiter* found no liquid water

Paragraph 4 is marked with an arrow (➡).

6   In paragraph 4, which of the following can be inferred about the water on Mars?

   (A) Nobody is sure how much of it there is.

   (B) Most of it can be found in frozen lakes.

   (C) There are only a few places it can be found.

   (D) More of it is being found every day.

Paragraph 4 is marked with an arrow (➡).

Most of the water on the planet today exists in the ice caps. The northern one is larger than the southern one. It is about two kilometers thick and 1,000 kilometers in diameter. It may contain more than 1.5 million square kilometers of ice. The southern one is only around 350 kilometers in diameter yet is around three kilometers thick. So it contains approximately the same amount of frozen water as the northern ice cap. Both grow and shrink as the seasons change. Like Earth, Mars experiences warm and cool periods each year. In the warm summertime, the frozen carbon dioxide in the upper layer of the ice caps melts. The carbon dioxide undergoes sublimation and transforms from a solid state to a gaseous one. The reverse happens in winter. Then, carbon dioxide in the atmosphere freezes, causing the ice caps to grow again.

➡ Mars also has frozen water underground. The *Mars Reconnaissance Orbiter*, a NASA space probe, took hundreds of ground-penetrating radar images of the Martian surface. It discovered a wide region that contains frozen water. It is between eighty and 170 meters thick and may be as large as Lake Superior. This frozen lake is fifty to eighty percent water. The remainder is dust and rock particles. It is located about halfway between the northern ice cap and the Martian equator. Other smaller patches of underground water have also been found, and more may be discovered in the future.

*Glossary

sublimation: the process through which a solid or liquid changes into a gas

7   In paragraph 5, the author's description of hydrated salts mentions which of the following?

A   How they may create liquid water on Mars's surface

B   Which chemical compounds they are created with

C   How many of them can be found throughout Mars

D   How warm the temperature should be for them to melt

Paragraph 5 is marked with an arrow (➡).

8   The word "sterile" in the passage is closest in meaning to

A   dangerous

B   dead

C   dry

D   damp

➡ New research indicates that if the proper conditions are met, liquid water flows freely on the surface. Many geological features on Mars appear to have been made by the carving action of flowing water. At first, astronomers believed this happened in the distant past. Yet continuous observation in recent years has shown some changes in the planet's geology. The *Mars Reconnaissance Orbiter* discovered dark streaks on mountain slopes that appear and disappear. They appear during warm periods and vanish in cool times. It is believed that these slopes contain high levels of hydrated salts. They are used on the Earth to melt snow and ice on roads. If a layer of frozen ice is located just below the surface, the hydrated salts could melt it in warm conditions. Then, the water flows downhill. When it gets colder, the temperature is too low for the salts to melt the ice.

The flowing of water on Mars may mean that there is life on the planet. It is likely that this will not be determined until more missions are carried out on the planet. They would most likely have to be manned missions. But nobody is sure when humans will ever set foot on Mars. Nevertheless, the possibility of there being free-flowing water on Mars increases the likelihood that the planet is not completely sterile but that it instead may have life on it.

*Glossary

hydrated salt: a type of salt that has some water in it which it crystallizes

9   Look at the four squares [■] hat indicate where the following sentence could be added to the passage.

It does not become a liquid because the atmospheric pressure and temperature are too low on Mars.

Where would the sentence best fit?

Click on a square [■] to add the sentence to the passage.

Most of the water on the planet today exists in the ice caps. The northern one is larger than the southern one. It is about two kilometers thick and 1,000 kilometers in diameter. It may contain more than 1.5 million square kilometers of ice. The southern one is only around 350 kilometers in diameter yet is around three kilometers thick. So it contains approximately the same amount of frozen water as the northern ice cap. Both grow and shrink as the seasons change. Like Earth, Mars experiences warm and cool periods each year. **1** In the warm summertime, the frozen carbon dioxide in the upper layer of the ice caps melts. **2** The carbon dioxide undergoes sublimation and transforms from a solid state to a gaseous one. **3** The reverse happens in winter. **4** Then, carbon dioxide in the atmosphere freezes, causing the ice caps to grow again.

*Glossary

sublimation: the process through which a solid or liquid changes into a gas

10 **Directions:** An introductory sentence for a brief summary of the passage is provided below. Complete the summary by selecting the THREE answer choices that express the most important ideas of the passage. Some sentences do not belong because they express ideas that are not presented in the passage or are minor ideas in the passage. **This question is worth 2 points.**

> Drag your answer choices to the spaces where they belong. To remove an answer choice, click on it. To review the passage, click on **VIEW TEXT**.

There is water in its liquid, solid, and gaseous forms on Mars.

-
-
-

ANSWER CHOICES

1. There is freely flowing water on Mars at times thanks to the presence of hydrated salts.

2. The *Mars Reconnaissance Orbiter* is looking for underground sources of water.

3. Most of the water on Mars is located in its northern and southern ice caps.

4. It is possible that life on Mars exists due to the presence of liquid water.

5. A manned mission to Mars is being planned to explore the planet's water sources.

6. There are large underground frozen lakes of water and other areas around the planet.

Honeybees and Bumblebees

A honeybee

A bumblebee

Honeybees and bumblebees are two insects that many people confuse with each other. While they share a few similarities, they also have a large number of differences. Their similarities tend to be general aspects. But the differences become apparent through a detailed examination of both.

The primary similarity between the two is that they are insects which live in colonies with different types of bees. The three types are the solitary queen, a few male drones, and the numerous female worker bees. The queens lead hives of both honeybees and bumblebees. For both insects, the majority of bees are involved in food collection. They mostly consume <u>nectar</u> and pollen from flowers, which they collect and return to store at their colonies.

As for their appearances, each of them has a black and yellow color. But their body shapes are different. Honeybees have longer, slimmer bodies and are similar to wasps in appearance. Bumblebees, on the other hand, have shorter, fatter, and hairier bodies. Honeybees have abdomen tips that are slender and tapering while bumblebees have more rounded ones. Honeybees also have short tongues, so they lap up nectar from open flowers. Bumblebees have longer tongues so can also get nectar from closed flowers.

The lifestyles of the two bees differ in many ways as well. Honeybees usually build nests, or hives, high above the ground in sheltered places. Bumblebees construct their nests close to or on the ground. Honeybees also live in enormous colonies with more than 20,000 bees per hive. Bumblebee colonies are much smaller as only around fifty to a few hundred bees live in a single nest. Honeybee queens can live for three to four years while bumblebee queens live for only one year. In addition, worker and drone bumblebees die when cold weather comes. The queen's eggs are fertilized by the male drones before they

die. She then hibernates underground all winter. In the spring, she starts a new colony and dies once the new queen hatches.

There are major differences in food production as well. Most honeybees are kept by beekeepers to produce commercial honey. They produce huge amounts which are more than they need to feed themselves. Most bumblebees live in the wild and produce only enough food to feed their colonies. Honeybees collect nectar and pollen and return to their hives. There, they pass on the food to receiver workers, which then store it in cells. There are no receiver worker bumblebees though. Each bee must collect and then store nectar and pollen by itself after returning to the nest since bumblebees are physically unable to transfer food to others. There are also fewer bumblebee workers due to the small sizes of their colonies. The worker bees must therefore toil hard to produce enough food for their colonies. While honeybees can store food for long periods of time, bumblebees can only store enough food for a few days. So they are in constant search of food sources.

When the bees attack others, their methods differ. Honeybees can sting their enemies only once. Their stinger is barbed and gets stuck in the animal they attack. When the honeybee moves away, the stinger rips off. The damage this does to the bee's body results in its death. Bumblebees rarely sting and only do so if they are aggravated. However, they are capable of stinging many times in a row. Their stingers have no barbs, so they do not die when they attack another animal.

Both bees communicate by using pheromones. These allow the bees to recognize members of the same colony and to tell other bees where some food sources are. Biologists also believe they have specialized pheromones that let them pass on the scents of certain flowers. This allows the bees to find good food sources. Honeybees also have a special communication method that bumblebees lack. This is called the waggle dance. When scout bees return from searching for food, they often fly around the hive. They fly in circles and make various movements that appear as though the bees are dancing. However, they are simply informing other bees where food sources are, what they are, and how far away they are. Other bees can then use the information gained from the dance to obtain new food.

*Glossary

nectar: something sweet a plant produces which attracts animals that pollinate it
pheromone: a chemical an animal gives off that can affect other animals of the same species

Beginning

Honeybees and Bumblebees

➡ Honeybees and bumblebees are two insects that many people confuse with each other. While they share a few similarities, they also have a large number of differences. Their similarities tend to be general aspects. But the differences become apparent through a detailed examination of both.

⇨ The primary similarity between the two is that they are insects which live in colonies with different types of bees. The three types are the solitary queen, a few male drones, and the numerous female worker bees. The queens lead hives of both honeybees and bumblebees. For both insects, the majority of bees are involved in food collection. They mostly consume <u>nectar</u> and pollen from flowers, which they collect and return to store at their colonies.

As for their appearances, each of them has a black and yellow color. But their body shapes are different. Honeybees have longer, slimmer bodies and are similar to wasps in appearance. Bumblebees, on the other hand, have shorter, fatter, and hairier bodies. Honeybees have abdomen tips that are slender and tapering while bumblebees have more rounded <u>ones</u>. Honeybees also have short tongues, so they lap up nectar from open flowers. Bumblebees have longer tongues so can also get nectar from closed flowers.

*Glossary

nectar: something sweet a plant produces which attracts animals that pollinate it

11 According to paragraph 1, which of the following is true about honeybees?

    Ⓐ They are the most unique of all species of bees.

    Ⓑ They have many differences from bumblebees.

    Ⓒ They look exactly the same as bumblebees.

    Ⓓ They are often confused with several types of bees.

Paragraph 1 is marked with an arrow (➡).

12 In paragraph 2, the author of the passage implies that female bees

    Ⓐ are more numerous than male ones

    Ⓑ protect the hive from attackers

    Ⓒ are responsible for making beehives

    Ⓓ do not engage in food collection

Paragraph 2 is marked with an arrow (⇨).

13 The word "ones" in the passage refers to

    Ⓐ shorter, fatter, and hairier bodies

    Ⓑ honeybees

    Ⓒ abdomen tips

    Ⓓ bumblebees

14 The word "sheltered" in the passage is closest in meaning to

- (A) defended
- (B) small
- (C) hidden
- (D) protected

15 According to paragraph 4, when does a bumblebee queen bee die?

- (A) After she lays her eggs
- (B) Before winter comes
- (C) Before the other bees hibernate
- (D) After another queen hatches

Paragraph 4 is marked with an arrow (➡).

➡ The lifestyles of the two bees differ in many ways as well. Honeybees usually build nests, or hives, high above the ground in sheltered places. Bumblebees construct their nests close to or on the ground. Honeybees also live in enormous colonies with more than 20,000 bees per hive. Bumblebee colonies are much smaller as only around fifty to a few hundred bees live in a single nest. Honeybee queens can live for three to four years while bumblebee queens live for only one year. In addition, worker and drone bumblebees die when cold weather comes. The queen's eggs are fertilized by the male drones before they die. She then hibernates underground all winter. In the spring, she starts a new colony and dies once the new queen hatches.

More Available ▲

16 In paragraph 5, all of the following questions are answered EXCEPT:

Ⓐ How long does it take honeybees to make honey?

Ⓑ Why must bumblebees work hard to produce food?

Ⓒ Why are there no receiver worker bumblebees?

Ⓓ How much food do honeybees produce?

Paragraph 5 is marked with an arrow (➡).

17 The word "aggravated" in the passage is closest in meaning to

Ⓐ annoyed

Ⓑ hunted

Ⓒ observed

Ⓓ attacked

➡ There are major differences in food production as well. Most honeybees are kept by beekeepers to produce commercial honey. They produce huge amounts which are more than they need to feed themselves. Most bumblebees live in the wild and produce only enough food to feed their colonies. Honeybees collect nectar and pollen and return to their hives. There, they pass on the food to receiver workers, which then store it in cells. There are no receiver worker bumblebees though. Each bee must collect and then store nectar and pollen by itself after returning to the nest since bumblebees are physically unable to transfer food to others. There are also fewer bumblebee workers due to the small sizes of their colonies. The worker bees must therefore toil hard to produce enough food for their colonies. While honeybees can store food for long periods of time, bumblebees can only store enough food for a few days. So they are in constant search of food sources.

When the bees attack others, their methods differ. Honeybees can sting their enemies only once. Their stinger is barbed and gets stuck in the animal they attack. When the honeybee moves away, the stinger rips off. The damage this does to the bee's body results in its death. Bumblebees rarely sting and only do so if they are aggravated. However, they are capable of stinging many times in a row. Their stingers have no barbs, so they do not die when they attack another animal.

18 According to paragraph 7, why do honeybees do the waggle dance?

Ⓐ To describe a potential site for a new hive

Ⓑ To point out food sources to other bees

Ⓒ To warn that enemies may be approaching

Ⓓ To indicate that another bee colony is nearby

Paragraph 7 is marked with an arrow (➡).

➡ Both bees communicate by using pheromones. These allow the bees to recognize members of the same colony and to tell other bees where some food sources are. Biologists also believe they have specialized pheromones that let them pass on the scents of certain flowers. This allows the bees to find good food sources. Honeybees also have a special communication method that bumblebees lack. This is called the waggle dance. When scout bees return from searching for food, they often fly around the hive. They fly in circles and make various movements that appear as though the bees are dancing. However, they are simply informing other bees where food sources are, what they are, and how far away they are. Other bees can then use the information gained from the dance to obtain new food.

*Glossary

pheromone: a chemical an animal gives off that can affect other animals of the same species

More Available ▲

19 Look at the four squares [■] that indicate where the following sentence could be added to the passage.

Many bees may sacrifice their lives in this way while protecting their hive from attackers.

Where would the sentence best fit?

Click on a square [■] to add the sentence to the passage.

When the bees attack others, their methods differ. Honeybees can sting their enemies only once. Their stinger is barbed and gets stuck in the animal they attack. When the honeybee moves away, the stinger rips off. The damage this does to the bee's body results in its death. **1** Bumblebees rarely sting and only do so if they are aggravated. **2** However, they are capable of stinging many times in a row. **3** Their stingers have no barbs, so they do not die when they attack another animal. **4**

208

20 Directions: Select the appropriate statements from the answer choices and match them to the type of bee to which they relate. TWO of the answer choices will NOT be used. **This question is worth 3 points.**

Drag your answer choices to the spaces where they belong. To remove an answer choice, click on it. To review the passage, click on **VIEW TEXT.**

STATEMENTS

1. Has queens that can live for six years

2. Makes nests that may be on the ground

3. Can sting enemies multiple times

4. Gives collected nectar to other bees in the hive

5. Can kill other animals when they sting them

6. Gets nectar only from open flowers

7. Has colonies with thousands of bees

TYPE OF BEE

Honeybee (Select 3)

-
-
-

Bumblebee (Select 2)

-
-

Electrical Systems and the Modern Home

In the present day, electricity is used in nearly every modern home all around the world. However, before scientists learned how to harness its power in the late 1800s, homes were quite different. People provided illumination in their homes with candles or lamps that burned whale oil or kerosene. They heated their homes with fireplaces or wood- or coal-burning stoves. They cooked with all of them as well. People normally rose when the sun came up and went to bed soon after it went down. There were no modern entertainment devices such as radios, televisions, and computers. The introduction of electricity into homes changed not only how people lived their lives but also the designs of their homes.

People have known about electricity since ancient times, but finding uses for it was difficult. It was not until Thomas Edison invented the light bulb in 1879 that there was a practical everyday use for electricity. Still, it took time for electrical systems to develop. Edison built the first power station in New York City in 1882. It used direct current, or DC, electrical power. At the same time, inventor Nikola Tesla was developing alternating current, or AC, electrical power. The first AC power station in the United States was built near Niagara Falls in 1895. It sent electricity to nearby Buffalo, New York. A power war between Edison and Tesla over which system was better began. In the end, Tesla's AC power proved that it was better able to send electricity over long distances and that it was safer than DC power. Over the next few decades, inventors developed more safety features to control it.

At the same time, electricians began to come up with ways to use electricity in homes. In older homes, they had to make modifications. In many cases, the wires for new electrical systems used the same pathways as plumbing pipes. This was necessary in old brick and stone homes that lacked easy access for the new system. In wooden homes, the electrical systems were installed alongside or through the homes' wooden frames. These early systems often used knob and tube wiring. Bare wires were run through the house. In places where the wire ran alongside wooden beams, ceramic knobs kept them from touching the wood. The wires were then pushed through the tubes. Both the knobs and tubes kept the hot wires from burning the wood. After a while, these systems were deemed unsafe. In many homes, they were later replaced with safer insulated copper wire. By the 1970s, most homes had modern electrical systems that were safe.

Over time, people used electricity to change their old way of living. The main change was in the lighting systems that they used. Instead of candles and lamps, people started using central ceiling lights. Almost every room had an electric light on the ceiling. Early electrical devices such as vacuum cleaners and fans had to be attached to sockets with a device called a lampholder plug. In 1903, Harvey Hubbell invented the two-pin electric plug and socket. Later, many plugs added a third pin to ground them. This made the plugs safer. Sockets were placed in rooms at low levels so that appliances could be easily used.

After a while, multiple sockets with two places for plugs became necessary since people bought so many electrical devices.

As electricity usage became normal in the early 1900s, there was an explosion in the use of these devices. They influenced the way that architects designed houses in the decades to come. Electric stoves and heaters became common in homes. Fireplaces were not needed, so they were no longer made in new homes. In places that had them, they became status symbols rather than practical devices for heating and cooking. Kitchen designs had to take into account the space and wiring needed for electric stoves, refrigerators, and dishwashers. Heavy-duty wiring was required for large power-hungry appliances such as clothes washers and dryers. Safety sockets were made for damp bathrooms. They let people use electric hairdryers and razors. Finally, room in homes was needed for large panels that controlled the flow of electricity to various rooms.

*Glossary

ground: to make an electric appliance safe by ensuring that electricity cannot harm a person
status symbol: an object that brings prestige or respect to its owner

21 The word "illumination" in the passage is closest in meaning to

    Ⓐ knowledge

    Ⓑ electricity

    Ⓒ light

    Ⓓ heat

Electrical Systems and the Modern Home

➡ In the present day, electricity is used in nearly every modern home all around the world. However, before scientists learned how to harness its power in the late 1800s, homes were quite different. People provided illumination in their homes with candles or lamps that burned whale oil or kerosene. They heated their homes with fireplaces or wood- or coal-burning stoves. They cooked with all of them as well. People normally rose when the sun came up and went to bed soon after it went down. There were no modern entertainment devices such as radios, televisions, and computers. The introduction of electricity into homes changed not only how people lived their lives but also the designs of their homes.

REVIEW

HELP

BACK

NEXT

HIDE TIME 00:54:00

More Available

22 Which of the sentences below best expresses the essential information in the highlighted sentence in the passage? Incorrect answer choices change the meaning in important ways or leave out essential information.

It was not until Thomas Edison invented the light bulb in 1879 that there was a practical everyday use for electricity.

(A) The invention of the light bulb was the first time that people found a way to use electricity.

(B) In 1879, Thomas Edison made his first invention, the electric light bulb.

(C) Until the light bulb, people had no way to see in their homes at night.

(D) There were few uses for electricity until Thomas Edison made an invention.

23 The author discusses "inventor Nikola Tesla" in order to

(A) state the reason for his rivalry with Thomas Edison

(B) discuss the differences between AC and DC power

(C) claim that he was a better inventor than Thomas Edison

(D) name his inventions that used electricity

24 Which of the following can be inferred from paragraph 2 about AC power?

(A) It is more commonly used than DC power.

(B) It is not as safe as most people believe.

(C) It cost more to use than DC power.

(D) It was developed by Nikola Tesla and Thomas Edison.

Paragraph 2 is marked with an arrow (➡).

➡ People have known about electricity since ancient times, but finding uses for it was difficult. It was not until Thomas Edison invented the light bulb in 1879 that there was a practical everyday use for electricity. Still, it took time for electrical systems to develop. Edison built the first power station in New York City in 1882. It used direct current, or DC, electrical power. At the same time, inventor Nikola Tesla was developing alternating current, or AC, electrical power. The first AC power station in the United States was built near Niagara Falls in 1895. It sent electricity to nearby Buffalo, New York. A power war between Edison and Tesla over which system was better began. In the end, Tesla's AC power proved that it was better able to send electricity over long distances and that it was safer than DC power. Over the next few decades, inventors developed more safety features to control it.

25 The word "modifications" in the passage is closest in meaning to

   Ⓐ decisions

   Ⓑ movements

   Ⓒ designs

   Ⓓ alterations

26 According to paragraph 3, which of the following is true about the electrical systems added to homes?

   Ⓐ They were impossible to add to brick homes

   Ⓑ They burned many wooden homes down.

   Ⓒ Their wires were often near water pipes.

   Ⓓ They were expensive for electricians to install.

Paragraph 3 is marked with an arrow (➡).

➡ At the same time, electricians began to come up with ways to use electricity in homes. In older homes, they had to make modifications. In many cases, the wires for new electrical systems used the same pathways as plumbing pipes. This was necessary in old brick and stone homes that lacked easy access for the new system. In wooden homes, the electrical systems were installed alongside or through the homes' wooden frames. These early systems often used knob and tube wiring. Bare wires were run through the house. In places where the wire ran alongside wooden beams, ceramic knobs kept them from touching the wood. The wires were then pushed through the tubes. Both the knobs and tubes kept the hot wires from burning the wood. After a while, these systems were deemed unsafe. In many homes, they were later replaced with safer insulated copper wire. By the 1970s, most homes had modern electrical systems that were safe.

27 In paragraph 4, the author's description of the electrical devices invented mentions all of the following EXCEPT:

Ⓐ what types of devices were made

Ⓑ why sockets were put low near the floor

Ⓒ how some of them were made safer

Ⓓ how much they cost to purchase

Paragraph 4 is marked with an arrow (➡).

28 According to paragraph 5, fireplaces became status symbols because

Ⓐ the price of bricks rose greatly in the 1900s

Ⓑ they were not necessary for heating or cooking

Ⓒ they were too big for most people's homes

Ⓓ architects no longer wished to design then

Paragraph 5 is marked with an arrow (⇨).

➡ Over time, people used electricity to change their old way of living. The main change was in the lighting systems that they used. Instead of candles and lamps, people started using central ceiling lights. Almost every room had an electric light on the ceiling. Early electrical devices such as vacuum cleaners and fans had to be attached to sockets with a device called a lampholder plug. In 1903, Harvey Hubbell invented the two-pin electric plug and socket. Later, many plugs added a third pin to <u>ground</u> them. This made the plugs safer. Sockets were placed in rooms at low levels so that appliances could be easily used. After a while, multiple sockets with two places for plugs became necessary since people bought so many electrical devices.

⇨ As electricity usage became normal in the early 1900s, there was an explosion in the use of these devices. They influenced the way that architects designed houses in the decades to come. Electric stoves and heaters became common in homes. Fireplaces were not needed, so they were no longer made in new homes. In places that had them, they became <u>status symbols</u> rather than practical devices for heating and cooking. Kitchen designs had to take into account the space and wiring needed for electric stoves, refrigerators, and dishwashers. Heavy-duty wiring was required for large power-hungry appliances such as clothes washers and dryers. Safety sockets were made for damp bathrooms. They let people use electric hairdryers and razors. Finally, room in homes was needed for large panels that controlled the flow of electricity to various rooms.

*Glossary

ground: to make an electric appliance safe by ensuring that electricity cannot harm a person

status symbol: an object that brings prestige or respect to its owner

29 Look at the four squares [■] that indicate where the following sentence could be added to the passage.

Their battle would eventually come to be known as the War of the Currents.

Where would the sentence best ft?

Click on a square [■] to add the sentence to the passage.

People have known about electricity since ancient times, but finding uses for it was difficult. It was not until Thomas Edison invented the light bulb in 1879 that there was a practical everyday use for electricity. Still, it took time for electrical systems to develop. Edison built the first power station in New York City in 1882. It used direct current, or DC, electrical power. At the same time, inventor Nikola Tesla was developing alternating current, or AC, electrical power. The first AC power station in the United States was built near Niagara Falls in 1895. It sent electricity to nearby Buffalo, New York. **1** A power war between Edison and Tesla over which system was better began. **2** In the end, Tesla's AC power proved that it was better able to send electricity over long distances and that it was safer than DC power. **3** Over the next few decades, inventors developed more safety features to control it. **4**

30 **Directions:** An introductory sentence for a brief summary of the passage is provided below. Complete the summary by selecting the THREE answer choices that express the most important ideas of the passage. Some sentences do not belong because they express ideas that are not presented in the passage or are minor ideas in the passage. **This question is worth 2 points.**

Drag your answer choices to the spaces where they belong. To remove an answer choice, click on it. To review the passage, click on **VIEW TEXT**.

Modern homes and lives changed greatly because of developments in electricity.

-

-

-

ANSWER CHOICES

1 Architects put plugs near the floor to connect easily to appliances.

2 Lighting systems added to houses altered the way that people lived their lives.

3 Many people's homes were renovated to have electrical systems added.

4 Nikola Tesla and Thomas Edison had a rivalry that lasted many years.

5 Numerous appliances, including heaters and stoves, were used in homes.

6 For centuries, people had woken up at sunrise and gone to bed at sunset.

Authors

Michael A. Putlack

- MA in History, Tufts University, Medford, MA, USA
- Expert test developer of TOEFL, TOEIC, and TEPS
- Main author of the Darakwon *How to Master Skills for the TOEFL® iBT* series and *TOEFL® MAP* series

Stephen Poirier

- Candidate for PhD in History, University of Western Ontario, Canada
- Certificate of Professional Technical Writing, Carleton University, Canada
- Co-author of the Darakwon *How to Master Skills for the TOEFL® iBT* series and *TOEFL® MAP* series

Allen C. Jacobs

- BS in Physics, Presbyterian College, Clinton, SC, USA
- BCE in Civil Engineering, Auburn University, Auburn, AL, USA
- MS in Civil Engineering, University of Alabama, Tuscaloosa, AL, USA

Decoding the TOEFL® iBT
READING Basic NEW TOEFL® EDITION

Publisher Chung Kyudo
Editors Kim Minju
Authors Michael A. Putlack, Stephen Poirier, Allen C. Jacobs
Proofreader Michael A. Putlack
Designers Koo Soojung, Park Sunyoung

First published in June 2020
By Darakwon, Inc.
Darakwon Bldg., 211, Munbal-ro, Paju-si, Gyeonggi-do 10881
Republic of Korea
Tel: 82-2-736-2031 (Ext. 250)
Fax: 82-2-732-2037

ISBN 978-89-277-0876-6 14740
        978-89-277-0875-9 14740 (set)

www.darakwon.co.kr

Components Student Book / Answer Book
11 10 9 8 7 6 5   24 25 26 27 28